The President and the
Management of National Security

The President and the Management of National Security

A Report by the Institute for Defense Analyses

EDITED BY
Keith C. Clark
AND
Laurence J. Legere

FREDERICK A. PRAEGER, *Publishers*
New York · Washington · London

FREDERICK A. PRAEGER, *Publishers*
111 Fourth Avenue, New York, N.Y. 10003, U.S.A.
5, Cromwell Place, London S.W.7, England

Published in the United States of America in 1969
by Frederick A. Praeger, Inc., Publishers

© 1969 by the Institute for Defense Analyses

Library of Congress Catalog Card Number: 77-79029

Printed in the United States of America

Preface

It is a commentary on our society and era that almost all states-men complain bitterly about how little time they can devote to reflection on even the most critical problems they confront—including those they can foresee long in advance. Perhaps time for thought has always been a scarce commodity for national leaders. Periods of history that seem to us to have been leisurely and simple no doubt seemed to the rulers and statesmen of the day to be fraught with pressing and difficult problems. But it is worth noting that only two decades have passed since our government found it necessary to create deliberate arrangements for "policy planning," to assign talent and resources within the government to this function, and to sponsor a special category of institutions outside the government called "think tanks."

Notwithstanding our national pace, every four years—by virtue of our Constitutional form of government—a season of reappraisal comes over us. Newspapers and journals devote space to such articles as "National Priorities" and "Whither the Nation?" Academic and institutional sages proffer advice and publish thoughtful agendas. Legislators heap guidance on Presidential aspirants. Official "position papers" flourish. In keeping with the season, in November, 1968, we at the Institute for Defense Analyses (IDA) made available both to officials of President Lyndon B. Johnson's Administration and to members of President-elect Richard M. Nixon's staff this report based on an intensive study of the national-security decision-making process.

The study was not commissioned by any agency of the U.S. Government. It was sponsored by IDA's Central Research Program and supplemented by a grant from the Ford Foundation, for which we express our thanks. The International and Social Studies Division of IDA initiated the effort in early 1968 on the assumption that, whatever the outcome of the autumn election, the next President and his Administration would find useful some informed reflections on decision-making in the difficult and important area of national-security policy.

The study does not concern itself with the role of Congress in national-security affairs and it addresses only tangentially the problem of improving communication with the public. Our approach to the task of preparing this work has been pragmatic rather than theoretical. We have tried to point out some broad options, within existing legislation and institutions, that might improve the quality of the national-security process. We have been influenced in our analysis more by what we thought possible than by what we regarded as ideal and we have been concerned more with rendering the process effective than with making it tidy. We hope that the study has profited from scholarly publications and that it is not lacking in imagination or informed speculation; however, it derives chiefly from the experience of many persons in the executive branch of the government.

Most of those engaged in this study have spent the major part of their careers in one or more of the principal departments and agencies charged with national security, including the White House staff in both Republican and Democratic administrations. They are Chester L. Cooper, Director of the Institute's International and Social Studies Division, who wrote the introductory chapter; Laurence J. Legere, project leader and editor, who was also co-author of Chapters II, VIII, and IX; Keith C. Clark, editor and author of Chapter III, as well as co-author of Chapter II; Vincent Davis, co-author of Chapters VIII and IX; Richard M. Moose, author of Chapters IV and V; John Ponturo, who wrote Chapter X; and Joseph A. Yager, author of Chapters VI and VII. In the course of the study, members of this group interviewed nearly 100 government officials—on active service and retired, Republican and Democratic, civilian and military, who hold or once held key positions in the White House or in the main departments and agencies involved in national-security affairs.

We have not identified any particular person with any particular view, and the records of our interviews have not been incorporated either in this book or in our original report. We did not, of course, encounter agreement among everyone on all questions. It would have been surprising and disappointing if we had. We have weighed and debated all differences but have not accepted all opinions. Although this book distills a vast reservoir of experience, it is not a compendium of every view expressed by everyone interviewed. The merits that the report may have are owing in great part to the officials and former officials who talked with us—but they are not to be held to account for the conclusions expressed here.

Nor do the conclusions necessarily express the individual opinions of the eighteen consultants whose names appear in Appendix B and who assisted us throughout the study by themselves submitting to interviews and by reviewing and commenting on successive chapter drafts. In addition to these consultants, Robert R. Bowie, Gordon Gray, and General Harold K. Johnson (Ret.), although not formal advisers, gave generously of their time at various stages of the study effort. We wish to thank them and also Delbert Arnold and Joseph Flader of IDA, as well as Joseph Lewis, formerly of IDA, each of whom made invaluable contributions to the research, the conduct and evaluation of interviews, and the shaping of the effort into the form that it has assumed in these pages. The contributions of General Maxwell D. Taylor (Ret.) far exceeded his responsibilities as President of the Institute for Defense Analyses. In particular, he assisted in the early conceptual stages and constantly helped the authors sharpen their thinking as work progressed.

The arrangement of our interviews with key officials of the Johnson Administration was handled through busy men in relevant areas of the government, and we express our appreciation to them. Among those unfailingly helpful were Bromley K. Smith, Executive Secretary of the National Security Council; Benjamin H. Read, Executive Secretary of the Department of State; George M. Elsey, Special Assistant to the Secretary of Defense, and his assistant, R. Eugene Livesay; Major General Norman S. Orwat, Deputy J-5, Joint Staff, Joint Chiefs of Staff; and, in the Central Intelligence Agency, Deputy Director for Intelligence R. Jack Smith and Special Assistant to the Director John A. Bross. To Assistant Secretary of Defense for Public Affairs Philip G. Goulding, our thanks for his personal help in expediting the security clearance of the completed manuscript.

Within IDA, our able editor Jean Mitson, together with Rockwood H. Foster, Robert A. German, Mary Z. Hoffman, and Howard N. Margolis, made important contributions toward moving the task to completion, supported by the project secretaries Sheila K. Myers, Patricia Cook, Sylvia Downing, Irene McManic, and Janice Morello, who recorded the interviews and prepared the manuscript in final form.

Washington, D.C.   K.C.C.
February, 1969   L.J.L.

Contents

The President and the
Management of National Security

I

Some Perspectives on the Art of Decision-Making in National Security

AN INTRODUCTION BY CHESTER L. COOPER *

In 1947, Congress passed the National Security Act, which created the National Security Council (the NSC) and the Central Intelligence Agency (CIA) and laid the foundation for a more effective organization of the armed services.[1] In the decades since, the world has changed in many important respects. The present international climate is by no means salubrious, but it is at least more temperate than it was in the frigid years following World War II. General peace still eludes mankind, but the threat of general war now seems reasonably remote.

One of the most difficult conceptual problems that has confronted each of our postwar Presidents is how best to use the national-security process he has inherited. Each often found that the NSC, created in the aftermath of World War II, fashioned at the onset of the Cold War, and organized against the possibility of an imminent World War III, was, as originally conceived, not an ideal instrument to cope with the international environment. Many of the world crises that have beset American policy makers have occurred in places and over issues scarcely foreseen in 1947. As President John F. Kennedy noted in September, 1963: "Countries which we had never heard of before, Vietnam, Laos, the Congo . . . countries which were distant names in our geographies, have now become matters of the greatest concern, where

---

* Chester L. Cooper was appointed Director, International and Social Studies Division of the Institute for Defense Analyses in 1969.
[1] See Appendix A for relevant excerpts from the National Security Act of 1947.

3

the interests of the United States are vitally involved." [2] The case of Vietnam, in which the National Security Council has played only a peripheral role, is a prime example. And yet there is an obvious and enduring need for the functions performed by such a council. Interdepartmental problems constantly arise and require attention at the highest level, so that the need for the National Security Council would still exist even if we were to achieve a genuine and long-lasting *détente* with the Soviet Union. Indeed, if there were now no NSC, something very much like it would have to be created.

Most of the formal changes to meet new national-security requirements of an evolving international situation have been made in the great departments of the government, rather than in the NSC, which has remained the same in structure, although wide variations have developed in its practice and importance. The Department of State has been expanded and given new responsibilities, largely through the creation of new subdepartmental organizations such as the United States Information Agency, the Agency for International Development, and the Arms Control and Disarmament Agency. The Department of Defense, established in 1949, immediately underwent formal reorganizations in 1949, in 1953, and again in 1958. These reorganizations have gradually diminished the authority of the departments of the Army, Navy, and Air Force and increased the centralized authority of both the civilian secretary of defense and the military joint chiefs of staff. The 1960's have witnessed increasing emphasis on rationalization of the defense-budget process, the introduction of tighter management tools and practices, and—most important—intensified efforts to harmonize military strategies, forces, and budgets, with military doctrines becoming more responsive to national-policy requirements and great strides being made in command and control, communications, intelligence, and information handling.

Over the past twenty years, the departments of State and Defense have been opened up to one another, and formal and informal communication between them has become the rule. Regular exchange of personnel between the two has deepened mutual

[2] Remarks at Billings, Montana, September 25, 1963.

understanding and broadened perspectives on both sides. Joint meetings and discussions at all levels have become commonplace. Collaboration on matters of mutual interest is now the customary way of doing business, and the amount of such business has mushroomed. Differences of special interest and outlook between these two major departments have not vanished, nor have friction and conflict disappeared, but they have been moderated, and these trends have all facilitated the integration of military- and foreign-policy considerations in formulating and carrying out our national programs.

Because each President has used the NSC in his own way, its actual role and responsibilities have varied widely. At a minimum level, the NSC has been used as a forum for announcing or discussing decisions already made by the President and requiring interagency coordination. More often, it has been used as the principal arena for debating alternative strategic courses of action and ensuring that all the relevant considerations were thoroughly considered in making a final decision. The NSC has sometimes provided one means by which the President and his principal advisers could ensure regular communication on a wide range of problems; at other times, it has been used as the central instrument for actual debate and resolution of critical issues.

Associated with the NSC have been subsidiary staff or committee arrangements, which have ranged from a loose and informal arrangement under one President to a highly structured set of interagency boards, staffs, and working groups under another. Paralleling the NSC, and often modeled upon it, have been other interagency organs, from formal broad-purpose "standing committees" to *ad hoc* "task forces" focused on specific issues. Over and above these arrangements, each President has also maintained an immediate staff in the White House which varied in size depending on his own needs and style and performed a consequential or relatively minor role in the management of national-security affairs.

Furthermore, we should note that no President has consistently used a single or rigid set of formal arrangements, neither NSC nor any other, to transact all of his interdepartmental business in national-security affairs. Each President in turn did a certain amount of organizational and procedural tailoring which varied according to the subject matter at hand, to special circumstances, and, of course, to the particular personalities and individual relationships involved. Each occasionally bypassed elements of the so-called system and sought the help of more detached outsiders. Some Presidents gave the appearance of much greater regularity and order than others, but none was either absolutely systematic nor completely unsystematic. Crisis decision-making, in particular, dictated faster, more streamlined, and more so-called leak-proof methods than those available through the formal NSC structure. Major crises have typically involved considerable direct participation by the President, bypassing standard procedures and relying on the counsel of a very few trusted advisers. The invasion of South Korea in 1950, the Quemoy–Matsu crisis in 1958, the Cuban missile crisis in 1962, and the Dominican crisis in 1965 are cases in point. Complex matters such as the annual budget or preparations for the nuclear test ban talks have required special arrangements and a wide variety of experts and staff support throughout the government. Politically sensitive or highly controversial issues such as prisoner exchanges and preliminary, secret contacts regarding the Vietnam negotiations, for example, had to be held closely in discreet channels. Less urgent, less controversial, or less sensitive issues have normally not required as much direct Presidential participation and have been handled at lower levels and by more people in a more deliberate or routine manner.

Over and above these general considerations, Presidents have differed in their preferences for large or small groups of associates, for reading or listening, for contemplation or action, for formality or informality, for reserve or intimacy. And, too, Presidents have had to take into account the variations in the personality and style of their principal advisers. Presidents rarely come to office rich with experience in managing vast organizations. And their principal lieutenants are not necessarily picked because of their long association with each other in common enterprises or even their compatibility as members of a team. Each new administration has gone through a shakedown period, when the President and his men were working into their jobs, taking one another's measure, adjusting to their respective capabilities and limitations, and developing their personal and working relationships. What finally emerged after this process frequently has been perceptively different from the blueprints of organization and procedure that a President had in mind on his inauguration day.

In spite of the many adjustments and adaptations in national-security arrangements during the last twenty years, there has been persistent dissatisfaction with and criticism of the management of affairs. There has also been considerable feeling on the part of students of government and government officials that major changes in the international climate may call for new approaches and that the organization and procedures devised to deal with old challenges may not be adaptable to the new. Some of this feeling has, no doubt, been partisan and directed more toward the substance of certain policies than toward the arrangements by which those policies have been carried out. Nevertheless, the experience of two decades clearly indicates that there is an inevitable relation between the content and quality of national-security policy and the manner in which it is made and implemented. The conduct of national security is an art, not a science. No two Presidents have practiced this art in the same way, although, broadly speaking, all our Presidents since Harry S Truman have had basically similar international aims, and all of them have become deeply involved in the day-to-day problems of national security.

This great personal involvement has occurred not simply because our law and custom have made Presidents the chief architects of the budget, commanders of the armed forces, and managers of foreign relations, nor simply because national-security issues have become so complicated that Congress and the people tolerate more Presidential latitude and presumably desire more Presidential leadership here than in other spheres of government. It has occurred also because national-security needs have absorbed huge amounts of our human and material resources, with profound implications for our way of life and have involved a proliferation of activities all over the world, with enormous potential for good or harm to the nation.

The tasks of providing for the common defense and promoting

the general welfare in the years since World War II have required an orchestration of interrelated political, economic, and military factors and resources, necessarily cutting across the traditional jurisdictions and functions of a number of major departments and agencies—none with authority over the others and most reporting directly to the President. Where the stakes were vital, consequences historic, and errors catastrophic, decisions were crucial. No President in the nuclear age could risk leaving them entirely to his subordinates.

The chapters that follow concentrate on how the process of decision-making in an important area of national policy has worked in the recent past and advance some suggestions that might make for a more effective process in the future.

But neither practitioners nor students of national-security policy should overemphasize the importance of the process or the procedures of decision-making. In the last analysis, the force of personality tends to override procedures. A strong President might (indeed, inevitably will) involve himself directly in even second-order foreign-policy or defense-policy decisions, regardless of how much responsibility he has formally assigned to the departments of State and Defense and regardless of the procedural arrangements set up to keep the White House role to a necessary minimum. Conversely, even the most ambitious procedural schemes for increasing the authority of the White House staff and the National Security Council will not bring meaningful power into the White House if the President basically is disinclined to concern himself with the day-to-day ebb and flow of national-security problems.

We should note that what is true of the President's active control over the heads of the great departments and agencies is true, also, at the level of the Cabinet secretaries and the agency heads. For example, no bureaucratic treaties, no formal interagency agreements, can guarantee that the Department of State will have primary responsibility in the field of foreign affairs unless the secretary of state and his principal subordinates play a strong personal role in interagency councils.

Thus, even the most ideally formulated process, conscientiously observed, cannot assure that national-security affairs will always be conducted with efficiency and wisdom. The better the process, however, the more likely it is to help the President and to give him a surer command of the resources at his disposal. Process cannot supply omniscience or perfection. It can help to minimize the risks of haphazardness in the formulation and implementation of policy.

II

The Main Issues

In making arrangements for national-security policy, any President will accept or reject what he finds at hand—the controlling factors being his own purposes and needs and those of his principal advisers. Without exception in modern times, each new administration has made changes in the way national-security policies are made and carried out and has acknowledged, one way or another, a relationship between what it wanted to do and the best arrangements for doing it. Procedures in this field are, in practice, built around particular men rather than abstract organizational theory; hence, this study is not a blueprint of machinery for churning out decisions. But testimony from a large number of participants in national-security affairs since World War II indicates that purposes of policy do bear directly on ways of making it or carrying it out, and vice versa. The job cannot all be done in kitchen-cabinet sessions, although it cannot be done without them, whether "national security" is widely defined as including virtually all our foreign and military affairs, plus many domestic matters, or whether it is given a narrower definition. This study avoids rigid definition and uses the term as it is normally used in government practice to include the range of matters which, over the past twenty years, have customarily occupied the attention of the National Security Council and its associated institutions or their successors.

A paradox is evident in the many interviews contributing to this inquiry. Veterans of the Eisenhower Administration usually argue for procedures along the lines of the NSC system of the 1950's, but they are also inclined to acknowledge that the structure became too rigid and given to routine. President Dwight D. Eisenhower himself has written that he shared this feeling in certain respects late in his second term. Many Kennedy and Johnson men show a converse tendency. They recall feelings of liberation arising from the quick and drastic dismantling of elements of the NSC structure in favor of less formal methods, yet many of them reflect that they may have dismantled too much too quickly and that they may have overlooked needs that went unfilled until something new had to be created to do a job. In short, testimony suggests that if there are pitfalls in elaborate process, there may be equal and opposite dangers in a very informal system.

SOME CENTRAL QUESTIONS

Certain main questions about the making and conduct of policy lend themselves to analytical assessment in light of experience, quite apart from matters of personalities or personal style. The first of these concerns the peculiar problems of any new administration's early months, the shakedown period, when a new President and his chief advisers must move quickly to integrate themselves and their institutions into an effective national-security team.

Beyond this, and in terms of the long haul, the following questions arise:

1. What implications do major domestic and international trends have for national-security policy arrangements?
2. What are the merits of the main alternatives for centering policy responsibility and initiative in the White House, the State Department, or other institutions?
3. What should be the functions of the White House staff and its relations with the departments and agencies, including the Bureau of the Budget and the intelligence community?
4. How are major defense questions affected by the relations of the civilian leaders with the professional military in the Department of Defense?
5. What are the relative advantages of a comprehensive codification of national-security policy versus *ad hoc* guidance?
6. What is the best way to assure performance and "follow-through"?

THE SHAKEDOWN PERIOD

Presidents have often referred to their chief advisers as a team, and any coach knows that even the best players he may have chosen will be handicapped until all have learned how to play their positions individually and together. In the first weeks or months of his administration, therefore, a President may want to take special precautions to cope with the problem of newness until his team has become familiar with the institutions at its command and the ways its members want to do business with one another. The testimony of veterans of both Republican and Democratic administrations emphasizes several peculiar needs of the shakedown period:

1. A new President or a new head of one of the great departments has a natural desire and an obvious right to do things in his own style and to avoid being a prisoner of his predecessor's ways. But much experience and many observers warn against dismantling arrangements unless and until the new leadership is sure that a useful function is not being lost at needless risk or expense.

2. In its early months, a new administration must also ensure that all concerned share the President's goals and perspectives and are familiar with each other's problems. This point received particular emphasis from many of those interviewed. Whether or not the President intends to use the National Security Council extensively during most of his administration, a number of useful purposes can be served at the outset by convening something like the NSC frequently. The President's main aim need not be to perfect policies but should be to educate his chief advisers on common problems and facilitate their guidance of their departments and agencies in a common direction, to identify and reassess policies or programs that he may want to change, and to familiarize himself and his associates with each other and with the institutions they represent. If such a procedure is used, most testimony indicates that the meetings should be restricted (as one veteran has phrased it) "to the top guys only." Large numbers of subordinates lining the walls would frustrate these purposes.

NATIONAL-SECURITY PROBLEMS: CHANGE AND CONTINUITY

Any new administration must take not only its own measure but also that of the world it confronts. The President taking office in 1969 faces domestic problems hardly less urgent than those of the Great Depression—and at a time when the world is undergoing transformations comparable in significance to those that occurred after World War II. Ways of conducting the Presidency appropriate to our problems and interests in past administrations will not necessarily serve well in the 1970's.

The implications of foreseeable trends and issues at home and abroad for national-security matters are fully discussed in Chapter III. Briefly stated, domestic considerations include some constraints likely to loom larger than heretofore—a mixture of reaction from the Vietnam War, a more general skepticism about how extensive America's foreign commitments ought to be and about the limits on our power, a decline in the strength of Cold War sentiments, and a number of more tangible factors arising from greater calls on resources to meet domestic needs, the balance-of-payments squeeze, and pressures to cut the foreign-aid and defense budgets.

The principal international trends and issues are harder to summarize, but they include the growing complexity and interdependence of relations between nations, a decline in Cold War bipolarity, the emergence of additional centers of power (indicated by erosion of both the Western and Communist alliance systems), and a mixture of threat and promise offered by trends in Russia and Eastern Europe and the expansion of Soviet nuclear and conventional military power. Perhaps even more important new dimensions in world affairs are the rapid advances in sophisticated weaponry, the problems of disarmament and nuclear proliferation, new uses of space and the oceans for both peaceful and military purposes, the ominous implications of population growth for world stability and well being, the gap between rich and poor nations, and the impact on us all of rising expectations or rising frustrations throughout the underdeveloped world.

If our international policies are subject to increasing domestic constraints and if we face a more intractable and complicated world, policy decisions on these matters become not less but more difficult and more crucial. We are not concerned here with recommending substantive policy, and certainly the trends now foreseeable do not, in themselves, dictate any one particular set of procedural arrangements over another. But whether or not domestic imperatives lead U.S. foreign policy to become less activist, the combination of domestic trends and international prospects suggests several major considerations with respect to ways and means of conducting national-security affairs.

First, any reassessment or new look at over-all U.S. security commitments, whether it leads to modification of policy or not, implies the need for close cooperation and communication among departments and agencies of the government. In an increasingly complex and interdependent world, tidy distinctions between politics, economics, military affairs, and technology become less and less realistic.

For similar reasons, the case is strong for steps to assure wider and more systematic awareness of trade problems, commodity-price considerations, international-monetary arrangements, and fiscal factors as these bear on our over-all international policies and position. Such matters are often central to our relations with particular states, yet they are often slighted or overlooked in 'discussions of political and military policy abroad.

By the same token, the growing importance of scientific and technological innovations as conditioners of our environment, offering threat and promise alike, suggests the need to bring expertise in these fields to bear on national-security problems in a more direct and sustained fashion than heretofore. This applies to both military and nonmilitary questions (ranging from population control and food production to space and oceanography), and the expertise involved must come both from within and outside the government. An especially important instance of the point just made arises in the field of advanced weaponry and the possibilities for arms control. Either an indefinite arms race or a real breakthrough toward arms control would place as great a premium on technological sophistication as on political skill and, either way, the need becomes more urgent and the stakes higher as time passes.

Another, quite different effect of technology on national-security policy problems is the sharp increase in the speed of communication and the volume of information flowing through the system. Often a mixed blessing, because more information is not always better information, this phenomenon is nonetheless a fact of life and calls for the best possible use of modern methods for processing information, analyzing and presenting it, and selecting what is important from what is not. There are distinct limitations on the application of computer techniques and various advanced methods of analysis to the subjective aspects of national-security affairs, but their usefulness for certain purposes is already demonstrated and their potential is likely to grow.

One final proposition deserves mention. If this study demonstrates anything, it is that we face a host of complex problems, with many variations and conceivable contingencies. Urgent problems and crises will not always occur one at a time at convenient moments. It is therefore desirable that national-security practices and procedures, however arranged over all, be capable of handling more than one matter of high priority at a time. Crises, by definition, strain any system. If they come in two's or three's, they can overload it.

THE BROAD CHOICES

From a President's point of view, probably that system is best which keeps him informed of present and prospective problems without overwhelming him with masses of information, which calls for him to deal personally only with the issues he must or wants to (when he should or wants to), and which disposes of the remainder efficiently and wisely. A number of schemes could be devised to serve these purposes, but experience suggests three broad patterns as the most feasible alternatives:

1. An arrangement in which the President and White House staff assume central initiative and active control of the national-security process, along with such direct extensions of the Presidential office as the Bureau of the Budget and the NSC staff

2. One which assigns primary responsibility to the secretary of state and the State Department and clearly affirms the secretary of state's responsibilities as the President's executive agent for directing the interdepartmental conduct of national-security affairs in Washington as well as overseas
3. An intermediate system which distributes the main functions among the White House, State, and other departments and agencies

Distinctions among these three systems cannot be made rigid. The most extreme variation of a plan to center responsibility in the State Department could not give that department final authority over the defense budget and a host of other military matters; a determined effort to centralize control in the White House would not relieve the State or Defense departments of some prime responsibilities for foreign or military policy, respectively; and, finally, a divided system, structured or loose, would never function as neatly as plans might call for.

It should be emphasized that these alternatives do not prejudice use of the National Security Council in any way and to any extent the President sees fit. Unlike most interdepartmental arrangements, the NSC has statutory status and could not be abolished without legislation, but it could be ignored if the President chose other ways of doing business. Or it could be revived and used more extensively than ever. The Council is often described as the highest authority in the national-security field, but it is in legal fact purely advisory to the President and can be adapted to any procedures or assignment of authority which he desires.

Its members by law are the President, the vice president, the secretary of state, the secretary of defense, and the director of the office of emergency preparedness. The director of Central Intelligence (who is also the director of the CIA) and the Joint Chiefs of Staff are statutory advisers to the NSC. The President can, of course, invite whomever he wishes to attend NSC meetings, either regularly or when a particular subject is under consideration. For example, during the Eisenhower Administration, the secretary of the treasury, the director of the Bureau of the Budget, and the chairman of the Atomic Energy Commission attended regularly.

Also, over the years, the practice has developed of having the chairman of the Joint Chiefs of Staff usually represent his colleagues at NSC meetings.

Ultimately, of course, any national-security system comes to a focus in the White House because of the President's over-all responsibility. The question is how closely he wants to hold active control and day-to-day responsibility in his own hands and those of his staff. A White House–centered system, of course, has advantages: It would assure the President direct communication and responsiveness from a personal staff accustomed to his style, familiar with his purposes, and endowed with Presidential rather than departmental perspectives and interests.

Proposals for enlarging the role of the White House have varied in conception, or at least in terminology. There have been suggestions for a Presidential deputy with such a title as first secretary of government or vice president for foreign affairs. There have been recommendations to institutionalize White House responsibility in something like an office of national security affairs, with a powerful Presidential mandate to oversee the planning and execution of policy, including directing the existing departments and agencies and arbitrating among them.

For the advantages of such centralized control, the President would pay a price. Inevitably, the arrangements implied would impose a layer of people between him and the heads of departments and agencies—at some cost in terms of initiative, sense of responsibility, and morale of the latter, as well as their direct feel for his needs. In theory, at least, none of these objections is fatal, but it should be clear that if this concept were followed, the organization and staffing required would be far larger and more elaborate than anything tried before. It might increase direct Presidential control, but it would not reduce Presidential burdens.

Many of the arguments against a White House–centered system are simply the obverse of arguments for a State Department–centered system. Under any system, the secretary and Department of State, as the President's agents for international relations, must necessarily be near the center of national-security affairs. Much could be done, however, to give the State Department a primacy often conferred on it in name, which has sometimes been enjoyed personally by secretaries of state but has never been fully realized by the department as an institution. The secretary (and under secretary) may and should enjoy the closest relationship with the President, but this has not, and probably would not, translate into effective leadership by the State Department as an institution without substantial reordering of the department in important respects. What are they?

Many observers inside and outside the State Department argue that it cannot hope to exert effective leadership in the national-security field without substantial strengthening of staff support for the top command and probably some other internal reorganization as well. Indeed, some of these steps would probably be salutary whether a State Department–centered system was desired or not, and, of course, the more authority and responsibility to be assigned to the department, the more important it would be to strengthen it. A renewed expression of Presidential intent to assign the State Department the primary role would be necessary but probably not in itself a sufficient precondition. It has been tried before with mixed results. To create the reality and to make it stick, certain organizational changes would be necessary.

Specific proposals and alternatives are assessed in Chapters VI and VII on the State Department. The principal recommendations include creating an under secretary for economic affairs and an officer of similar rank to serve as a general manager or chief of staff of the department in the interests of freeing the secretary and under secretary from operational burdens. Farther down the ladder, measures to strengthen the interagency authority and departmental staff support for both the top command and for the regional assistant secretaries would be important. Finally, much could be done to build on inherited instruments. One is the Senior Interdepartmental Group and the subordinate Interdepartmental Regional Groups (the SIG/IRG system). This arrangement has the advantage of having been designed to facilitate interdepartmental leadership by the State Department and of being a fairly new and pliable system, in operation long enough to show promise but not long enough to ossify. There are also less formal arrangements by which the State Department already exerts leadership in interagency deliberations on foreign policy. All of these (or adaptations) could be employed to give the State Department a more central role than before; in any case, many of them have proved their usefulness in practice and perhaps ought to be maintained and improved, whatever the system.

Since no conceivable arrangement is likely to be schematically pure, the third prototype—an intermediate or mixed system—may prove most realistic. More often than not, it has been the way things were done. The real question here is along what lines initiative and control might be divided among the White House, the State Department, and other institutions. Perhaps the most useful analytical distinction between functions is along the lines of resource allocation, policy planning, and the coordination and monitoring of operations.

There is substantial agreement among most observers that overall direction of *resource allocation* belongs primarily in the White House (and by extension, the Bureau of the Budget and perhaps other parts of the Executive Office of the President, including the National Security Council and its staff). The biggest allocation by far is for the defense budget, a question on which the State Department is scarcely equipped to have the last word, even though its views on the issue should obviously be given weight. There are, of course, resource-allocation issues of primary or at least considerable interest to the State Department. State should join with the Bureau of the Budget in reviewing the budget submissions of the principal civilian agencies operating overseas. Recent experimental efforts to develop a foreign-affairs planning, programing, and budgeting system should be continued, not because they will bring a magical solution to the problems or turn them successfully over to the computer but because it is useful to explore the extent to which the new disciplines involved in this approach may be of use.

The second major function—*coordination and monitoring of operations*—refers chiefly to overseas operations. There is a clear case for the State Department's primacy in this respect, unless one rejects the concept of the ambassador as head of the country team and the established leadership of the regional assistant secretaries in coordinating day-to-day operations in Washington. A number of ways for strengthening and improving this system are discussed in subsequent chapters on the Department of State, but the fundamentals of the approach appear sound.

The case is more moot with respect to the remaining major function—*policy planning.* Obviously, the planning of broad national policies, in this as in any field, must be sensitively responsive to the President's guidance; in theory, this might argue for assigning a high degree of White House control over the planning function. The President will, no doubt, take greater interest in some national-security questions than in others, either because he wants to or because he has to. And as a general proposition, the more a matter involves interdepartmental and interagency interests, the more the authority and perspective of the White House may be useful or necessary.

At the same time, national-security policy planning in depth is a time-consuming task. If centered in the White House, it would imply collecting more manpower and area expertise directly under White House control than has heretofore been thought desirable. It would also require positive action to alter present arrangements, which would weaken such primacy as the State Department now enjoys in this function through the Policy Planning Council, the SIG/IRG system, and a variety of less formal working arrangements.

The key questions concerning policy planning in an intermediate system are: How deeply into the planning effort does the President want to inject himself and the White House staff? How much and what kind of planning is appropriate for the State Department or interagency bodies led by the department? What assignments of authority and initiative are proper for the other principal departments and agencies?

The roles of these other institutions of course add further dimensions to any system. The secretary and the Department of Defense are of central importance, as are the Joint Chiefs of Staff, their chairman, and the director of Central Intelligence and the CIA. For many purposes, the secretary of the treasury and his department have, to some extent, critical interests and responsibilities, and the same is true of agriculture, commerce, and others. In terms of allocating money, of course, the problems of the Department of Defense are far and away the most important.

Major Issues in the Department of Defense

The Defense Department is vastly different from what it was ten years ago, both internally and in its relations with other departments and agencies. Most observers believe that the McNamara Revolution—notably its planning and budgetary innovations —was necessary if the secretary of defense was really to gain control of the department and that its essentials are here to stay. Other experts, who would not necessarily disagree with that proposition, nonetheless feel strongly that Secretary of Defense Robert McNamara and his staff went too far in downgrading professional military judgment, particularly the impact of systems analysis by civilians on critical issues of weapons and research and development.

These differing views have not given rise to serious controversy during the past several years of increasing defense budgets. However, if an end to the Vietnam War or other causes should lead to a period of decreasing defense appropriations, then improved coordination and communication between the office of the secretary and the Joint Chiefs of Staff would become more important than ever.

Probably the first thing about which the new President and his secretary of defense will want to satisfy themselves is that the administration is not deprived of needed military judgments from the professionals, and that, at the same time, there is no weakening of the secretary's control over the department, its budget, and similar critical matters. Certain modifications of present arrangements and encouragement of present trends in the Pentagon (discussed in Chapters VIII and IX on the Department of Defense), should prove useful in meeting this need. Essentially, they include the following propositions:

1. The new President and his secretary of defense may want to consider changes in Pentagon organization and procedures that

would integrate the professional military contribution more effectively into defense decision-making, including the budget cycle. The process of extending the writ of the secretary of defense over the department during the past ten years or so has necessarily given the secretary authority at some expense to the professional military—notably the service departments and the Joint Chiefs of Staff. Much of this was inevitable if the secretary of defense was to do his job. The process may have gone too far, and a case can be made for giving greater weight to advice from the military professionals for certain purposes.

2. Whatever the limitations on systems analysis as a discipline and an approach, the joint staff of the Joint Chiefs of Staff would probably benefit from some of its techniques and insights to improve its ability to prepare and defend its own positions. The joint staff, and the chiefs as a body, would also benefit from encouraging recent trends toward greater "openness" or lateral communication with civilian opposite numbers elsewhere in the executive branch.

3. The chain-of-command principle should not be so rigidly applied as to prevent the President from receiving "unfiltered" military advice when appropriate, and the growing use of the chairman as representative of the Joint Chiefs of Staff points to reliance on the chairman for this purpose.

WHAT KIND OF WHITE HOUSE NATIONAL-SECURITY STAFF?

The selection and assignments of the President's immediate staff for national security are, of course, peculiarly individual matters. From his point of view, discussion of the subject'may sound like gratuitous advice about personal preferences for office management. Yet, from the standpoint of the departments and agencies, the President's staff is a matter of central concern; in almost any system, much national-security business between the President and the rest of the government is bound to pass through the hands of this staff one way or another. The staff's responsibilities and size, how it operates and is organized, will be functions both of the President's personal style and of the broad scheme of national-security arrangements he chooses. In recent years, the staff has been a relatively small, action-oriented structure, having continuous but informal relations with the permanent departments and agencies. It is still called the NSC staff, but the fact is that in the Kennedy-Johnson period, support for the National Security Council as such occupied only part of the time of a few members.

The new President may settle on something more or something less as his White House national-security staff, but, unlike President John F. Kennedy, he inherits little by way of formal organizational structure to either dismantle or add to. He does, however, have the legacy that the bureaucracies are fairly well accustomed to dealing with the President through his staff for many purposes, and if this procedure has not always rested easy on them, it has provided a ready means of useful liaison in both directions.

Quite obviously, the more the President wishes to vest primary responsibility for national-security affairs in the departments and agencies, the less his need for immediate staff; and the more he desires active White House initiative and control, the larger his staffing requirements will be. And the mix, of course, will also be a matter of what kinds of national-security functions or responsibilities he wishes to delegate and what he does not. The variations are assessed in detail in later chapters on the White House and NSC staffs. To summarize the essentials:

1. At a minimum, the President's staff should be responsible for maintaining an orderly flow of information and action papers to and from the President and for conducting liaison with departments and agencies. This function is not routine paper shuffling. In the very process of deciding whether to send the President a departmental memorandum today or delay it, to endorse it or say something else about it, the White House staff can exercise formidable influence.

2. Beyond the minimum of secretariat-type functions, the President would probably find even a limited staff useful for occasionally reaching out or down into the process to bring Presidential interests and perspectives to bear on selected issues, either well before they reach the top or after they have received Presidential attention and require special followup and monitoring. (The latter function is discussed separately in the final paragraphs of this chapter.)

Over and above these minimal functions, White House or NSC staffing depends on over-all national-security arrangements and is treated in appropriate chapters of this study. There is, however, one area, related both to White House perspectives and to the over-all national-security process which merits separate consideration—intelligence.

THE PRESIDENT AND INTELLIGENCE

At any given time, the President may be sure that a vast volume of information is headed straight his way from many sources, and he will want it to sustain him without inundating him. He can most easily adjust the flow by reliance on his immediate assistants and on his principal intelligence officer, the director of Central Intelligence (DCI). By statute and practice, the director has a dual function as head of the Central Intelligence Agency and the President's chief intelligence adviser. In the latter capacity, he chairs the U.S. Intelligence Board (USIB); this board is composed of the chief intelligence officers of the State and Defense departments, the deputy director of Central Intelligence, the director of the National Security Agency, and the intelligence chiefs of the FBI and the Atomic Energy Commission. The heads of the army, navy, and air force intelligence components sit as observers and have the right of dissent. As chairman of the USIB, the director is responsible for coordinating the efforts of the intelligence community.

The director of Central Intelligence is an appointee of the President and serves at his pleasure. Over the past twenty years, different incumbents have carried out their functions in somewhat different ways and have varied with Presidential needs or desires. Some have given greater emphasis to presiding over the intelligence community and others to running the CIA. Some have permitted themselves greater latitude than others with respect to the distinction between intelligence and policy advice. By all testimony, the present director is rigorous in observing this distinction and in confining his role to that of intelligence adviser.

Probably no President is going to rely exclusively on official channels of information, but, within the official system, he may wish to hear more or fewer voices. President Eisenhower relied on a fairly tight system of coordination; the flow of intelligence came through channels in a highly coordinated way. He also attached great importance to regular systematic intelligence briefings, both for himself and for the National Security Council. Presidents Kennedy and Johnson both tended to reach out, or down, for information on their own, sometimes bypassing the central system. This practice has attractions and risks. The advantages derive from contact with intelligence near the source and from exposure to a variety of views. The dangers are those of getting flooded with hot news, unscreened by expert analysis, and of permitting the immediate to crowd out important but less obviously relevant matters. An absence of system can also invite confusion if the President and other officials act on the basis of different information.

Most observers believe that the intelligence community now works well and that it has improved over the years, with the maturing of career professionalism and sophisticated techniques. Overall, most of those interviewed consider the intelligence community capable of flexible adaptation to requirements imposed on it by the President or others on his top team. One important consideration is that the President make known what he wants from intelligence, both at the outset and through a continuing process of feedback. Presidents have done this in recent years in various ways (one was the regular attendance of the director of Central Intelligence at President Johnson's Tuesday lunches), including continuous, often informal exchanges between the director and the special assistant for national-security affairs. Presidential supervision of the intelligence effort is reinforced by institutions such as the President's Board of Advisers on Foreign Intelligence and a special committee that has been chaired by the President's special assistant for national-security affairs and oversees a number of designated matters in the intelligence field.

STRUCTURE VERSUS INFORMALITY

There is no inevitable correlation between the formality of the structure and the extent to which the system formulates policy guidance comprehensively or otherwise. But experience suggests that the more elaborate it is, the more the system favors comprehensive policy codification; the less structured it is, the more it tends toward *ad hoc* policy guidance.

Arguments for and against each approach involve trade-offs between two sets of values—each good in itself. On the one hand, systematic propagation of policy—in written form—can help the President and his top advisers control the bureaucracies and assure common understanding of goals and programs. This approach may be more useful in the early part of a new administration than later. Furthermore, the process of formulating and examining policy will often be of more help than the documentary products, because the process itself involves some healthy educational and analytic discipline. It forces those involved to define and think through issues; it smokes out differences of view or of interest between departments or agencies; and it provides a body of explicit, agreed doctrine, which large bureaucracies by nature need. This need is not limited to tidy-minded bureaucrats at lower echelons; Winston Churchill recorded that one of his first acts as Prime Minister was to instruct that his decisions be promulgated in writing and that this seemingly simple step, not always practiced before, had a salutary effect.

For the benefits of codification, there is a price. Formalized procedures, particularly elaborate compilations of policy guidance, can easily reduce a President's flexibility of action and foreclose his options prematurely. A President sometimes will not want to decide policy matters in advance; ambiguity can be useful or necessary to him for external or domestic reasons, or both. There is also the danger of routinization; organizations and systems sometimes lose vitality and a sense of purpose in the very process of perfecting smooth machinery. This is not serious where problems are routine or repetitious, but that is seldom the case in questions of national security—and certainly not for issues demanding Presidential attention.

How strike the balance? Formality has been defended for avoiding confusion and criticized for ponderously producing generalities too abstract for practical use. Informality has been urged for its flexibility and derided as producing confusion and making it difficult to know where the action is or why, even for those with a need to know.

There is probably some truth in each set of criticisms, as there is in the rebuttals. The first rebuttal is that each approach was what the people responsible wanted and that this alone is sufficient justification. The second is that the charges are exaggerated: President Eisenhower's system involved more flexibility than appears from NSC organization charts, and both Presidents Kennedy and Johnson used the substance of the NSC machinery even though they tended to avoid the terminology. Finally, there is the matter of different environments. The 1950's were chiefly a time of Cold War confrontation with the Soviet Union; in the 1960's, the Cold War continued but became more complex, and a number of other crises came to a head as well. A new environment called for different procedures, and so, probably, will the 1970's. Nonetheless, there is a substantial consensus among informants from each of the past three administrations that the President's own interests, as well as the national interest, would benefit from somewhat more systematic procedures in policy making and guidance in the national-security field. To be specific, the following criteria emerge from inquiries on the issue:

1. A President intent both on controlling the bureaucracy and benefiting fully from its professional skills will probably want to use *both* institutionalized and informal ways of accomplishing this. Neither approach alone would do what has to be done.

2. So far as remedial measures can be suggested in advance, they lie chiefly in tightening up institutional procedures; others will spring from the President's personal interests and style.

3. Procedures should observe three general principles, not easily made compatible: They should channel major policy questions, adequately staffed, to the President; they should direct most operational matters elsewhere; and they should provide opportunity for the President himself (at least through his staff) to keep aware of what is going on and to intervene on any matter, at any time, before it gathers a momentum of its own.

4. There is a desirable middle course between codifying all policy guidance and codifying none of it. To attempt the former would almost guarantee routinization and overload the system with secondary considerations. To settle for the latter would invite confusion and burden the President needlessly. The key to the middle course is selectivity, determined by certain test questions.

a. Is the matter of truly national importance?
b. Does it involve the interests and responsibilities of several departments and agencies?
c. Does it, by nature, lend itself to (or require) advance planning and policy lead time, or is it a bridge to be crossed only on arrival?
d. Is it a matter already well and satisfactorily understood in the government? (If it is, codification would be extraneous.)
e. Does it involve reassessment or redirection of standing policies? If so, explicit codification is more useful than in cases where policy is already clearly known. This factor may be more important early in an administration than later.
f. Is it a matter on which U.S. policy can have an effect or should try to have an effect? Some matters are beyond our influence, and pronouncements on them are not policy but statements of aspiration or attitude not requiring codification.

ASSURING PERFORMANCE

Ideally, there should be no need for concern about whether Presidential policy is carried out and continues to be carried out. Nevertheless, every President since Franklin D. Roosevelt has expressed his frustration at finding that this is often not so and that he needs some means of following up or monitoring to assure sustained performance. Similar observations were made by many of the men interviewed in the course of this inquiry. In the real world, any sharp distinction between planning and performance is necessarily somewhat artificial, because the same problems and (to some extent) the same people are necessarily involved in a continuing process. To a considerable degree, monitoring is part of the continuing responsibility of anyone involved in operations. It is also a cyclical process, as monitoring may lead to reassessment of earlier decisions in the light of success or failure. But as a need of successive Presidents and many of their advisers, the monitoring function deserves separate attention.

In the heyday of the NSC's full structure, monitoring was the particular province of the Operations Coordinating Board (OCB), established early in President Eisenhower's Administration and summarily abolished early in President Kennedy's. Most of those who served on the board or knew it well consider it the least satisfactory part of the NSC system, as did President Eisenhower himself. The burden of criticism is that it soon degenerated into a paper mill, into which the departments and agencies fed self-serving reports showing that they were doing what they were paid to do and designed to demonstrate that this constituted progress toward agreed-upon national-security goals. A kind of logrolling developed, which was incompatible with clear assignments of responsibility and crisp assessment of interagency differences.

The Kennedy treatment was swift amputation of the Operations Coordinating Board *in toto*. This was coupled with a mandate to the White House staff to monitor such national-security questions as necessary to keep the President informed and a reminder that most of the work was expected to be done, and that expeditiously, by the departments and agencies. This new, free-swinging style, with variations, prevailed throughout the Kennedy-Johnson years. Under it, the President's needs for followup and monitoring were met in various ways with varying effects. Presidents Kennedy and Johnson did some of it themselves, no doubt at the cost of considerable personal expenditure of time and energy; both delegated some of it to a few highly trusted subordinates.

Recognizing that planners and operators are not always the best critics of plans and operations, the President may wish to effect new arrangements for this function—to relieve himself of some burdens and to do so without undermining his control of the matters important to him. Whatever the arrangements, one essential feature is to fix continuing responsibility clearly on either particular individuals or institutions. The operating departments and agencies will necessarily do much of the job as part of their regular functions. If additional arrangements are established, those given primary responsibility should be close enough to the President to know his perspectives, should have a clear Presidential mandate to assure their authority, should enjoy sufficient detachment from departmental interests to overcome logrolling and protective tendencies, and should possess sufficient self-restraint to avoid undue interference in what properly belongs to the departments and agencies.

Some of this job could be done by an individual close to the President or by people of adequate stature and energy on the White House national-security staff. Or it could be assigned to existing institutions, subject to the qualifications just mentioned. It may be that no one department could or should want to accept responsibility for monitoring other agencies on such a broad basis. (Certainly if the job were vigorously discharged, the opportunities for making bureaucratic enemies would be ample.) In any case, even if primary responsibility is not centered in the White House, there is no substitute for giving members of the President's own staff a direct and active role—if only as his eyes and ears.

III

Future Domestic and International Influences

Some eras have been notable for calm and continuity, but not ours. Far-reaching change in our national life and international environment has become more the rule than the exception. Even if domestic and international politics were to stand still, which they never do, technology and economics are working irresistible alterations, which cannot be ignored. In these circumstances, one can assess the future with great apprehension or with high hope. Probably the best course is to accept that we face both threats and opportunities and must guard against the one and make the most of the other.

As a study of national-security procedures, this is not an inquiry into the whole range of our foreign and domestic affairs. If the present chapter dwells chiefly on problems and dangers, the emphasis is deliberate. The essential concern of national-security policy is to guard against threats and to manage risks. Those we face in the coming years may grow or diminish in various ways, but they will not disappear. There will also be opportunities arising from new technology and any number of political possibilities, and these have not been entirely ignored. But unless the term "national security" is stretched beyond all useful meaning, it must be accepted as primarily related to the defense and safety of the United States at home and abroad, not to every concern of the U.S. Government. This limitation has been observed in what follows.

NATIONAL PURPOSES AND INTERESTS

The most general objectives of the United States change little, if at all. They are to assure the survival and the well being of our

31

own society and to do it without sacrificing those values which underlie and must in the long run guide our national and international policies. But if these broad purposes remain constant, two kinds of change go on apace: One is in the world environment —the international context in which America must play its role; the other is in our national attitudes—official and public—about what we can do, must do, or should do at home and abroad. Both, of course, interact all the time, and the interaction is central to the never-ending process of deciding how our national-security interests are to be protected and promoted.

The concept of national security rests on the proposition that most foreign and military affairs, and some major domestic matters, are bound up, each with implications for the others. Prior to World War II, there was a prevailing assumption that the country was either at peace or at war and that this distinction called for a compartmentalizing of responsibilities within the government as between civil and military affairs and domestic and foreign matters. World War II and U.S. assumption of a global role ended the sharp distinction. In the modern world, political, military, economic, and technological considerations all affect each other closely, and a major power can only ignore the fact at its own risk. Moreover, twenty years of the Cold War and the Korean and Vietnam conflicts have demonstrated that in the nuclear age our most pressing national-security problems consist less of sharp choices between war and peace than in making fine adjustments in ambiguous areas between. The nation is still learning what it means to fight limited war, where the stakes are not clear cut, the objectives are something less than classical military victory, and public support is less than overwhelming.

The Vietnam experience will condition American attitudes for a long time, whatever its ultimate outcome. It will do so in contradictory ways. In some quarters—not confined to the irresponsible fringe—there will be strong skepticism about any U.S. commitments which carry risk of even limited military involvement. Others will draw different lessons, arguing that Vietnam shows the need to be better prepared than ever to bring power quickly and decisively to bear against threats to peace, stability, our friends, or our interests. Many will be influenced both ways and will feel not only that we ought to be more selective about commitments but also that power should be used more decisively if and when we do use it. The middle view may contain contradictions, but contradictions have been characteristic of the Vietnam experience.

National-security policy is thus likely to be the subject of continuing and searching debate. People who believe that needless restraint prevented success in Vietnam and people who believe that the whole venture was mistaken to begin with are not likely to reconcile their differences easily or early. Crosscurrents of sentiment will flow in both public and official opinion on those questions. Decisions about future situations resembling Vietnam in any way will have to be made against a background of these sentiments. The kind of national consensus that prevailed in the 1950's about what threatened us and how we should meet threats may prove harder to realize in the future.

Our complex of urban ills, racial tensions, protests against poverty, and the generation gap would probably have developed if the Vietnam War had never occurred, but the unpopularity of the war has intensified these problems and linked domestic dissensions with opposition to some established foreign policies and assumptions about national interests. Slogans about getting our own house in order and not trying to police the world contain implicit challenges to some long-standing attitudes about our international interests.

In these circumstances, questions of whether U.S. power should or can prevent or contain trouble in certain cases may loom larger than before. Evaluation of national interests and the limits of power may come under increasingly searching scrutiny. Some interests, once defined almost unquestioningly as vital, may be demoted to important; some, which were once considered important, may be downgraded to preferable; some may be ranked as marginal. This trend is not necessarily retrogression or a retreat from reality; within limits, it may prove a mark of greater maturity. But for good or for ill, such self-questioning seems likely to be a more important constraint in national-security policy than heretofore.

There will also be more tangible constraints. The urgency of domestic demands as a political matter has been mentioned. In addition, the balance-of-payments problem loomed larger in the 1960's than before and came more and more to condition decisions about what the nation was or was not prepared to do abroad. It will doubtless remain an important constraint. The pinch might be eased but would not be solved by an end to the Vietnam War and by other measures to economize abroad. In short, the problem of measuring the financial costs of the U.S. national-security commitments against domestic calls on resources will probably become more difficult in the years ahead.

The trend is already apparent in U.S. foreign-aid policy. The past few years have seen the Congress less and less hospitable to the program—both in its economic and military aspects—and more inclined to cut the costs involved. Perhaps this change was inevitable, given tighter economic constraints and competition for resources, the decline of Cold War bipolarity, and cumulative disillusion or skepticism about the results and advantages of foreign aid. Inevitable or not, the trend undercuts one instrument of U.S. foreign policy that has been very important for two decades. It will no doubt bring some diminution of U.S. influence with recipient countries, although much experience suggests that economic and military aid do not automatically translate into political influence, and the political effects of a reduction may prove less than might be expected. Nonetheless, any substantial cut would lend credence to the thesis that the United States was withdrawing from world responsibilities. These effects would be mitigated but not entirely offset by a policy of greater support for and reliance on international institutions and arrangements for assistance to underdeveloped countries.

A reduction in U.S. aid programs would not affect Europe and Japan economically but would tend to weaken U.S. efforts to encourage participation by European governments and the Japanese in programs of assistance to the less-developed areas. What would have a direct and critical effect on U.S. relations with the industrialized nations would be any indications that the United States was moving back to protectionism in trade policies. There is already some apprehension about this in Western Europe and Japan, and any changes in U.S. policy that lent substance to these fears would be taken as evidence that the United States was abdicating responsibilities and objectives which it has pursued, and urged others to pursue, for a quarter-century. The United States would pay some political price if this took place.

THE INTERNATIONAL SCENE

No short formula serves to describe the pattern of international developments ahead—even those which now seem reasonably predictable. It is a truism to observe that the bipolar world of the 1950's has given way to one in which international problems are more complex, and many of the old postulates no longer serve as realistic bases for analysis and action. Nothing unifies like a clear and unambiguous external danger, and not many years ago the monolithic power of international Communism had just such an impact on U.S. and general Western policy. Communism is still a threat but a more complicated one—in some respects greater and in other respects less than it appeared to be ten years ago. A divided Communist world does not mean an impotent or pacific one.

The Role of the Soviet Union

The Soviet Union presents the spectacle of an imperial power seeking with some success to expand its influence in some parts of the world while trying with mixed results to prevent dissolution of the empire closer to home. The invasion of Czechoslovakia was a brutally efficient move of military aggression. It was also, from Moscow's point of view, a politically defensive act, born of fears that liberal and nationalist trends in Czechoslovakia and elsewhere in Eastern Europe threatened Soviet hegemony there, if not the system in Russia itself. Having seen the left wing of international Communism turn hostile through the Sino–Soviet split, the Russian leaders apparently decided that drastic action was required to prevent erosion of their right flank, and they took it.

The Russians have flexed their military muscles impressively over Czechoslovakia and demonstrated a degree of toughness which may inhibit or even reverse the East European trends they feared. In doing so, they have paid no small price—at home, in the Communist world, and elsewhere. The process clearly produced—or reflected—divisions within the Soviet leadership, increased the dislike of the regime among the intelligentsia within Russia and Eastern Europe, and split the Western European Communist parties like nothing since the Nazi–Soviet treaty of 1939. It has also had some reviving and reunifying effect within the Western alliance, as it has seemed to slow if not reverse disintegrating trends within the North Atlantic Treaty Organization (NATO). Finally, it produced reaffirmations of the U.S. commitment to Western Europe's defense.

Whatever the long-term result of the invasion of Czechoslovakia and trends within the Communist world, the U.S.–Soviet military equation remains a central issue of our national security, because the Soviet Union is the only power able to threaten our national survival and is increasing its military capabilities through augmented missile forces on land and in submarines. The rapid growth of Soviet strategic forces probably dates from decisions taken after the Cuban missile crisis of 1962, a confrontation that led many to conclude that the United States enjoyed effective superiority over the Soviet Union. This belief may have served us and our allies in the years since, but what has comforted us must have done the reverse for the Soviet leaders. From their viewpoint, to invest billions for strategic forces and end up not only inferior but widely *considered* to be inferior could hardly make either strategic or economic sense. Some such calculations must have figured in the decisions that led to the expansion of Soviet strategic offensive forces over the past few years.

We do not know how far the Soviet programs will go nor what the ultimate political and military effects will be on the over-all strategic relation between the United States and the Soviet Union. Obviously, the Russians have domestic economic constraints and calls on their resources that constitute inducements for avoiding an indefinite strategic-arms race with the United States. Some Soviet military thinkers have registered awareness of the futility of over-kill and unfeasibility of achieving a reliable "first strike" capability. Obviously, too, what the United States does, on its own or in response to Soviet programs, constitutes part of the equation and will affect Soviet calculations. The sincerity of their willingness to discuss arms-limitation agreements may be open to question, but it should not be dismissed out of hand. Preoccupation with only worst-case possibilities could serve to prevent mutual steps in directions serving the real interests of both sides.

The Soviet Union is not only bent on strengthening its strategic attack and defense forces vis-à-vis the United States and NATO but it is also developing means to apply other forms of military power in areas heretofore beyond its reach. Soviet general-purpose forces, particularly their long-deficient sealift and airlift capabilities, are being improved. New military-transport aircraft and helicopter carriers will enter service within the next few years and will provide the Soviet Union with a capability for distant action it has not previously had. The increased Soviet naval presence in the Mediterranean, negligible in the mid-1960's, demonstrates support for the Soviet Union's friends in the Arab world and generally underlines the Soviet role as a great power in the region; these forces are not likely to be withdrawn and may very well be augmented. Thus, the monopoly of naval power that the U.S. Fleet once enjoyed in the Mediterranean has been ended. This is one of several factors pointing to the Middle East as a notable source of future troubles and tensions, a subject discussed more fully below. Here, it is sufficient to say that, with improved Soviet distant-action capabilities, outbreaks of trouble in such areas could lead to some form of actual or threatened military intervention by the Russians before the United States decides whether it should employ force. Such a contingency has not previously occurred except near the Soviet homeland, but it is becoming a more realistic possibility than it once was.

All this is not to say that the United States faces an infinite series of military confrontations with Soviet forces around the globe. It does mean that a number of new options may open up for the Russians. The result need not be all bad for international peace and order; involvement in remote, troubled areas could even bring with it an accompanying sense of caution to the Soviet leaders (they did, for example, in 1968, counsel caution to Arab militants who would renew war with Israel, and they took new initiatives in seeking U.S. cooperation to move the Arab–Israeli controversy toward some kind of settlement), but Soviet involvement may also do the reverse. In any event, one result will probably be a compounding of the risks and a sharpening of the dilemmas facing both the United States and the Soviet Union, as and when local conflicts threaten to break out between their respective friends or clients.

The chief constraint on both the superpowers in such local conflicts is a mutual apprehension that confrontation might escalate to general or nuclear war. This constraint will probably continue indefinitely; it helps to preserve peace between the superpowers, but it does not guarantee it. The system is neither foolproof nor failsafe. Both powers have learned the painful lesson that a small state's dependence on a great one for military, economic, and political support does not always give the larger power commensurate influence over the lesser. A proliferation of independent power centers among states of second, third, or fourth rank may even be healthy in the long run, but it would pose some new problems for both the superpowers. In some respects, these would be greater for the United States than for the Soviet Union, because we have more commitments.

In time, this trend may increase the incentives for the United States and the Soviet Union to achieve *détente*. In addition to the advantages of toning down the Cold War and trying to avoid an arms race, an accommodation might also serve to limit both the expense of supporting lesser allies and the risks of confrontation arising from conflicts between the latter. Such a *détente* would be greeted with mixed feelings by other states, including some of our allies, who would fear that a deal between the superpowers was being made behind their backs and possibly against their interests. It would, nevertheless, simplify life for the superpowers and perhaps help eliminate one of the most critical kinds of threat to general peace.

Obviously, the chances of a U.S.–Soviet *détente* depend not only on our policies but also on those of the Soviet leaders. Movement toward accommodation can easily be vetoed or terminated by either side, but it takes two to ease tensions. Any *détente* with the Russians, if it occurs at all, is going to proceed from calculations of advantage by both sides and not from sentiment or ideological compatibility. In their over-all foreign policy, the Soviet leaders are reasonably prudent if not always predictable. They have shown a disposition to limit tensions, despite the Vietnam War and cease-less charges from the Chinese that they are soft on the United States. Until Czechoslovakia, they felt compelled to accept a very substantial loosening of Russian control over Eastern Europe, and, despite Czechoslovakia, they may have to accept even more. At home, the collective leadership has scarcely demonstrated efficiency in running the society or the economy, but it has shown some degree of responsiveness to domestic demands for better living standards. As the Soviet economy becomes more sophisticated and as the people become more educated, more aware of the outside world, and more interested in the good life, these demands are likely to be more insistent. Western observers, and some Soviet citizens as well, increasingly emphasize the alienation of Soviet intellectuals, technocrats, and economic managers from the party ideologues and suggest that the latter are becoming less relevant and in time may therefore become less powerful.

A return to Stalinism in the Soviet Union may not be likely, but it is not inconceivable. Processes for the transfer of power in the Soviet Union are uncertain and unpredictable; in view of the age and ill health of the present top leadership, the early 1970's are likely to bring important changes in its makeup, with effects now unpredictable. Long-range trends in Soviet society offer some grounds for optimism, but such trends are neither irresistible nor automatic in their effects, at least in relation to Soviet policies affecting U.S. security. They certainly are no guarantee of improve-ment in the early 1970's. There could indeed be a continuing, internal liberalization of Soviet society, which would have little effect on Russia's foreign and military policies or which might even be accompanied by a tougher posture in these respects. Periodic Russian expansionist tendencies were a fact of history long before Communism was.

The Far East

Even after the Vietnam War ends, the Far East promises to be a major source of U.S. national-security problems, and it is likely to compel some difficult policy decisions. The biggest question mark in the long run is, of course, China, whose leaders are locked in a struggle over ideology, power, and policy, the outcome of which defies confident prediction. At best, China will always be a major concern for U.S. foreign policy; at worst, it may become a growing threat—initially to our friends and interests in Asia, eventually nearer to home. Certainly its present leaders are working hard to achieve the latter capability with their nuclear program. There are, of course, very severe limits on U.S. ability to affect the course of events in China, and the United States has little choice but to work for the best and be prepared for the worst. Our assertions of readiness to establish good relations with Peking have had little effect so far and may never have, but it does little harm to keep the offer open. Mao cannot last forever, and his successors may be quite different—though we cannot yet know. In the event of some U.S. *détente* with China, one effect might be to exacerbate tensions with the Soviet Union, just as the reverse could be true. It is hard to conceive of successfully improving relations with both.

Meanwhile, it is important to keep the Chinese convinced that the United States would resist their encroachments against its own interests and against those independent Asian states which rely on U.S. power for their security. Yet it is also important to do this without unduly contributing to Chinese beliefs that the United States is implacably hostile to China. The outcome of the Vietnam War will of course affect the calculations of the Chinese, as well as of other Asians, concerning the U.S. role in the area. The Chinese have customarily talked tough and acted with caution; one major reason, no doubt, is their fear of U.S. strategic power, because China's massive land armies, formidable as they may be for certain purposes, offer little hope for protection against U.S. strategic force. It will probably be years before China achieves significant intercontinental strategic capabilities, and it will be a long time, if ever, before it comes near to matching those of the United States or the Soviet Union. But the Chinese need not match U.S. or Soviet strategic capabilities to get mileage out of their nuclear potential. To exploit Asian fears of China's nuclear capability does not require 1,000 ICBM's. Meanwhile, Communist China remains an inwardly troubled, isolated, and dogmatically hostile state. One must hope that eventually China can become a responsible member of the world community, but right now it is difficult to see how or when.

There may be some comfort in the fact that China is at least as troublesome to the Soviet Union as to the United States. So long as the Sino–Soviet split continues—and it is unlikely to end at any early date, if ever—the Russians may find their interests corresponding to those of the United States in some respects; we both, for example, have supported India against China. A termination of the Vietnam War would remove one obstacle to this kind of parallelism, but, barring a more drastic change in Soviet policies than now seems likely in the next few years, any mutuality of U.S. and Soviet interests in containing China would probably have to be indirect and tacit.

The relations with the United States of the non-Communist states around China's periphery vary widely. There is a comparatively healthy sense of partnership in Japan, South Korea, and Thailand, a kind of sullen dependence felt by the Nationalist Chinese, the erratic ambivalence of Sihanouk in Cambodia, and a largely unspoken awareness by the governments of India, Pakistan, and Burma that U.S. power is needed in the area. Whatever their public pronouncements, none would contemplate a withdrawal of U.S. power from the Far East without lively apprehension over their vulnerability to Chinese power.

This is not to say that the United States can expect open gratitude if it continues to assume a major security responsibility in the Far East. Whatever they say publicly about Vietnam, most pro-West and even neutralist government leaders in the area are less distressed over the fact of U.S. intervention than over its failure to produce decisive results. The kind of militant moral opposition to the Vietnam War that runs strong in Europe and in many quarters in the United States is less noticeable among non-Communist Asians, who feel the threat of Communist expansionism close to home, whether in the form of subversion and insurgency, the potential of China's massive armies, or the coming threat of its advanced-weapons program. Anything in the nature of a clear Communist success in Vietnam would increase their fears that the United States, its fingers burned, was pulling back from the area and preparing to cut its commitments.

One of our main problems in the Far East will be how to accept the responsibilities that our interests demand and yet avoid shouldering more of the burden than we should or successfully can take on. It is part of the price of U.S. military and economic strength that other nations are too willing to let the United States do most of the job. This has been a lesson of the Vietnam War. Because similar tendencies have been reflected in the defense appropriations of our European allies for many years, it is hardly surprising that our Asian allies do the same. To encourage some of them to accept greater responsibilities will be no easy task.

Our Far Eastern position is not, of course, purely a matter of defense and security commitments. The non-Communist states of the region have lives of their own, interests of their own, and some have particular strengths of their own. This is most notably true of Japan, whose phenomenal economic growth in the past twenty years places it third among 'he great industrial nations of the world. It has consistently avoided the kind of military role that might be considered commensurate with this status, preferring to rely on the U.S. defense commitment and for the most part to concentrate on trade rather than politics in the Far East. Popular Japanese opposition to assuming a military role remains strong, but the price—clear dependence on the United States—is also not entirely compatible with Japanese national self-respect. The Japanese Government, sensitive to this contradiction, may move in time to develop a military potential and assume greater security responsibilities, but it will be an uphill task in view of public sentiment in Japan and a national preoccupation with economic and commercial pursuits rather than participation in security affairs. Thus, a significant role of this sort for Japan is probably years away, desirable as it might be for U.S. interests to have Japan assume it. Meanwhile, Japan has begun to play a useful part in regional economic development and political cooperation among non-Communist Asian states—a salutary trend for U.S. interests and for stability in the Far East.

Western Europe and Canada

The historic success of the Western alliance in giving Western Europe security and the unprecedented economic progress of the

Western European states owe much to U.S. assistance and strength. This does not mean, however, that U.S. policies with respect to Europe, which have worked well in the past, are all viable and relevant for the future. After twenty years, NATO is far from dead, but it is hardly in good health. Many Europeans have long been convinced that the Soviet threat to Europe is not serious, and, although Czechoslovakia led to some second thoughts on this score, Western Europe's concern for its defense can hardly be described as urgent. Indeed, many Europeans are less worried about the Soviet Union than about what they view as excessive U.S. power deriving from U.S. economic and technological influence in European economies. These sentiments are not confined to President Charles de Gaule or the Marxists.

For Americans accustomed to a leading U.S. role in Western Europe, such attitudes may be difficult to accept, but they represent a major fact of European political life, one not likely to disappear. Whether Europe moves toward greater political integration —a stronger possibility once de Gaulle goes than it is now—or abandons the effort except perhaps in the fields of economic and technological cooperation, a general European impulse to assert independence is probably with us to stay. There can be many variations on this theme, but almost all of them imply readjustments of one kind or another in the political relations and security arrangements between the United States and the Western European states—individually and collectively.

Meanwhile, however one assesses the Soviet threat to Western Europe, one danger point stands out as deserving special attention —the German problem, generally, and Berlin, in particular. If there ever were grounds for equanimity concerning the troublesome potential of Berlin and the two Germanys, they have been dispelled in the wake of Soviet behavior in Czechoslovakia. In the case of Berlin, an overt Communist grab still appears unlikely, but salami tactics,[1] pressures below the kind of threshold which would clearly stimulate a vigorous Western response, may prove a very real problem.

Attitudes in Europe have altered in other ways important to our

[1] "Salami tactics" is a term used to describe the achievement of one's objectives by small steps, as in cutting up a salami one slice at a time.

security interests. The time has all but passed when the United States could count on significant military help from its European allies in any effort to cope with trouble in areas once dominated by European imperial power. The end of the French, British, Dutch, and Belgian empires has put an end to the willingness and ability of the former metropolises to accept responsibility for peace and order in former colonial areas. They are eager to do business with the new states, they are willing to extend a certain amount of economic and military aid, and they still enjoy and occasionally exert some residual political influence there. They are, however, largely unprepared to incur the price or risks of forceful action to avert or to cope with threats to peace in these regions.

A different kind of trend is evident in Canada, whose new government is reassessing the international role Canada has played for two decades. Whatever its final decisions, the net effect is likely to be in the direction of some reduction in Canada's commitment to European defense and some greater assertiveness of an independent Canadian voice in world affairs.

The United States has customarily sought to act in cooperation with its major allies when considering action in situations of this sort, but the possibilities of securing such cooperation are much diminished. The result is likely to sharpen our dilemmas, because it may be assumed that conflict will break out in these volatile and unstable areas, i.e., insurgent and factional conflict within states as well as local wars between them, sometimes with Communist or other support unfriendly to U.S. interests. In such circumstances, the United States will have to decide whether to take unilateral action, to rely on U.N. efforts (an often useful course but one that, to be effective, normally requires the cooperation or acquiescence of the Russians), or to stand aside. If it is decided that U.S. interests or questions of peace and security require some form of U.S. intervention, it is probably going to be more difficult than before to enlist active help from our Western allies.

The Middle East

The long-standing problems of the Middle East offer little hope of early solution, and some new ones will probably appear. The area is of particular importance because it is the scene and target of sustained Russian efforts to expand the Soviet Union's influence and weaken that of the West. The Soviet Union has been particularly successful with the radical Arab nationalists controlling Egypt and Syria. The struggle between radical and conservative Arabs, dampened in the wake of the June, 1967, war with Israel, is almost certain eventually to break out again. The Arab–Israeli conflict is hardly close to solution, despite Israel's smashing victory and Soviet overtures to the United States to join in imposing a peace, under great-power sponsorship. The 1967 war has speeded polarization in the Middle East—heretofore resisted with some success by the United States—with the Russians championing the Arabs, while the United States is more and more looked on as Israel's backer.

United States influence with the moderate Arab states will be more difficult to maintain. These states control Arab oil. Mutual interest in selling and buying oil, as well as the desire of Iran and the moderate Arabs for U.S. support, may help preserve our influence, but the outlook is not bright. And in any future conflicts, whether between Arabs and Israelis or between moderate and radical Arabs, the Russians may play a more active role than before. They probably will want to avoid direct military intervention if this risks direct confrontation with the United States, but their presence in the area is expanding, Arab dependence on them is increasing, and their capabilities for employing force in the area are growing. Certainly the Soviet Union's naval force in the Mediterranean, whatever its real capabilities, has its political effects on all states in the area. The Soviet Union is presumably not anxious to incur the risks of another Arab–Israeli war, but there can be no assurance that its influence will in all circumstances be decisive in this respect nor that it would play quite such a passive role as it did in 1967 if Arab–Israeli hostilities broke out again.

The Persian Gulf is one area of the Middle East which has been largely tranquil but promises to be far less so in the future. British withdrawal from the region will create a kind of vacuum, and local nationalists, backed by Arab governments elsewhere, will probably begin campaigns against the traditional local rulers well before the

British depart, seeking to gain credit for speeding the process—as happened in Aden and South Arabia. Efforts by local rulers to create a federation and build security forces may have some success, but similar attempts after British withdrawal from other areas do not suggest that their chances are great. The Russians—working directly or, more probably, with radical Arab forces on the spot or in Cairo, Damascus, and Baghdad—are not likely to ignore this chance to bid for influence. In such circumstances, the United States would have to decide whether to counter these efforts, and if so, how—whether to throw its weight on the side of incumbent regimes of uncertain viability, to try to accommodate to nationalist forces claiming to represent reform and modernization but more or less antipathetic to the West, or simply to let events take their course.

The Particular Problem of Latin America

Geography, history, and economics combine to make Latin America a special problem for U.S. national-security policies. What happens in this area often affects us more quickly and directly than more remote events, and, like it or not, the United States and Latin America can scarcely avoid a kind of close embrace, conditioned though it may be by ambivalent attitudes on both sides.

This brief survey can hardly attempt even summary treatment of Latin America's political, social, and economic problems. Nevertheless, it is important to note that the states of this area, disparate as they are, share in one degree or another most of the problems common to other underdeveloped areas—poverty, growing over-population, dependence on one or two crops or mineral products for foreign exchange, political extremism of both left and right, and a shortage of the time, capital, organization, and skills required for the process of modernization. With a few notable exceptions, accelerating popular demands for improvement in living conditions conflict with conservative resistance to change. In many countries, there is no reliable political means to cushion the shock between these conflicting pressures nor to make an orderly transfer of political power. To these problems must be added fear and envy of U.S. power, resentment at cuts in U.S. economic and military assistance, and extreme sensitivity to U.S. trade- and commodity-import policies. The rise of Fidel Castro in some respects weakened Communist strength in Latin America by splitting the Moscow wing from the more militant elements and by alarming conservative and moderate forces. At the same time, it encouraged advocates of violence. Since the death of Ernesto "Che" Guevara, a new approach to insurgency in Latin America can be expected, perhaps some kind of synthesis of previously competing rural and urban techniques. In any case, there is likely to be continuing political instability in a number of states, conflict and violence within some of them, and perhaps occasional serious controversies between certain of them. One way or another, U.S. interests will be affected by these developments, and the nature and extent of U.S. involvement will be a continuing policy problem.

Despite our leading position in the Western Hemisphere, there are limits on U.S. ability to influence events in Latin America, especially in the larger and more distant countries. In reviewing or undertaking commitments in the area, it is important to assess, country by country and problem by problem, exactly what our interests, objectives, and capabilities are. The benefits of U.S. involvement as well as the costs and risks will vary from one case to the next. The diversity that prevails from Tijuana to Tierra del Fuego makes the search for any panacea in Latin American affairs as illusory as the quest for El Dorado.

Many Latin American governments count on U.S. help not only to resist Communist threats (fractionated as these may be) but also to protect or strengthen them against their domestic opponents and regional rivals. Policy-makers in the fields of arms aid, security cooperation, and the like face the continuing problem of reconciling our political and military interests and purposes with those of the recipient government. In addition, it is not always easy for the United States to distinguish Communist or other irretrievably hostile movements from other brands of dissidence or to gauge the chances of local insurgencies being captured by Communist, or equally unfriendly, forces.

In helping Latin American national and regional economies, the task will be to alleviate hardship and broaden opportunity without attempting to transform societies overnight and without raising such high popular expectations that dissatisfactions and political disturbances become explosive. Cuts in U.S. aid of course make this task more difficult and may require redefinition of common economic goals (e.g., of the Alliance for Progress), if these goals are to be made realistic.

The principle of supporting representative governments is central to our spirit, our policy, and our long-term interests; but, at the moment, about two thirds of the countries of Latin America are ruled directly or indirectly by the military, and it would be self-defeating to shun them out of principle. Furthermore, military governments have no monopoly on misrule in Latin America, and some may be relatively responsive to certain popular needs.

It is not inconceivable that the United States may at some time be asked or feel required to use force in Latin America to defend a vital interest. In such a contingency, it would be important for the United States to work through the Organization of American States, if at all feasible. This move would help to mitigate the adverse political repercussions of any such intervention.

The Underdeveloped World

Certain areas or issues stand out as particular sources of concern because they are already the source of active troubles and tensions still far from resolved. The Middle East tensions and the implications of the Vietnam problem in the Far East have been emphasized, but this does not mean that other parts of Asia, Latin America, and Africa will be free of trouble. In the underdeveloped world generally, each year is almost certain to bring its quota of domestic turbulence and international strife. Many of these problems will be of concern to U.S. national-security policy—but not all. One continuing problem will be not only to anticipate where and how conflict and instability may occur but also whether it will affect U.S. interests, and if so, how.

In making these assessments, the government does not, of course, start with a blank slate. Its freedom of action is circumscribed by a number of treaties or other commitments. Policy makers may want to reassess or modify some of these, but they cannot ignore them. Nor are the problems only those of threats or pressures on ourselves and our friends from avowed Communist adversaries. South Korea faces danger from the North, but it also has antagonisms with Japan which have been ameliorated but not eradicated. Hostility between Indonesia, Malaysia, Singapore, and the Philippines is much less intense since Sukarno was removed from power, but controversies over territory and other issues continue to trouble the relations of these states with each other and could take a turn for the worse, with awkward implications for the United States. Security problems among or involving these states are likely to increase with the prospective British withdrawal from Singapore. Hostility between India and Pakistan is another case in point. Pakistan's progressive alienation from the United States in recent years has in one sense simplified the painful problem of trying to avoid siding with either of these adversaries, but this hardly constitutes an over-all net gain—for either U.S. interests or the Indian subcontinent's peace and stability. The Greek–Turkish controversy over Cyprus presents comparably difficult problems, made more so by the fact that both are NATO allies. Similar problems loom ahead in sub-Saharan Africa, where black-nationalist movements have been and continue to be on collision course with white governments or the remnants of European empires. The United States has reasons of national and domestic interests to avoid alienating either side, but the choice between supporting one party or staying aloof can be difficult.

U.S. concerns in the underdeveloped world are not confined to anticipating or coping with volence. Conflict in these regions, whether insurgency, revolution, or war between states, is often as much a symptom as a cause of trouble. If some miraculous atmosphere of political tranquility settled over them for the next few years, these areas would still pose a host of problems, some of which directly or indirectly affect U.S. interests and security.

Essentially, these problems are mostly concomitants of the historical process through which these societies are pushing toward twentieth-century norms, i.e., modernization. The process carries mixed blessings—both for the societies involved and from the standpoint of U.S. interests. It is typically turbulent, messy, and disruptive of traditional patterns of authority to which we have long been accustomed. Not infrequently, it brings to the surface forces hostile to the United States and its principal allies. It often provides the Communists with opportunities they lacked in calmer eras. They have had some successes in their efforts to exploit nationalist and revolutionary discontent, as well as some setbacks. They have invested substantial economic and military aid in the campaign, and in time they may come to wonder if it is worth the price—although they are still clearly willing to pay it in selected areas. For the United States, these patterns pose a recurrent dilemma. Realities dictate that we work with established authorities in the conduct of diplomatic and other relations, and U.S. interests frequently come to be identified, locally and at home, with incumbent regimes. Yet the latter often have but a tenuous hold on power and are sometimes out of touch with the times. Hence, when and if they are turned out, their successors may repudiate cooperation with the United States or other Western powers as part and parcel of the evils of the old regime.

Whatever the benefits and the disadvantages, the process of modernization is going to go on inexorably, although with wide, local variations in scope and pace. The chief manifestations are familiar enough in broad outline: The gap between rich nations and poor nations not only persists; it is probably becoming greater as the economies of the industrial societies of the Northern Hemisphere grow at a rapid pace, while most of those in the Southern Hemisphere limp unevenly along. The growth of population, unchecked and already reaching critical proportions in many of the less-prosperous states, is, of course, a major contributing cause of their failure to make progress. Demographers can argue over whether the outlook is catastrophic or merely grim, but, if it is not to be considered hopeless, effective action is urgently needed.

Accompanying these conditions is the phenomenon often called the "revolution of rising expectations" or, more ominously, the "rising frustrations" in the underdeveloped world. This development has been intensified by advances in communications that have put transistor radios, if not television sets, into even the remotest villages. Invidious comparisons between the lot of most inhabitants of the poor nations and that of the rich nations become more obvious, producing resentment in the former and some unease in the latter. As well as expanding literacy and political awareness at the lower levels of most underdeveloped societies and, proportionately, increasing the numbers of educated and semi-educated people at the middle levels, the result has been revolutionary and promises to be more so. All over the world, people whose fathers could be called politically unaware or downright primitive have become more concerned and sensitive about what goes on in the twentieth-century world—both near home and far abroad. Sophisticated or not, they are active and alive in ways not previously seen in world history. For the United States, the results may be good, bad, or indifferent, but they will be impossible to ignore.

NEW TECHNOLOGICAL DIMENSIONS

The political and military problems discussed above are in many respects variations on the familiar. The next few years will bring change in these problems, but much of it will be evolutionary degrees of difference rather than radical alterations in our environment. There are other aspects likely to change more rapidly and more drastically, most of them stemming from the rapid advance of modern science and technology. The destructive power of modern weaponry may have made the world a potentially more dangerous place, but the technological skills underlying sophisticated weapons have also opened up unparalleled challenges and opportunities for mastering our environment. Space exploration, oceanography, weather manipulation, new modes of instant communication and supersonic transport—these and other frontiers of technological advance—have a direct relevance to our national safety. Yet they also have implications and applications going well beyond the customary concerns of national security, opportunities for improving the quality of our existence and for building better cooperation between interdependent nations.

Some promising starts have already been made in international efforts along these lines. The International Geophysical Year of 1957–58 was a beginning, and the U.S.–Soviet treaty of 1968 on the recovery of astronauts is the latest step. The intervening ten years, for all their political up's and down's, have seen a continuing growth in communication between the scientists and the political leaders of both major camps concerning matters of mutual scientific and technological interests which would have been unthinkable in the 1950's. Limited moves toward understanding along these lines have not ended the competition in arms and may never do so, but they may contribute to a climate of potential understanding which could in time do just that. Many scientific and political leaders in the West have long pressed urgently for this kind of understanding, and there are signs that a significant body of Russian individuals, if not official bodies, are thinking and even speaking along the same lines.

There is indeed a discernible impulse—in scientific and other intellectual circles throughout much of the world—of impatience, even boredom, over the kind of political conflict associated with the Cold War and a marked decline of the kind of evangelical fervor that characterized both sides in the 1950's. It is increasingly viewed, especially by young people, as sterile and irrelevant to the real demands of today's world. So far, these sentiments are much more in evidence in the free atmosphere of the West than in the Communist world, but they are far from absent there—despite official efforts to suppress them. We are no doubt a long distance away from any international system devoted to a cooperative advance toward the better life through scientific mastery of all our problems. We may never get anywhere near it, but there are some grounds for arguing that the force of circumstances may impel us in this direction sooner than we believe. The rational inducements on all sides are strong; the will is by no means absent, and it may be growing.

Some Implications for National-Security Arrangements

If the foregoing assessment of our national and international prospects is anywhere near the mark, it remains to ask: What of it? What do these trends and problems imply for the ways in which national-security policy can best be made and carried out? This study is not concerned with substantive policy recommendations, and it can hardly be argued that foreseeable trends clearly dictate one scheme of procedural arrangements over another, but it is obvious that *what* has to be done affects the question of how best to go about doing it. In terms of the environment, then, what elements of continuity and, more especially, of change, have particular implications for procedures? No short inventory can be complete, but the following discussion suggests some of these implications.

In the domestic context, one important trend is a widespread impulse to reorder some long-established national priorities. It arises from a combination of pressures, but the net effect may be to reduce the relative amount of time, attention, and resources that the President can or wants to devote to foreign affairs. Even the President and his top advisers have only twenty-four hours in each day; even in an expanding economy, a tax dollar spent on urban renewal is not available for foreign aid; even if an end to the Vietnam War removed a major issue of national contention and debate, we would still be far from a clear national consensus on how our real interests and responsibilities in the world should be defined.

This is not to say that international problems are on the way to becoming unimportant. It has been rightly said that the world will not stop and we cannot get off. Indeed, a period of increasing domestic constraints and a greater disposition to acknowledge the limits of national power in a complex and intractable world would render decisions in this area more difficult, more delicate, and more crucial than ever. In terms of defining national-security goals and realistic means of achieving them, subtraction can be a more difficult process than addition. At least on paper it is often easier to describe a particular national interest as vital rather than merely important or even marginal, and there is a human temptation to hope that U.S. power will be decisive in some situations where it may have only limited effect.

But new approaches need not be simple subtraction. They can sometimes take the form of substitution. For example, if economic constraints and political realities make U.S. overseas bases less feasible in certain cases, which may prove true, the loss may be offset by increasing U.S. strategic mobility through improved airlift and sealift capacity. Similarly, if such military alliances or arrangements as the Central Treaty Organization (CENTO) and the Southeast Asia Treaty Organization (SEATO) are in disarray and unlikely to be revived, their place and purpose may be served, at least in part, by other regional approaches, even though the latter would probably be more oriented toward economic and other cooperative action rather than conventional military defense.

IV

The White House National-Security
Staffs Since 1947

Experience suggests that a President's view of the White House national-security staff is likely to be conditioned by his assessment of the practices of his predecessors. Each President brings to office his own style of doing business, his own concept of what was wrong with the previous system, and his own view of what is needed. President Eisenhower, for example, believed that the Truman Administration had "failed to bring into line its crisscrossing and overlapping, and jealous departments and bureaus, and agencies." [1] To correct this situation, he created an elaborate staff mechanism which, in President Kennedy's view, generated needless paperwork between the President and his principal advisers. President Kennedy, in turn, "liberated" himself from the Eisenhower system but emphasized that his staff was not to interpose itself between him and his Cabinet. Within the White House, he had created what some called a "little State Department," which President Johnson, in turn, quietly sought to de-emphasize.

The evolution of national-security staffs since the passage of the National Security Act of 1947 reflects a progressive increase in Presidential involvement in national-security affairs. With each succeeding administration, the amount and depth of the information available to the President through his staff has increased, both with respect to the external international environment and the internal operations of the government. The vital nature of national-security affairs and the President's exposure to them in greater detail have led to Presidential efforts to reach deeper in order to gain control

[1] Speech by Dwight D. Eisenhower, San Francisco, California, October 8, 1952, as printed in *The New York Times*, October 9, 1952.

of a wider range of issues at earlier stages in the process. In general, the successive White House national-security staffs have been prime instruments of this effort.

Whether or not a President elects to continue this trend, he will need help. Experience indicates that he will be faced with the following kinds of problems:

Acquiring information. How can the President be kept fully enough informed to "stay on top" of his job in all senses of the phrase? What is happening? What does it mean in terms of the national security? What does it mean to him as the political leader of the administration? This involves, above all, the availability and analysis of information, and it is indispensable for directing the departments and agencies.

Identifying issues. How can the President ensure that his views will be brought to bear on issues affecting his interests in important ways? Some questions come to the President because of their weight or their sensitivity or because of his known interest in them. The more difficult problem is to identify among all other issues those which are of potential concern to him. In their daily operations, the departments and agencies deal with many matters which the President should know about. He needs some assurance that his interests will be recognized and, that if his views are not known, they will be sought and taken into account in a timely manner. In addition, the President should be able to take a long view of national interests in the context of likely future issues or emerging trends; this raises the question of the role of policy planning as a potential tool of Presidential direction and the ancillary question of its relation to operations.

Making decisions. How does a President ensure that he knows and can weigh all aspects of a problem before making a decision? At a minimum, he needs the relevant facts and the recommendations of his principal advisers and other responsible officials. The President must have some way of exploring alternatives and evaluating consequences. He needs to understand not only the substantive background of the issues but also their bureaucratic and

political implications. Because few problems are the sole concern
of one department, the President is inevitably surrounded, in the
words of a former White House staff member, "by advocates with
strong, often institutional, and nearly always conflicting views." In
some cases, these views can be useful to the President, but, whether
they are or not, many advocates are likely to represent important
constituencies—within the executive branch, in the Congress, or
in the nation at large—and he should be able to sort out the perspectives and motives of these constituencies.

Coordinating. How can the President share managerial responsibility with his department and agency heads and be assured
that their individual decisions result in a coherent and responsive
pattern of actions? Action responsibility on most important issues
is shared by several departments and agencies whose views and
priorities very often, and quite rightly, diverge. The President cannot make all the decisions, and it is neither possible nor desirable
for him to deal separately with each of the various agencies on each
question. Even when the departments and agencies are guided by
explicit Presidential directives, they will differ over interpretations
and responsibilities. It is in the President's interest that many of
these differences be resolved below his level without compromising
his objectives, but it is equally in his interest that some means
exist for distinguishing between what can be settled below and what
must come to him.

Assuring performance. How does the President ensure that
appropriate and expeditious action will flow from his decisions?
Just as his interest does not begin at some theoretical point of
decision, neither does it end at signing a piece of paper. His decisions must be communicated to, and understood and acted upon
by, all concerned, both inside and outside the government. Problems will arise in implementation and interpretation, adjustments will be required, and, not infrequently, so will some prod-
ding.

The various approaches of Presidents to these problems have
been evident in their respective staff organizations, with the dis-

tinctions turning largely on the extent of the President's active involvement, the methods he has employed to manage the system, and the performance and responsiveness of the various departments and agencies. President Eisenhower used his White House national-security staff primarily for the promulgation of rather formal policy guidance designed to lend direction and coherence to the activities of a system within which relevant Cabinet officers bore heavy responsibility for policy formulation and implementation. Presidents Kennedy and Johnson, on the other hand, charged their staffs to maintain much more active contact with the ongoing activities of the government and to help influence direction at various stages of the process.

PRESIDENT TRUMAN: 1947–53

President Truman initially looked on the National Security Council as an institution which might encroach upon his constitutional prerogatives. Accordingly, he approached its use with caution and selectivity. Between the passage of the National Security Act in 1947 and the outbreak of the Korean conflict in 1950, President Truman did not attend council meetings regularly, and the executive secretary and the NSC staff remained at the periphery of his relationship with his Cabinet officers and departments. Nevertheless, by the end of the Truman Administration, certain precedents and usages had been established which were followed and elaborated upon by his successors.

President Truman's use of the council emphasized its strictly advisory nature. The NSC produced a series of papers which were approved by Truman and which represented the first attempt to formulate explicit national objectives and to provide guidelines for actions by departments and agencies. With the outbreak of the Korean conflict, the need for better means of coordinating policy and action became more apparent. President Truman, recognizing the value of the council's prior work in mobilization planning and in appraising U.S. strategic interests, then directed that all major national-security policy recommendations should come to him through the council. He continued to stress, however, that the council did not share his decision-making responsibility. As he later wrote: "I used the council only as a place for recommendations to be worked out. The policy has to come down from the President, as all final decisions have to be made by him." [2]

From the outset, President Truman considered that the NSC staff belonged primarily to him rather than to the council. He used the first NSC executive secretary, Sidney Souers, as a briefing officer and, to a limited degree, as a channel for relaying reactions obtained in briefings to the departments and agencies. In 1950, Truman designated James Lay, Souer's successor, as chairman of the "Senior Staff"—the original interagency planning group and the forerunner of President Eisenhower's NSC Planning Board. Lay replaced the State Department representative who had previously chaired the group. The official "Organizational History of the NSC" explains the change as follows: "Over time the feeling grew that other departments and agencies would cooperate more effectively in the work of the council in matters directly affecting their own responsibilities if the major interdepartmental staff groups were chaired by someone without departmental ties." [3]

By contrast, President Truman rejected a proposal that the executive secretary be given authority to see that the President's NSC decisions were carried out. Toward the end of his full term, a small unit was created within the NSC staff to ensure that reports from the departments and agencies on the status of national-security programs were readily available to the President and the council.

In 1951, President Truman established the Psychological Strategy Board (PSB) and charged it with responsibility for guiding and evaluating the psychological (such as foreign information programs) activities of the government. The PSB reported to the council, but it was never fully incorporated into the NSC structure and had a short life.

[2] Harry S Truman, *Memoirs*, II, "Years of Trial and Hope" (New York: Doubleday and Company, Inc., 1956), 59.

[3] U.S. Congress, Senate, Report of the Jackson Subcommittee, *Inquiry on National Policy Machinery*, II, "Studies and Background Materials" (Washington, D.C.: U.S. Government Printing Office, 1961), 432.

PRESIDENT EISENHOWER: 1953–61

President Eisenhower took office deeply convinced of the need for a "national strategy for the Cold War." In a campaign speech in San Francisco on October 8, 1952, he had said that this would require "the selection of broad national purposes and the designation within purposes of principal targets. . . . We must bring the dozens of agencies and bureaus into concerted action under an over-all scheme of strategy." [4]

This theme was given an organizational framework by Robert Cutler, who, under a Presidential mandate, elaborated the skeletal NSC structure of the Truman era into a comprehensive "NSC system." This system thereafter became the central vehicle for formulating and promulgating policy and was designed to be the primary means of imparting Presidential direction and over-all coherence to the activities of the departments and agencies.

The focal point of the system was the council itself. The system has sometimes been called "policy hill," with planning going up one slope for approval by the NSC and followup coming down the other side. The council's subsidiary elements—the Planning Board and the Operations Coordinating Board (OCB)—were in supporting positions. The Planning Board examined policy recommendations of the departments, resolved interagency differences wherever possible, and prepared policy papers for the council's consideration. The OCB translated broad policies into more specific operational guidelines and sought to assure, primarily through a system of reports from action agencies, that policies were being implemented and coordinated.

President Eisenhower's staff organization cannot be fully understood without bearing in mind the careful distinction that was made within the staff between the handling of policy and operations. A "policy" question was one which involved the formulation or revision of an NSC policy or an operational matter which suggested the need for revision or clarification of a policy. If a proposed action or recommendation did not fall into either of those

---

[4] Eisenhower, *op. cit.*

categories, it was not a "policy" matter and did not fall within the purview of the NSC system.

Thus, in national-security affairs there were two staff channels to the President: (1) the NSC system, presided over by the special assistant for national-security affairs and including the Planning Board, the NSC, and the OCB, together with their officers and staffs and (2) a channel involving day-to-day flow of operations and intelligence matters, which went through the hands of Brigadier General Andrew J. Goodpaster, President Eisenhower's Staff Secretary. These two staff channels worked closely together, but a careful distinction was made between their respective responsibilities.

General Goodpaster's service to President Eisenhower has been compared to that performed by the secretary of a military general staff. In the evolution of national-security staff institutions, his job represented an expansion of the earlier role of the NSC executive secretary. In handling the daily flow of informational and operational memorandums to and from the President, Goodpaster exerted a discipline which sought to assure proper coordination and to avoid ex parte proceedings. In addition, one of his prime responsibilities was to keep the President informed of pending and completed actions, including those which did not come to the President's personal or institutional attention. Through his daily information and intelligence briefing to the President and his attendance at most of the President's meetings, including those with Cabinet officers, Goodpaster was thoroughly familiar with the President's views and interests, and he served as an active channel for conveying them to the departments and agencies through formal points of contact.

General Goodpaster's briefings were a principal source of President Eisenhower's information on current developments. The briefings consisted primarily of an oral presentation of material contained in CIA, Department of State, and military intelligence and operational summaries. To the extent that Eisenhower required additional information on briefing items, it was obtained by Goodpaster from the original institutional sources. In all matters, Goodpaster took care not to come between the President and his principal advisers. Thus, he was a critical link in the operational chain but was not a substantive contributor to it.

Early in his Administration, President Eisenhower directed that the National Security Council review all existing national-security policies. He placed his own man, Robert Cutler, in charge of this undertaking, conferring on him the new title, Special Assistant for National Security Affairs. It was anticipated that the incumbent would change with succeeding administrations, while the NSC staff, headed as before by the executive secretary, would remain, providing continuity in council operations.

Initially, the special assistant's major responsibilities were to preside over the activities of the Planning Board and to assist the President in the conduct of council business. In 1960, the special assistant, then Gordon Gray, was also made chairman of the OCB (until then chaired by the under secretary of state). However, for most of the Eisenhower Administration, as mentioned above, a distinction was maintained in the NSC staff structure between formulation of policy in the Planning Board and the coordination of operations under existing policies through the OCB.

The National Security Council, of course, reached the summit of its importance during the Eisenhower Administration. President Truman had used the council as an important but supplementary advisory body, while President Eisenhower determined that—except in special cases of urgency—responsibility for national-security policy formulation was to run from a department, agency, or individual through the NSC mechanism and not go outside its framework.

The NSC met on an average of once a week during the first two years of the Eisenhower Administration and less frequently thereafter. Unless otherwise directed by the President, sessions dealt primarily with the making or revising of broad policies—either in anticipation of future eventualities or in response to a current situation. Much less frequently, it considered reports from the OCB about the implementation of existing policies. The council did not, according to Gordon Gray, "concern itself with interagency conflicts not involving policy considerations." [5]

[5] Report of the Jackson Subcommittee, *op. cit.*, p. 182.

The deliberations of the council were usually based on written papers prepared by the Planning Board. Following each meeting, a record of council actions was prepared under the supervision of the special assistant and circulated to the council participants for comment before it was submitted to President Eisenhower. The President's action on this record, including his resolution of any differences not settled in the council, constituted his decisions on the matters involved. The Presidentially approved record was then sent to the council participants.

President Eisenhower also used the council for considering matters of current importance. He did not, however, formally consult the council on every issue; and he did not, observers note, use the council to decide what to do "tomorrow." It was not unusual for council meetings to be immediately followed by more intimate rump sessions. Furthermore, President Eisenhower often convened select groups of advisers on important issues rather than call a regular NSC meeting. These were referred to as "special NSC meetings." A record of action was made of such sessions, but attendance was on a more select basis, somewhat similar to the later "Ex Comm" [6] format of President Kennedy. Thus, President Eisenhower was more flexible in his attitude toward the council than many critics have alleged or, for that matter, than his defenders themselves have implied.

The NSC Planning Board was essentially President Truman's "Senior Staff" under a new name. Members, generally at the assistant-secretary level, were expected to have the personal confidence of their agency heads and to devote their primary attention to the board's activities.

The special assistant was the presiding officer of the Planning Board. Under his supervision, and with guidance from the President and the NSC agencies, the Planning Board drew up the agenda of policy matters to be discussed by the council and prepared the papers which were the basis for the council's deliberations, and Planning Board members briefed council principals on the issues. A former member of the Planning Board who was interviewed for this study described his role as "two-edged": He had an obligation

[6] See below, page 80.

both to the President and to his own department. He could not be purely an instructed delegate; he had to do some freewheeling as well. The same interviewee saw the board member's functions to include, first, mobilizing talent in his own department; second, debating with his Planning Board colleagues; and third, promoting effective subsequent debate among the principals in the NSC.

A distinction must be drawn between the Planning Board members, who inevitably tended toward institutional advocacy, and the special assistant for national-security affairs and his staff, who acted as moderators and managers but not as substantive contributors. As chairman and a nonvoting participant, the special assistant could express his views on the presentation of issues, but he sought primarily to ensure that the board's papers were adequate and that they satisfactorily reflected the views of the members. When "splits" could not be avoided, the special assistant was responsible for presenting them to the council as clearly and accurately as possible. On occasion, in order to sharpen differences between positions, the special assistant would reformulate a department's position (subject to its approval) before presenting a policy paper to the council.

The special staff was a small group of NSC staff professionals under the direction of the deputy executive secretary. Its originator, Robert Cutler, described its functions as follows: "It analyzes, summarizes, and probes, from an *unbiased* point of view, the work produced in the departments and agencies concerned with a particular issue." [7] [Emphasis added.] One of its specific duties was to make an independent analysis and review of each Planning Board paper at each stage of its development.

These analyses were used by the special assistant both in the refining process which took place in the Planning Board and in briefing the President before council sessions. The function of the special staff was a delicate one because it bore on the substantive content of a department's position. At the very least, its existence meant that there was available to the President (through the special assistant) an independent source of analysis of departmental recommendations. It is impossible to know what value President Eisen-

[7] Report of the Jackson Subcommittee, *op. cit.*, p. 178.

hower placed on the work of the special staff, but at least one special assistant found it "indispensable."

Until the Operations Coordinating Board was created in September, 1953, one department or agency—usually State—had been designated as primarily responsible for coordinating implementation of NSC policy papers. Although other agencies were almost invariably involved, arrangements for coordination were of an *ad hoc* nature.

The purpose of the OCB, as described by Robert Cutler, was "to coordinate, 'ride herd on,' and report to the council on the performance by the departments and agencies charged with responsibility to carry out national-security policies approved by the President, and to be constantly mindful of such policies' and such performances' psychological implications. . . ." [8] The OCB membership roughly paralleled that of the NSC itself, with each agency represented on the board at sub-Cabinet level. The board worked primarily from papers prepared by working groups from the departments and agencies. It was a cooperative body with no voting procedures or directive authority. Theoretically, the rank of its members was such that they would have sufficient authority to implement their own agreements. Substantive disagreements were supposed to be reported to the council, but, in practice, this was rarely done.

The board has been roundly criticized for what it did not do, but its positive aspects have received very little attention. Many of those who worked closely with the OCB and who still favor a structured process of coordination concede that it had many faults; they frankly refer to it as a paper mill. Others have characterized its reports as "self-serving bromides" designed to demonstrate that the agencies were doing what they were being paid to do. One perceptive insider noted, however, that some of the complaints about the paper mill may have served to disguise the disinclination of an agency to be skewered for dragging its feet.

The paper-mill charge focuses primarily on the formal working-group and reporting aspects of the OCB and does not take into

[8] Robert Cutler, *No Time for Rest* (Boston: Little, Brown and Company, 1966), p. 311.

account what many who were intimately involved consider its more important contribution—the informal means of coordination and exchange of information which it provided. Secretary of State Christian Herter, for example, in testifying before the Jackson Subcommittee in 1960 said: "The members of the OCB eat lunch together every Wednesday. In those discussions where there is very little staff, anything can be brought up and those discussions are extraordinarily useful." [9] Implicit in such remarks, however, may be a tacit acknowledgment that the remainder of the OCB process represented a questionable expenditure of bureaucratic energy.

Until 1960, the chairman of the OCB was the under secretary of state. A respectable body of opinion holds that some chairmen were less than even-handed in their direction of the OCB. Some observers hold that occasionally they may even have been more interested in excluding from the agenda matters which the State Department did not wish to have discussed than in making the board an effective institution. Other agencies had similar concerns; for example, the Treasury Department and the Bureau of the Budget tended to resist the OCB because they feared its deliberations might be used against them in budgetary matters. On balance, it would seem that there was substantial logrolling in the OCB and a reluctance among agencies to find fault with each other.

These problems were recognized by the NSC officers responsible for the board's operation, and in the later years of the Eisenhower Administration a series of steps were taken to enhance its effectiveness. In 1957, President Eisenhower issued an executive order formally placing the OCB within the structure of the NSC. Later in the same year, the President appointed a special assistant for security-operations coordination and named him vice chairman and principal Presidential representative on the board. In 1959, the board's elaborate reporting schedules were simplified. And in 1960, as noted earlier, the special assistant for national-security affairs replaced the under secretary of state as chairman, a move which strengthened the staff's position and reflected the President's desire to be able "to look to one office for staff assistance in the whole range of national-security affairs." [10] The special assistant for secur-

---

[9] Report of the Jackson Subcommittee, *op. cit.*, I, *Hearings*, 725.
[10] *Ibid.*, II, 143.

ity-operations coordination remained as vice chairman, with special responsibility for initiating new programs of implementation and for seeing that board actions contributed to a favorable "climate of opinion" abroad.

Unfortunately, in the opinion of many involved, these adjustments came too late for a fair trial. In retrospect, it seems that what the OCB most needed was a chairman who could cut through agency points of view and report to the President when serious matters were not being resolved. In the absence of this, and given the negative attitude of the State Department toward the board, it is hardly surprising that it was not more effective. The conclusion of those who knew the OCB best is that effective coordination of interagency operations requires either White House direction or, at a minimum, active Presidential backing.

In terms of formal organization, President Eisenhower's NSC staff system was the most comprehensive yet known. Its elements provided a framework for orderly relationships between the President and the responsible officials of his executive branch and for systematic attention to all aspects of national-security affairs. Each of the problem areas outlined at the outset of this chapter was specifically addressed by one or more elements of the Eisenhower staff system. General Goodpaster organized the flow of information and national-security correspondence and maintained liaison with the operating departments and agencies. The Planning Board systematically looked ahead to prepare the President for issues which would confront him in the future, and, together with its parent body, the National Security Council, provided a way of formulating policy to meet them. The Operations Coordinating Board addressed the problems of translating broad policy into guidelines for action and of assuring that it was implemented and coordinated.

There are two schools of thought concerning the Eisenhower system. Some grant that it may have been ponderous and that perhaps the bureaucracy tended to run away with the system, but they still favor something like it because of the protection it afforded the President and the assurance it provided that all views would be heard. Others perceive in the system's characteristics a sluggishness and routinization that made it difficult for the system to respond to challenge or to deal selectively with central issues. One of those intimately involved with the system makes the point that President Eisenhower thought the issues would be brought up to him out of the system and that his decisions on them would be almost automatically carried out. Nothing could be more wrong, this observer argued: The President must concern himself with forcing issues up for decision and with seeing to their execution thereafter.

President Eisenhower's staff organization did not impose Presidential priorities on Cabinet officers. Although the Planning Board and the OCB were located in the White House or the Executive Office Building, and although their activities were supervised by Presidential assistants, they were not instruments of direct Presidential control. The departments and agencies furnished most of their staff work and were able to exercise substantial influence over their agendas. In chairing the Planning Board, for example, the special assistant was not expected to represent a Presidential view but to ensure that policy proposals satisfactorily reflected the views of its members. If one believes, as many of those who were involved in it now do, that the NSC system could have been strengthened by giving greater authority to NSC staff officials, it must also be borne in mind that a cardinal tenet of the system was respect for departmental authority and responsibility.

Adherence to this tenet was also evident in Eisenhower's reluctance to accord his staff officers a more assertive role in OCB activities. President Eisenhower himself appears to have recognized the consequences of this. In the concluding section of his memoirs, he wrote of the OCB: "It functioned fairly well. However, I came finally to believe that this work could have been better done by a highly competent and trusted official with a small staff of his own, rather than by a committee whose members had to handle the task on a part-time basis." [11] Eisenhower summarized the role he envisioned for this individual (whose title he suggested might be "secretary for international coordination" or "first secretary") as follows: "In short, he could help insure that the President's policies

[11] Dwight D. Eisenhower, *Waging Peace* (New York: Doubleday and Company, Inc., 1965), p. 634.

were scrupulously observed and that the actions of one department would not negate those of another." [12]

In a subsequent passage, President Eisenhower recounts the opposition of Secretary of State John Foster Dulles to the concept of a "secretary for international coordination"—even after the President told Dulles that he had him in mind for the job. The President never pushed the idea, but he noted that Dulles later "came to agree to the wisdom of such a plan. He said that he would like to give the bulk of his time to assisting in developing policy and making certain the government moved as a unit in all its foreign relations." [13]

President Eisenhower acknowledged that his first-secretary proposal would have required "a great deal of educational work." Apparently, Robert Cutler was among those who would have needed persuasion. Writing after President Eisenhower had advanced his suggestion, although without reference to it, Cutler said: "No arrangement should be proposed or put into action that will tend to cut across the lines of responsibility which run directly from the President to his responsible departments and agency chiefs." [14]

One of the most significant aspects of the Eisenhower NSC staff was its concentration on the activities of the National Security Council, the Planning Board, and the Operations Coordinating Board. Business transacted in those forums was thoroughly—some would say exhaustively—staffed, albeit with the limitations noted. On the other hand, business arriving on the President's desk through other than NSC channels, as well as orders emanating from the Presidential office in forms other than as NSC policies, did so with minimum staff handling. As one observer put it, President Eisenhower's staff work in this area was largely done in the departments. To make this observation is not to imply that President Eisenhower was bound by departmental advice, that such advice was bad, or that substantive staff review would have added anything. Rather, it was a matter of personal preference. Given

[12] *Ibid.*, p. 635.
[13] *Ibid.*, p. 637.
[14] Report of the Jackson Subcommittee, *op. cit.*, I, 592.

his relationships with his Cabinet advisers, any other course would have been unlikely.

PRESIDENT KENNEDY: 1961–63

President Kennedy took office believing that vigorous Presidential initiatives were required in order "to get America moving again." In the national-security field, he considered that the bureaucratic constraints embodied in the NSC system were partially responsible for what he viewed as an accumulation of unresolved problems inherited from the Eisenhower Administration.

Three weeks prior to his inauguration, President-elect Kennedy appointed McGeorge Bundy Special Assistant for National Security Affairs and indicated his intention to consolidate, in simplified form and under Bundy's direction, the various components of the existing arrangements in order to achieve a "single, small, but strongly organized staff." The purpose of the staff would be, in Kennedy's words, "to assist me in obtaining advice from, and coordinating operations of, the government agencies concerned with national security." [15]

Under President Eisenhower, the Planning Board, the NSC, and the OCB had been used to obtain advice from and coordinate the actions of the departments. The NSC staff had related primarily to the operations of these bodies rather than to President Eisenhower in a more personal sense. Thus, the Kennedy phrase, "to assist me," takes on particular significance.

President-elect Kennedy also declared his intention to seek advice from members of the council, both collectively and individually, but the council itself was to be de-emphasized. Bundy would facilitate the work of the council but only as "part of his assignment." As Bundy himself later wrote to Senator Henry Jackson, "the business of the staff goes well beyond what is treated in the formal meetings of the National Security Council." [16]

In announcing Bundy's appointment, Kennedy noted that he had been "much impressed" by the staff reports of the Jackson Subcommittee on National Policy Machinery, and he indicated that

[15] Press release by President-elect John F. Kennedy, January 1, 1961.
[16] Report of the Jackson Subcommittee, *op. cit.*, II, 1337.

they would provide the starting point for a review by Bundy of the NSC organization. The review was duly carried out, but, in a sense, it had already taken place during the Jackson Subcommittee hearings of 1960 and in the thinking of many of those who were to serve in the Kennedy Administration.

On February 19, 1961, as part of his program "for strengthening the responsibility of the individual departments," President Kennedy issued an executive order abolishing the Operations Coordinating Board. This move, while not unexpected, nevertheless came as a disappointment to many former NSC officials. The latter, keenly aware of the OCB's shortcomings, had sought to overcome them in order to leave its machinery in good working order for their successors. Many of the board's responsibilities were to be centered on the secretary of state, who would in turn rely on his assistant secretaries to "consult closely with other departments and agencies." The President would assure responsiveness to his direction by maintaining direct communication with the responsible agencies, and the Bundy staff would be expected to follow up on White House decisions.

A fundamental feature of the new Administration's approach to national-security staffing was, as Bundy informed the Jackson Subcommittee, the elimination of "the distinction between planning and operations that governed the administrative structure of the [Eisenhower] NSC staff." Bundy went on to explain: "This distinction, real enough at the extremes of the daily cable traffic and long-range assessment of future possibilities, breaks down in most of the business of decisions and action. This is especially true at the level of Presidential action." An unstated corollary to this concept was de-emphasis of the concept of policy per se, though not necessarily of planning directly related to operations. The discontinuation of the Planning Board under President Kennedy was evidence of this attitude, which was also reflected in the new Administration's general commitment to action.

Under President Eisenhower, policy had been conceived as a major managerial tool of the President; as such, it absorbed large amounts of top-level personal and institutional energies. By viewing policy as a tool, the Administration intended to cover a wide range of matters coherently, making its goals and general means clear enough so that lower levels of the government could operate without constant, specific direction from the top. Under President Kennedy, policy tended to be viewed more as the set of reasons lying behind an action program undertaken, or simply as a description of an action program; the action itself was the focus of interest.

By late February, there had emerged the "single, small, but strongly organized staff" Kennedy had envisioned. It was indeed quite small, and it consisted originally of a few Presidential appointees, such as Walt W. Rostow and Carl Kaysen, plus a very few holdovers from the Eisenhower NSC staff. During 1961, several other members were added to the staff, three or four of whom dealt directly with the President within their areas of specialization. In addition, several Presidential assistants not specifically assigned to national-security affairs took a substantial interest in them. While not responsible to Bundy, they maintained a degree of contact with him.

The functions of this staff were never formally defined and are therefore more difficult to delineate than those of the Eisenhower staff. They were evolved in practice rather than having been prescribed in advance as Cutler had designed the Eisenhower NSC staff. One of the Jackson Subcommittee staff reports of 1960 contained a passage that anticipated the functions Bundy and his staff later came to perform:

> The President should at all times have the help and protection of a small personal staff whose members work "outside the system," who are sensitive to the President's own information needs, and who can assist him in asking relevant questions of his departmental chiefs, in making suggestions for policy initiatives not emerging from the operating departments and agencies, and in spotting gaps in policy execution.[17]

The manner in which the staff's role evolved was not—and probably could not have been—anticipated in early 1961. The factors that most significantly affected its development were probably (1) the extensive and continuing personal involvement of the President

[17] *Ibid.*, III, *Staff Reports and Recommendations*, 40.

—both by choice and of necessity—in national-security affairs, (2) the nature of the State Department's response to its new responsibilities, and (3) the generally informal methods that characterized the Kennedy Administration.

At President Kennedy's request, General Goodpaster remained at the White House for a few weeks to ensure an orderly transfer of his duties to the new staff. Bundy took over the staff responsibilities connected with day-to-day operations previously performed by Goodpaster; and Brigadier General Chester V. Clifton, Kennedy's new defense liaison officer, assumed the daily briefing function. It soon became apparent that the President would not be satisfied with the oral-briefing format preferred by his predecessor or with summary presentations. Clifton's briefings were therefore supplemented by additional material prepared by Bundy and his staff. When Kennedy called for back-up or source material, the staff often provided it because the speed with which the State Department responded rarely matched the President's expectations. As one White House aide put it: "We were very quickly in a 'real time' situation which would have dismayed our predecessors." Kennedy's now-renowned telephone calls to State Department desk officers were a reflection of his impatience with regular channels and of his desire to immerse himself in the details of his problems.

This quest for more and better information also led to a requirement for more intelligence data and reflected a reluctance—particularly after the Bay of Pigs—to rely entirely on the bureaucracy's selection and analysis of information. According to one Kennedy assistant, without the facts they could not ask the right questions —or evaluate the answers.

In April, 1961, following the Bay of Pigs, the Situation Room was set up in the old "Map Room" in the West Basement of the White House, adjoining offices created for Bundy and the executive secretary of the National Security Council. The purpose of the Situation Room was to enable the President to stay on top of fast-breaking events, and it quickly proved itself in a series of international crises. Although it remained under the nominal control of the naval aide de camp's office until after President Kennedy's assassination, its focus from the very outset was on Bundy's operation. Its primary virtue was its ability to locate and move more information to the President more quickly than had previously been possible.

Some former Kennedy aides, in retrospect, believe that, more than any other factor, it was the effort of the Bundy staff to fill the "information gap" which initially led to its extensive involvement in the internal activities of the departments and agencies. The staff closely followed those activities through an extensive range of personal contacts at all levels of the bureaucracy.

A pattern of close cooperation on matters of mutual interest developed between the Bundy staff and the staff of the Budget Bureau. The bureau staff's contacts within the departments made it a valuable source of information for the NSC staff. In return, the NSC staff officers were able to provide their counterparts in the bureau with a window on many top-level matters. This relationship continued into the Johnson Administration and proved particularly valuable in dealing with such matters as foreign developmental assistance.

Similar collaboration took place between the national-security staff and that of the special assistant to the President for science and technology. The latter office, created during the Eisenhower Administration, had been useful in many ways—augmenting scientific staff resources of the Office of the Secretary of Defense, the State Department, and the Bureau of the Budget; advising the President on long-term scientific planning; and acting as technical auditors of agency programs and projects. During the Kennedy Administration, the science adviser and his staff worked closely with McGeorge Bundy, Carl Kaysen, and other NSC staff members on a broad range of military–scientific issues and provided President Kennedy with valuable insights on their complex technical aspects.

Interagency coordination, instead of being primarily a State Department responsibility as President Kennedy had indicated, became a mixed enterprise in which the Bundy staff was often a principal element. The relations of the staff with the two principal departments are therefore of particular interest.

Many of those involved at the time assert that both President Kennedy and Bundy made a determined effort to get the State Department to assume the role of interagency leadership outlined for it. But there are also many who believe that the President always intended to be his own secretary of state. In the course of the "committee-killing" operation which accompanied the abolition of the Operations Coordinating Board, primary responsibility for an extensive range of matters was vested in the State Department. Despite official misgivings over a lack of enthusiasm within the State Department for emphasizing the political and developmental aspects of foreign assistance, the reorganized foreign-assistance program was kept under the control of the secretary of state. The Peace Corps was also placed under the State Department's jurisdiction, and in the field of development-lending an effort was made to strengthen the Department of State's position in dealing with the Treasury Department. The intent of these and other similar decisions was to provide the secretary of state with authority to match the leadership role expected of him.

According to many, the State Department was slow to assume its new responsibilities, although this varied from bureau to bureau within the department, with much depending on the individual assistant secretaries. Theodore Sorensen described President Kennedy's reaction to this as follows:

> The President was discouraged with the State Department almost as soon as he took office. He felt that it too often seemed to have a built-in inertia which deadened initiative and that its tendency toward excessive delay obscured determination. It had too many voices and too little vigor. It was never clear to the President . . . who was in charge, who was clearly delegated to do what, and why his own policy line seemed consistently to be altered or evaded.[18]

More than any other factor, this impression of sluggishness within the State Department shaped the nature and role of the Bundy staff. In those instances where the Department of State's response did not measure up to the President's expectations, the

[18] Theodore Sorensen, *Kennedy* (New York: Harper & Row, 1965), p. 287.

NSC staff moved in. The result was a slow but perceptible increase in the size and activity of the staff.

Although Bundy himself and Deputy Special Assistant Kaysen were deeply involved in important early decisions concerning force levels and weapons systems, as well as in subsequent defense-related questions, the Bundy staff never developed a defense-oriented component comparable to its depth in foreign affairs. There were several reasons for this—including the presence in the White House for fifteen months of the President's military representative, retired General Maxwell Taylor (discussed below). Many of the most important issues in the defense area were one-time items or were tied to the annual-budget cycle, whereas foreign affairs presented a continuing barrage of *ad hoc* problems in which the President was instinctively interested and with which he and his staff were very familiar. More important, however, was the fact that Robert S. McNamara, the new secretary of defense, soon asserted his authority to settle most defense matters within his own department while keeping the President informed. According to some observers, an added explanation for the apparent smoothness of White House–Defense Department relations was the manner in which the department's memorandums were prepared. When these came to the White House, they bore Secretary McNamara's personal imprint, and, unlike the more impersonal State Department memorandums, they almost never required supplementary analysis or information.

The appointment of General Taylor as the President's military representative in June, 1961, following the Bay of Pigs, reflected a substantial diminution of the President's confidence in the joint chiefs and in the intelligence community. General Taylor served primarily as a military adviser and worked to repair relations between the President and the chiefs. He also kept an eye on the intelligence community and served as chairman of an interagency committee that reviewed sensitive, clandestine matters for the President. (A similar committee had existed under President Eisenhower but initially had been allowed to lapse by President Kennedy.)

The military representative worked closely with the special

assistant, and his presence greatly enhanced the President's ability to deal with military questions. When General Taylor was named chairman of the joint chiefs in October, 1962, he recommended to the President that he not be replaced in the White House.[19]

A prominent feature of the Kennedy Administration was the use of Presidentially designated interagency task forces such as those on Laos, Berlin, and Cuba, to coordinate the efforts of several departments and agencies. These task forces, which reported to the President, often covered the spectrum of activities from formulating over-all policy recommendations to the detailed management of crises in the areas of their concern. They were often headed by assistant secretaries of state or defense, but a key member of all such groups was either a Presidential assistant or one of the Bundy staff. It was through these individuals that the President kept in touch with the groups' activities and provided guidance.

There were great varieties of more informal *ad hoc* committees, as well as continuing ones—such as the Cuban Coordinating Committee, over which a State Department officer presided and which included representatives from several departments, some with primarily domestic responsibilities. Another major committee was the Special Group for Counterinsurgency (CI). The latter was chaired by the President's military representative and also included Attorney General Robert Kennedy and McGeorge Bundy. The driving force within this and other groups invariably came from those closest to the President.

This process of experimentation with *ad hoc* coordinating mechanisms was to continue into the Johnson Administration, before a more formal and comprehensive approach to the problem of interagency coordination was attempted.

President Kennedy's approach to making decisions was first to immerse himself personally in the issues at stake. In addition to meeting with the various department and agency heads, he often

---

[19] Nevertheless, at Bundy's request, one of Taylor's military assistants remained as a senior member of the NSC staff, partly in order to provide liaison with the office of the chairman. This practice was continued during the Johnson Administration.

talked with working-level specialists and—of particular relevance here—he drew on the resources of Bundy and his staff. During the formative stages of a problem, staff officers were expected to know the status of work in the appropriate departments and what final positions were likely to emerge. The availability of such information made it possible for the President's views to be taken into account before departmental positions hardened. Because several of the staff, in addition to Bundy, dealt personally with the President, the feedback process was both direct and energetic.

Bundy's ordering of the President's business and the information he furnished orally or in memorandums gave the President additional assurance that all relevant views were presented and all consequences and alternatives considered. The purpose of these presentations was not to superimpose staff judgments, but to analyze departmental or other positions and to provide the President with a full understanding of conflicting views. By all accounts, staff analyses were scrupulously fair, but searching in their examination.

The Presidential decisions that followed were enunciated in various ways—during or after formal or informal meetings, by memorandums, or in direct conversation with the Cabinet officers having primary interest. Most decisions were recorded, either by letters or by notes—sometimes from the President himself —by Bundy memorandums, or by National Security Action Memorandums (NSAM's), which were a key instrument of White House direction in the Kennedy period.

The Kennedy Administration developed no equivalent of the OCB requirements for departmental reporting on the implementation of policies, although a system was instituted for keeping track of Presidential directives and requests and the implementation of NSAM's. Bundy expressed confidence that the State Department would act just as fast as it could to respond to the President's directives and that he would query the department "only if in the normally brisk dispatch of business we are not in the position to tell the President what is happening." Although some systematic accounting was continued throughout the Kennedy Administration, it was never as important as the more informal and continuous contacts of the staff with all levels of the bureaucracy.

Another device introduced to enhance White House knowledge and control of ongoing actions was the requirement that important outgoing State Department telegrams be cleared with the White House. This procedure, relatively unknown in earlier administrations, began very selectively with respect only to designated issues, but the requirements were progressively broadened to include a wide range of subjects.

At the same time, the simple fact that the staff had virtually unlimited access to departmental communications meant that it was not as dependent upon formal departmental accounting as the Operations Coordinating Board had been. While the staff's monitoring could be more selective than that of the OCB, there was, of course, no assurance that Bundy and his associates would be able to stay on top of everything. Indeed, many observers and participants of the processes of the Kennedy–Johnson period believe there were great gaps between the articulation of policy objectives and the implementation and verification of coordinated action in furtherance of those objectives.

President Kennedy's attitude toward the National Security Council was perhaps best expressed by McGeorge Bundy when he wrote to the Jackson Subcommittee in late 1961: "The National Security Council is one instrument among many; it must never be made an end in itself." [20] Although President Kennedy met with the full council much less frequently than President Eisenhower had, he did use it to discuss long-term matters such as basic U.S. policy toward particular countries, as well as selected national-security problems that did not require urgent decision. Formal meetings were prepared for in advance by agendas and papers. In general, however, the President preferred to make major decisions with fewer people present than would have been involved in a full-blown NSC meeting. Just as his predecessor had done, he held many informal meetings which might otherwise have been labeled NSC meetings, because all or most of the statutory mem-

[20] Report of the Jackson Subcommittee, *op. cit.*, I, 1336.

bers and advisers were present. As President Kennedy himself expressed it:

> We have averaged three or four meetings a week with the Secretaries of Defense and State, McGeorge Bundy, the head of CIA and the Vice President, but formal meetings of the Security Council which include a much wider group are not as effective. It is more difficult to decide matters involving high national security if there is a wider group present.[21]

President Kennedy also occasionally used council meetings as a means of getting his advisers to commit themselves and of assuring each his day in court—purposes that had been well served by council sessions during his predecessor's administration. Finally, some formal NSC meetings were probably held in order to reassure those who, as Theodore Sorensen described them, "equated machinery with efficiency."

The clearest manifestation of the *de facto* NSC gathering was the "Ex Comm" (Executive Committee) group which met during the Cuban missile crisis. The President assembled an initial group of thirteen advisers and experts of his choosing (the number and attendance subsequently fluctuated), and he relied heavily upon them for advice during those critical two weeks of October, 1962. As testimony to the power of the NSC image, Kennedy went to the trouble of having the Ex Comm arrangement approved by the full NSC and enshrined in a NSAM—on October 22, 1962, when the existence of the crisis was first made known to the country.

In perspective, then, during the Kennedy Administration, the Bundy staff became a distinct element in the national-security process, closely related to the expanded Presidential scope of interest and activity. Without President Kennedy's intensive personal involvement in national-security affairs, the staff would not have developed and existed as it did—largely independent of the bureaucratic forces surrounding it. It was often referred to as the "NSC staff," but this title was a misnomer—it became, in fact, a Presidential staff. The action orientation of President Kennedy

[21] Sorensen, *op. cit.*, p. 284.

was manifested in the importance that the staff attached to information handling and to the timely identification of issues. As soon as an issue of concern to the President had been identified, the staff became an active participant in its management. Such participation, coupled with the staff's direct ties to the President, made possible the more or less continual exertion of Presidential guidance and often served to broaden the President's options in decision-making. Finally, the contacts of the staff within the bureaucracy and its access to internal, departmental information enabled it to monitor selected departmental operations intensively.

The staffing practices of the Kennedy Administration contrast sharply with those of the Eisenhower Administration in several major respects: First, the Kennedy staff devoted very little energy to the National Security Council per se, and the council's supporting mechanisms were abolished; second, the staff concentrated heavily on what was happening at the moment, in part because so many critical situations arose which demanded the President's personal attention, but primarily because the President himself reached down and out for so many issues; and third, many staff members had direct and personal access to the President, and thus became channels for a type of guidance that had previously flowed through traditional channels from the President to his department and agency heads.

Although these staffing practices offered advantages to the President in terms of direct responsiveness and immediate feedback, they also tended to diminish the initiative of the State Department and to disturb its already none-too-strong internal organization. This in turn made it more difficult for the department to afford the President the support he desired. Had the State Department pulled together the threads of the responsibility intended for it, the national-security staff might not have developed as it did. When the State Department did not appear to be responsive, the staff moved in—not in a deliberate effort to acquire power but, in their view, in order to do the President's work.

In retrospect, President Kennedy probably had two alternatives, either to take steps to strengthen the State Department or to rely increasingly on a staff of his own. The latter course was easier.

Although many of those most intimately involved in this experience reaffirm the need for some national-security staff, they nevertheless believe that strengthening the State Department was—and remains—a long-term necessity.

Experience has also led some of the original Kennedy people to have second thoughts about the wisdom of their wholesale abolition of the NSC system. As one of them phrased it: "We aimed at Eisenhower and hit Kennedy." Or as another put it: "We did away with the old and didn't put anything in its place."

PRESIDENT JOHNSON: 1963–69

Before the functions of President Johnson's national-security staff are examined, it will be instructive to note some general characteristics of the national-security process during his administration. Taken together, these characteristics shaped the conduct of affairs far more than statutes or organization charts. They included the following:

1. More than his predecessors President Johnson had facilities readily at hand that enabled him, when he chose, to dominate the process—a vast array of information and intelligence, a sophisticated communications system, and an in-house staff which lessened his dependence on the bureaucracy and greatly increased his knowledge of its activities.

2. The President frequently chose to participate actively in decisions—big and small—which he believed would significantly affect U.S. interests or his position as political leader of the administration. He often assumed tactical control of issues while engaging in a wide-ranging, informal, and closely held process of consultations.

3. Decisions emerging from this process often did not become matters of formal record, nor were their rationales always necessarily explicit; written decisions for policy guidance were the exception rather than the rule.

4. A strong desire for "open options" characterized decision-making, often depriving the departments of preliminary guidance on Presidential thinking, restricting their operational latitude, and complicating the planning process.

5. As a corollary to the preceding, individuals—particularly those whom the President had personally "calibrated"—were more important than institutions.

6. Beginning in 1965, Vietnam occupied a major portion of the time and energy of the President and his principal advisers, sometimes at the expense of attention to policy problems in other areas of the world. The demands of the war affected the President's way of doing business with his principal advisers in a number of ways, drawing them together in a tightly restricted inner circle—from the secretary of state alone with the President, to the four or five who normally attended the Tuesday lunch at the White House.

The special assistant, the deputy special assistant, and the executive secretary of the National Security Council, supported by the NSC staff members and the Situation Room personnel, together made up the Presidential national-security staff. In form and function, the staff changed less at the time of transition from the Kennedy to the Johnson administrations than it did later, when Walt W. Rostow succeeded McGeorge Bundy as special assistant. Even before Bundy left, however, there were marked changes in the staff's relationship with President Johnson as well as with the departments and agencies. Presidential contact with staff members—with the exception of the special assistant and deputy special assistant—gradually became less frequent, and fewer memorandums went to the President on the responsibility of individual staff members. Toward the end of 1968, most of the staff were officers on loan from the departments—largely the Department of State—and their approach to the bureaucracy was less aggressively activist than that of many of their predecessors. With certain exceptions, few of the staff were closely identified with the President.

Although President Johnson did not exhibit, especially initially, his predecessor's wide-ranging, in-depth interest in foreign affairs, he did exercise very tight control over selected issues, Vietnam above all. In many cases, he looked to the staff more for ongoing information and monitoring of operations than for independent initiatives. The staff's role was to see that the President's options were protected and that coordination took place among the agencies. Only on selected matters of overriding and specific concern to the President (such as Vietnam, foreign assistance, or balance of payments) did staff members exercise a strong personal role in interagency matters.

In most instances, the transaction of business between the President and the bureaucracy took place through the special assistant and the staff. The high informality of the early Kennedy era settled into general patterns which, if not always efficient, were usually predictable. The staff and the departments became accustomed to doing business with each other—the bureaucrats having come to accept the idea that the staff and the White House could be useful to them, and the staff more frequently pursuing its objectives through normal channels. Much of this change apparently resulted from a conscious effort by the President and the special assistant to deemphasize, at least to the public, the staff as a factor in the President's relations with his principal officers. This de-emphasis began immediately after President Johnson's succession to office; it became more pronounced after the departure of McGeorge Bundy in early 1966, followed by Walt W. Rostow as his replacement. President Johnson initially indicated that Rostow was not "replacing" Bundy, although in substance he did. Nevertheless, the President's close personal relationship with the secretaries of state and defense, and the staff members' more indirect relationships with the President, had the effect of restricting their activities in areas other than those where significant Presidential interests were involved.

As will be noted later, President Johnson's decision in 1966 to give greater interagency authority to the secretary of state had the effect of orienting some of the staff's activity toward new arrangements centered in the State Department. To the extent that the State Department picked up the lead in this and other less formal means of coordination, the activism of the staff diminished. In selected geographical and functional areas of particular Presidential interest, individual staff members remained quite prominent, but by 1968 they had become the exception.

The special assistant's contacts with the President were more frequent than those of any Cabinet officer, and he and his staff sat astride and coordinated formal communication with the President. He often had both the first and last shot at bringing matters to the President's attention and was usually the first to know the President's reactions. As the person often first charged with meeting the President's requirements and carrying out his instructions, he was at the very nerve center of the process.

The special assistant attended most important meetings between the President and his principal advisers, traveled abroad with him, and often spoke for him. He sat as the White House representative on the many principal, interdepartmental committees, such as the Committee of Principals, the Senior Interdepartmental Group, the various Vietnam coordinating committees, and the committee that supervised clandestine-intelligence activities.

The special assistant's duties do not lend themselves to neat organizational analysis, but in general he performed duties in one or more of the categories listed below.

1. The special assistant coordinated and, as appropriate, supplemented the flow of information and intelligence to the President from the departments and agencies, devoting particular attention to items of potential concern to the President, and providing additional depth of coverage on selected items of particular interest, importance, or sensitivity.

2. He ordered and coordinated the flow of decision papers to the President, ensuring that priority items were promptly handled and that the President had available not only all the relevant information and recommendations required to make a decision but also the underlying bureaucratic and political considerations.

3. He followed the daily operations of the government to help ensure that matters touching the President's interests received appropriate attention, that adequate interagency coordination occurred at Cabinet level or below, and that the President's directions were being followed and his options protected.

4. He often communicated Presidential decisions and instructions to the departments and agencies.

5. He provided a point of liaison with Cabinet officers on matters which, although important, did not require the President's personal or immediate attention.

6. He acted in a close personal sense as adviser to the President, and, together with his staff, provided the President with independent substantive analysis as requested or as deemed appropriate.

During most of the Kennedy and Johnson administrations, an important role was played by the deputy special assistant. His responsibilities included international financial and economic matters (excluding aid policy), as well as the related problems of alliance politics in Western Europe. Because of the urgent nature of problems in this field—French troop withdrawals from NATO, the trilateral negotiations with the United Kingdom and West Germany on troop levels and burden-sharing, post–Kennedy Round adjustments, and international-monetary reform, the deputy special assistant frequently dealt directly with the President. The fact that the deputy special assistant was concerned with powerful domestic interests and dealt extensively with powerful domestic departments also tended to separate his activities from other national-security problems within the general cognizance of the special assistant.

The deputy special assistant (initially Carl Kaysen and later Francis Bator) represented the President in top-level interagency committees such as the Cabinet committees on the balance of payments and textiles. Bator's successor, Edward Fried, assumed substantially all of his responsibilities, but without the title of Deputy Special Assistant.

The executive secretary of the NSC throughout the Kennedy and Johnson administrations was Bromley K. Smith, who was appointed to that position in early 1961. Because of the relative inactivity of the National Security Council, his work, like that of the NSC staff officers, related primarily to that of the special assistant. He filled in for the special assistant in his absence, but was somewhat handicapped in such instances because he did not have the special assistant's personal relationship with the President.

The executive secretary assisted the special assistant in handling the flow of communication to and from the departments, and he provided over-all direction to the White House Situation Room. Directly related to these functions was the executive secretary's continuous liaison with the departments and agencies and with elements of the White House staff outside the national-security area.

When the National Security Council did meet, the executive secretary conferred with the special assistant on the selection of agenda items, supervised preparations for council sessions, and maintained the NSC records. Working with the special assistant, and in collaboration with points of contact in the offices of the secretaries of state and defense and the director of Central Intelligence, he assembled the suggested agenda for the Tuesday lunch meeting.

The composition of the Rostow NSC staff is best illustrated by the attendance at the staff meeting that Rostow held three times a week. In addition to the special assistant, the deputy special assistant, the executive secretary, and the director of the Situation Room, there were usually about a dozen other staff and liaison officers. Some of the staff members had fairly specific assignments, although their responsibilities in some instances overlapped. The clearest assignments were those corresponding roughly to geographical divisions of the State Department, i.e., one officer for each of the following: Asia generally, but Vietnam in particular; Southeast Asia, less Vietnam; China–Korea–Japan; Latin America; the Near East; Africa–South Asia; and Eastern Europe–Soviet Union. Some of these officers also carried additional functional portfolios; for example, the Africa–South Asia officer exercised a major staff responsibility in foreign-assistance matters.

The Bureau of the Budget was usually represented at staff meetings by an assistant director. The responsibilities of some NSC staff officers were oriented toward other agencies or White House offices; for example, one followed matters concerning the National Aeronautics and Space Administration (NASA) and the Atomic Energy Commission (AEC), and another maintained liaison on national-security affairs with the White House Press Office. In addition, there were those who functioned as integral parts of the staff, but who belonged to other entities and performed liaison functions. Among these were representatives of the Science Advisor's Office, the Central Intelligence Agency, and the Office of the Chairman of the Joint Chiefs of Staff. During the height of the Vietnam War, the latter was active in White House monitoring of Vietnam military operations and in the interpretation of related intelligence.

President Johnson's use of and attitude toward the National Security Council was similar to that of his predecessor. The council met fairly often, but the agenda rarely included the big issues of the day. Council sessions were frequently used, in the words of some of those familiar with them, for "educational, ratification, or ceremonial" purposes.

Regularly scheduled council meetings—as opposed to those convened in crisis situations or for the purposes mentioned above —occasionally served as forums for discussing selected upcoming problems on which coordinated advance planning was desirable. While several courses of action may have been discussed in the council, specific decisions were rarely requested of, or made by, the President during the sessions. Such meetings provided an opportunity for the President to express his general views on agenda topics, which were useful in guiding the subsequent handling of the problems. Occasionaly, the President gave his agreement "in principle" to a course of planning and action outlined in the council, but he instructed that specific questions be later brought to him for decisions as necessary.

The most important regular, high-level meeting in the national-security process during the Johnson years was not the National Security Council, but the Tuesday lunch. Even this arrangement was not, strictly speaking, comparable to the NSC, the agenda being primarily devoted to operational decisions—mostly on Vietnam—rather than to broad questions of national policy.

The Tuesday lunch began as an informal meeting of President Johnson, Rusk, McNamara, and Bundy. Gradually, it became a predictable occasion, which the participants could count on for dealing with the most pressing issues of the week. Participation was later enlarged regularly to include the Presidential press sceretary, the director of Central Intelligence, and the chairman of the Joint Chiefs of Staff, with others added as the occasion suggested. The format of the lunch was fully compatible with the President's personal preferences, as described, for example, by former Press Secretary Bill Moyers: "He is generally more satisfied with small groups of people he knows well. As Kennedy before him, he learned that the NSC is not a live institution, not suited to precise debate for the sake of decision. President Johnson chooses to call in a handful of top advisers, confidants, close friends." [22]

The Tuesday lunch came to be regarded as a useful, and by many an indispensable, institution, given the President's preferred way of operating. It was a place where critical advice was proffered, key decisions made, and major guidance issued. It was flexible enough to include whomever the President wanted and felt he needed for the work at hand. The importance attached to it in many quarters suggests that in its absence the processes of the Johnson Administration would not have provided adequate opportunities to obtain firsthand Presidential thinking on important subjects.

Several problems arose in connection with the Tuesday lunch. The agenda was sometimes hurriedly prepared and, as a result, adequate staff work was not always available to the participants. Furthermore, decisions were sometimes reached on matters that had not been scheduled for discussion and therefore were not fully reviewed in advance or coordinated with all interested parties. Because no written record was kept, each of the advisers was somewhat on his own in interpreting and carrying out decisions. Although this situation did not appear to worry the principals, their subordinates sometimes found it difficult to piece together a reasonably good version of what had been decided at lunch.

The Situation Room staff, the executive secretary, and the special assistant screened an enormous intake of intelligence and military and diplomatic reporting in order to supplement the regular reporting to the White House by the departments and agencies.

[22] Interview with Michael Janeway, *Atlantic Monthly*, July, 1968, p. 35.

They looked primarily for the new, fast-breaking events, for items that involved Presidential concerns of which the bureaucracy might not have been aware, and for matters which the departments, left to their own devices, might not readily have brought to the President's attention.

Some of those familiar with President Johnson's information intake believe he received too much information too fast. They argue that in many cases it would have been better to slow the process down in order to put new developments into better perspective. Preferences in this matter, however, naturally were determined by the President.

Liaison between the NSC staff and the departments and agencies on information and intelligence handling was quite close. The White House Situation Room was linked by teletype and other means with the State and Defense departments, the CIA, and the National Security Agency. In addition, each of these organizations had a "watch" operation similar to the Situation Room, and together they formed an efficent network that assured the President ready access to information anywhere in the system.

At a higher level, the executive secretary and the special assistant were in frequent touch with their points of contact in the departments. The State Department executive secretariat was an important element at this level of liaison because much of the significant information in the system derived from its reporting and daily activities. The channel worked in both directions, of course, and through its White House contacts, the State Department secretariat was able to keep abreast of Presidential interests and to supply information from the State Department when it appeared necessary or desirable. From the State Department's point of view, these arrangements would probably have worked better if the department had had a better idea of what information the President was receiving.

Much of what has been said regarding White House–State Department relations in the information area also applied to the Central Intelligence Agency. The agency's regular summary and special reporting to the President moved to him through the special assistant without delay. In addition, the special assistant, and occasionally members of his staff, relayed requests to the CIA for additional information which would be of use to the President. From time to time, the special assistant, aided by members of his staff, furnished the President with in-house analyses of intelligence data. While this was a source of concern to some, those responsible saw the problem as one of getting the product of the intelligence community to the President in a more useful form. In any event, such analyses were in addition to, and not substitutes for, the regular products of the intelligence community.

The President also received a continuous flow of reports from the departments and agencies in the national-security field concerning their current operations. Some of this was transmitted in conversations between Cabinet officers and the President, and some in the form of memorandums or regular reports such as the State Department's nightly report of each day's activity. Not all such memorandums reached the President. The NSC staff screened out some because they had been overtaken by events, while others were incorporated into staff memorandums elaborating or commenting on the department's reporting, on the basis of the staff's independent familiarity with the President's knowledge of the subject matter. The bulk of such material went into the President's "night reading."

The implications of the President's exposure to this wealth of information were considerable. He was probably better informed across the board—if not in depth—than many of his Cabinet officers, and his reactions to what he received constituted a continuing source of stimulus and guidance to the staff, the departments, and the agencies. Although most information went to the President in written form, his reactions were usually passed on to the bureaucracy orally by the special assistant or a member of the NSC staff.

Many of those involved in national-security affairs during the Johnson Administration believe that one of the most persistent problems was identification of interagency issues requiring coordinated planning and management. During much of the time, there was no functioning interagency mechanism charged with locating such issues and bringing them under centralized management. Responsibility thus rested both on the departments and on the NSC staff, with no clear division between them.

In some areas of the State Department, this function was well carried out, but, as in other matters, much depended upon the effectiveness of individual assistant secretaries. Much also depended upon the nature of the issues themselves; in international financial matters, for example, and in questions of alliance diplomacy with heavy economic and military overtones, the natural tendency toward independent departmental decision-making was simply not appropriate. In such instances, the relations of staff members with senior departmental officers were the President's best assurance that his interests and options were being protected.

There was no fixed pattern to such activity. Some members of the staff, for example, the deputy special assistant, often operated at both Cabinet and sub-Cabinet level across three or four departments. Only a staff officer with substantial access to the President could do this, and by late 1968 few of the staff were in this category. Other staff members, operating primarily at the assistant secretary level and below, were nevertheless able to initiate activity within a department or bureau and to stimulate the exchange of information within and between the agencies—all directed toward the identification and management of issues. Their assets in this type of activity were their wide perspective on issues, their access to information across a broad range of problems, and their relatively neutral status. When results could not be obtained by the staff member within established channels, it was possible for him to bring potential trouble spots to the President's attention through the special assistant.

Coordination of operations in the Johnson Administration continued for the most part to be an *ad hoc* endeavor involving an uneven exertion of initiative by the State Department, reinforced and supplemented by the NSC staff. The coordination of certain large issues, such as Vietnam, and of some lesser, but politically sensitive issues, was centered in the White House, often in the hands of the President himself.

Nevertheless, following Rostow's appointment as special assistant, an obvious effort was made to reduce the visibility of the

NSC staff. One manifestation of this was the approval by President Johnson in March, 1966, of NSAM 341. By this action, President Johnson assigned to the secretary of state "authority and responsibility to the full extent permitted by law for the over-all direction, coordination and supervision of interdepartmental activities of the United States Government overseas." The principal organizational feature of NSAM 341 was the creation of a permanent interdepartmental committee, the Senior Interdepartmental Group (SIG), headed by the under secretary of state exercising the power of decision, subject to appeal. Subordinate to the SIG were the Interdepartmental Regional Groups (IRG's), chaired by the regional assistant secretaries of state.[23] In explaining the need for the President's action, General Maxwell D. Taylor, who conducted the study which led to the issuance of NSAM 341, said, "I will say that always the White House is going to be a focal point of activity and there is going to be a lot of necessary coordination in this building regardless of what takes place outside. I think it would be fair to say if this new system works as I visualize it, that a Mr. Bundy would not be faced so frequently with the need for *ad hoc* coordination between departments." [24]

In preparing his recommendations, General Taylor had found little enthusiasm among senior officials for refurbishing the National Security Council. Thus, the remaining choices, as reported by General Taylor in a press conference, were to set up "some new organization stemming from the President himself," or to "give more specific authority to the Secretary of State." The latter course was chosen. In theory, the benefits to the President could not have been clearer: coordination at a high interdepartmental level, thus reducing the role of the White House staff, and achievement of greater selectivity in bringing matters of top priority to the President. More than a year elapsed before there was any significant progress in making the SIG/IRG system operational. During that period and to the end of the Johnson Administration, the staff

[23] NSAM 341 and the SIG/IRG system are more fully described and discussed in Chapter VI.

[24] Transcript issued by the White House of press briefing by General Maxwell D. Taylor, March 4, 1966.

remained active, *inter alia*, in the task of assuring interagency coordination.

Rostow himself was an advocate of the SIG/IRG system and frequently indicated his desire that the State Department assume a more vigorous role in coordination. The official position was that the staff would seek to ensure that coordination took place, preferably outside the White House. In practice, however, it was difficult to establish the distinction between encouraging coordination and being an agent of coordination. This was complicated by the fact that President Johnson frequently handled issues himself, or placed them in the hands of his own staff, as a means of ensuring coordination. One notable instance of this was the Indian food problem in the winter of 1966–67, and a continuing example was the President's requirement that his approval be obtained for all foreign assistance loans over $5 million or $10 million (depending on the nature of the loan) and on all Public Law 480 authorizations. This requirement was designed to provide the President with assurance—which he needed because of Congressional and other domestic pressures—that such loans had been fully coordinated and that the relevant Cabinet secretaries had personally approved them. The instruments of the President's personal control in these latter instances were the members of the Budget Bureau and national-security staffs who handled the final processing of the decision memorandums.

The mixed nature of the coordinating process was also illustrated in the handling of the trilateral negotiations with the British and the West Germans during the spring of 1967 on several subjects affecting the balance of international payments. The over-all management of this problem was vested in an *ad hoc* committee composed of the secretaries of state, defense, and the treasury. Tactical control, however, actually was exercised by an informal sub-Cabinet group representing the three departments and including the deputy special assistant. The latter illustrates one of the most frequent coordinating devices of the Johnson Administration, i.e., the *ad hoc* group formed around a particular issue and including a member of the national-security staff who was the connecting link between the tactical group and the President. Many of those most familiar with this practice point out that it was considered particularly well suited to a situation in which the President wished to emphasize his preference for "open options." Even if "open options" had not been the rule, some of these same individuals would have argued against standing committees on the grounds that their membership often is not relevant to specific problems in terms of expertise, and that, because of their built-in institutional positions, they are less likely to get down to serious business.

Nevertheless, many of the adherents of the *ad hoc* approach do believe that something like the SIG/IRG mechanism could be effectively used as a means by which special issues are identified and carefully chosen groups designated to deal with them. Even if this were possible, however, they believe there would still be a significant, indeed indispensable, role for a White House national-security staff in maintaining "a dialogue" between the President and the operators and in "lubricating" the wheels of coordination.

President Johnson disposed of the vast majority of questions which reached him—and a very large number did—on the basis of decision memorandums prepared by, or coming through, the special assistant. Larger and more critical decisions, however, rarely came to final decision on the basis of a single, written presentation. President Johnson usually discussed them with the special assistant and the relevant Cabinet officers and often asked for additional work to be done, such as exploring a particular alternative or a suggested new approach. He frequently engaged in a wide range of personal consultations both inside and outside government through individual conversations, phone calls, or *ad hoc* meetings. There was no predictable pattern to such consultation, and even the closest members of the President's official family were unable to follow it. At the end, a decision emerged. Many well-qualified observers believe this approach to decision-making substantially impaired the bureaucracy's understanding of the President's views and its ability to implement his wishes.

A memorandum signed by the special assistant, the deputy special assistant, or occasionally by other staff officers, was the usual vehicle for presenting recommendations to the President. Practically nothing, even from department and agency heads, went to the President without some indication that it had been at least noted by the staff.

State Department memorandums normally underwent review either by the special assistant, or his staff, or both, the operative portions often being recast in a summary or covering memorandum in order to sharpen the presentation, to supplement or elaborate the alternatives, and to analyze the latter in terms of political or tactical considerations of a Presidential nature which the basic memorandum had not addressed. In short, the staff sought to assure that when a problem was presented to the President, the covering memorandum highlighted the questions he might be expected to ask before making his decision.

The process described above was a source of substantial discomfort to the State Department during the Kennedy–Johnson period. The State Department lost control of its paper when it reached the White House, and its officers were troubled by uncertainty concerning the terms in which its recommendations had reached the President. Most national-security staff members defended this procedure as being beneficial to the President. First, and most important, the President preferred it. He was accustomed to having choices presented in a particular format and style, one with which his staff was familiar and the regular bureaucracy was not. Second, President Johnson, like President Kennedy, valued independent review by his own staff. Finally, the State Department generally lacked sufficient top-echelon staffing to review memorandums with corresponding thoroughness or breadth of perspective.

During the Johnson Administration, most significant decisions were either communicated by the President directly to the principals concerned, individually or in a group, or relayed by telephone calls from the special assistant or other staff officers. As noted above in discussing the Tuesday lunch, this informality occasioned concern and, not infrequently, problems in the bureaucracy. Even those who stressed the practical limitations on how much could or should be formally recorded believed that a greater effort by the President and his staff to provide better guidance—in whatever form—would have been repaid in better understanding at the middle levels of government and in an enhanced capability for departmental planning. However, not all of the responsibility for this situation rested with the White House. Internal communication and discipline within the State Department appeared—from the White House—to have been less than adequate. When State Department officers could not obtain guidance or a hearing within their own organization, they very often turned to staff officers in the White House.

The information flow to the White House and the constant contacts of the staff with all levels of the bureaucracy constituted President Johnson's primary means of assuring himself that his decisions were carried out. Very little a department did or did not do could long escape the notice of the national-security staff. The bureaucracy's knowledge of that fact provided a certain amount of discipline within the system.

As in the field of coordination, the staff inevitably concentrated on the more important matters and followed departmental actions closely to ensure that instructions were faithfully executed. In the absence of a much larger staff and a more systematic followup, probably not much more than that could have been done.

The telegram-clearance procedure mentioned earlier provided another means of follow-through and monitoring. When a Presidential decision required instructions to a diplomatic mission, for example, the proposed instructions were passed to the White House for clearance. Either the special assistant or the staff officer most familiar with the issue reviewed the draft message to verify its consistency with the President's instructions or known position. Frequently this process was expedited by the actual participation of the special assistant or a staff officer in the drafting of the message. On occasion, the outgoing instructions were drafted in the White House and referred to the State Department for comment prior to transmission.

At the end of the Johnson Administration, the national-security staff appeared to stand at a crossroads in its evolution. Under President Eisenhower, the NSC system and its corresponding staff organization provided an elaborate formal framework for integrating the government's national-security activities. During the Kennedy and Johnson administrations, the staff evolved primarily as an extension of the President's direct interest and role in national-security affairs. Because of the President's frequent involvement in the detailed direction of the process and the absence—or nonuse—of more formal procedures, the integrating functions performed earlier by the NSC system of interdepartmental committees were often performed by the President himself or through the informal intermediary efforts of his national-security staff.

Although there are continuing differences of opinion concerning the proper limits of the staff's role, there is general acceptance of the President's continuing need for his own national-security staff. The climate of working relations between the staff and the departments and agencies has mellowed. The bureaucracy has found that it can frequently use the staff to good advantage and has become less fearful of being used by it.

Late in President Johnson's Administration, the national-security staff had dwindled to a rather small group of officers, most of them detailed from the departments and agencies. It was neither a highly structured staff organization like that existing in January, 1961, nor the assertive and highly personalized staff inherited by President Johnson. It was, instead, a staff which largely limited itself to monitoring the national-security process from the President's perspective, making sure that the various elements of the process were in touch with each other when other means proved insufficient, and providing the President with whatever in-house advice and support he felt he needed.

V

The Future of the
White House National-Security Staff

Any President is going to need a White House national-security staff. The chief questions are: What kind? How much? For what purposes? The answers depend not only on the President's personal style and preferences, but also on the amount of time and attention he wants to devote to foreign affairs as against domestic matters, on the degree to which he wants to involve himself in day-to-day management of national-security affairs, on the extent to which he wants to delegate responsibility to department and agency heads, and on his over-all concept of the best national-security arrangements. In some sense, these considerations are all independent variables; none of them is necessarily determined by the others. The President might, for example, want to retain quite close personal control over major functions of the system, but to do so through his Cabinet officers or through interdepartmental arrangements, rather than through a dominant, White House national-security staff. Or he might wish to assign very active initiative to the State Department and still seek strong staff support from his own official household. The Presidency itself and the corporate entity usually called the White House staff or national-security staff are not institutionally synonymous unless the President chooses to make them so.

Regardless of his over-all arrangements for national-security affairs, there is an irreducible minimum of staff functions that any President will require in the White House. A staff will be needed for the following purposes:

1. To impose coherence and order on the formidable flow of paper (whether it requires action or simply conveys information) to and from the President

2. To provide working contacts between the President and the departments and agencies
3. To fill certain needs which for any number of reasons the President will prefer to have handled with assured discretion and tight control in his immediate official household

Most of those interviewed for this study agree that these minimum essential functions should be discharged by a single staff and that it is desirable for that staff to be under the direction of one person enjoying the President's fullest confidence. Without such single direction, the President would have to deal with a number of staff subordinates for national-security matters, and his burdens would probably be increased rather than decreased. In addition, senior officials in the departments and agencies need a single point of contact in the White House, short of the President himself, for conducting business of concern to the President, but which need not or should not immediately occupy his time. Whether the man in charge is called the special assistant for national security affairs, or something else, is less important than that there be one man in charge of carrying out these functions. (He will be referred to hereafter as "the special assistant.")

It almost goes without saying that the special assistant must be thoroughly familiar with the President's views, priorities, and interests, as well as privy to national-security operations across the board. He must also have the confidence of the principal department and agency heads as well as that of the President himself. Much testimony emphasizes how important it is that the special assistant take care to represent departmental views to the President accurately and fairly, to distinguish clearly between his opinions and theirs, and—in dealing with the bureaucracies—to distinguish between his personal suggestions and the expressed wishes of the President.

The flow of information and action documents to and from the President must be managed by someone with an intimate knowledge of the President's interests and constraints and a grasp of the over-all activities and concerns of the national-security community. Priorities must be established and enforced by someone with a keen sense of what the President must, should, or would want to see—to determine what needs to be handled when, and in what order, and whether the necessary staff work is complete.

Timeliness is vital in providing the President with what he needs when he needs it. In this connection, the White House Situation Room, with its facilities for the rapid exchange of information, is one of the President's most valuable assets. Because of the turnover of staffs and the removal of Presidential records and correspondence following each administration, the national-security staff lacks corporate memory other than that embodied in one or two specific individuals. It may therefore be desirable to develop a more effective information storage and retrieval system.

Effective contact between the White House and the national-security departments and agencies cannot be confined to the flow of documents. In order to assure close mutual communication among the White House, the State Department, the Defense Department, the Joint Chiefs of Staff, and the Central Intelligence Agency, the special assistant must establish close working arrangements with the heads of those institutions and their principal staff officers. Among the latter, the executive secretary of the State Department is a particularly important contact because of the constant pressure of foreign-affairs problems.

The ability of the State Department, the Defense Department, and the CIA to support the President will be greatly enhanced if, in addition to the contacts of their own senior officers with the President, the special assistant is able to keep them informed, not only about the President's specific requests and inquiries, but also about the concerns uppermost in his mind—all the things which might enable them to anticipate his needs and desires.

There are many tasks related to the President's personal requirements in national-security affairs that he will want handled by his official household, but which require a broad knowledge of current national-security operations. These would include, for example, making discreet inquiries outside bureaucratic channels, arranging the details of foreign visits, dealing with the domestic political aspects of national-security affairs, drafting sensitive correspondence, or preparing speeches bearing on national security which the President may wish particularly to bear his personal imprint.

Even if the White House national-security staff is confined to performing the minimum essential functions, there will inevitably be the problem of enabling it to work without interfering with the effectiveness and authority of the departments and agencies. The experience of past administrations indicates that there is no simple solution to this problem, but it does suggest a few guidelines, which would be helpful to all concerned:

1. The departments and agencies should recognize that the President's interests, priorities, and constraints do not on every issue coincide with their own.
2. Department and agency heads—and their institutions—should acknowledge that the national-security staff has a legitimate function to perform on behalf of the President.
3. The White House staff should recognize that, although they are often closer to the President's perspectives than the departments and agencies, nonetheless the latter do have viewpoints that are themselves important to the President and may serve him better.

White House Staffing Under Alternative Systems

Beyond the minimum requirements discussed above, Presidential staff needs and functions will depend on over-all choices in the organization and conduct of national-security affairs. Elsewhere, this study has delineated three broad choices or prototypes for such organization—a State Department–centered arrangement, one based on close White House control, and one described as "intermediate."

It is assumed that any concept of national-security organization will, in one way or another, take into account basic functional requirements such as policy planning, resource allocation, and operational coordination. Except perhaps in the most highly centralized system, responsibility for these functions will be shared among the President, his staff, and the departments and agencies. What is important is to distinguish between the form and the substance of this allocation. In the Eisenhower Administration, the major functions were allocated to a series of NSC committees: The form was that of a system centered in the White House. Nevertheless, the influence of the secretary of state and the Treasury secretary predominated in these bodies. In the Kennedy Administraton, the prestigious Planning Board and the OCB were dissolved and their responsibilities transferred to the individual departments, particularly the Department of State. Nevertheless, on the frequent occasions when President Kennedy chose to do so, his personal involvement—supported by the efforts of an activist national-security staff—had the effect of centering the process in the White House. This pattern continued well into the Johnson Administration, and it was not until 1967 that a new form began to emerge—that of the SIG/IRG system. Although this system gave some form to interagency relationships, the locus of substantive power remained uncertain and shifting. Had the secretary of state exercised the full measure of his authority under NSAM 341, the system would have been centered in the Department of State—in reality as well as in theory. In practice, however, when the President or his staff officers assumed the initiative on a given issue, the existence of the system was of little significance. When a new administration takes office, the future of the SIG/IRG system is uncertain. A strongly supported secretary of state could make it an instrument for the exercise of broad, delegated authority. On the other hand, if the SIG/IRG system, or something like it, were placed under White House chairmanship, it would then become the organizational framework of what would be, in effect, a White House–centered system. Implicit in the latter move, of course, would be a revocation of NSAM 341's delegation of authority to the secretary of state.

The use of the National Security Council—either more or less than in the past—is perfectly consistent with any of these alternative systems. In any case, each of these systems, and any variation on them, would imply different requirements and roles for the White House national-security staff.

At various times in the past—even within the span of a single administration—the National Security Council has been peripheral, important, central, or irrelevant to the national-security process, its role dependent on issues, personalities, and the problems of the time. Its significance has sometimes depended primarily upon the individuals present and how they interacted with one another.

Among President Kennedy's other objections to formal and regular use of the council was his feeling that the statutory membership included more officials than were needed to do the job or were compatible with his way of doing it; his complaint was compounded by the custom of members who brought subordinate advisers with them to the council's deliberations. In other eras, the council commanded attention because it was the organizational focal point of the entire national-security process. But even under those circumstances, many agree that what took place outside the council was of equal and sometimes greater importance than its formal meetings. Nonetheless, Presidents Kennedy and Johnson, without regard to their opinion of the council's practical utility for decision-making, found its symbolic value useful in times of crisis.

If the council is to be employed in a continuing role as the forum for the deliberation and promulgation of policy, some systematic means should be employed to select and prepare proposals for its consideration. This could be accomplished either by providing it with its own supporting mechanism, something comparable to the Planning Board of the 1950's, or by linking it to the operation of something resembling an active SIG/IRG system, charged, among other things, with specific responsibility for identifying problem areas and preparing policy recommendations for the council's consideration.

In either case, the President and the council should continue to have the benefit of a secretariat as well as an independent staff capable of dealing with substantive issues. Historical precedents for both are to be found in the Eisenhower NSC "Special Staff" and the Bundy–Rostow staffs. The Special Staff, which worked through the special assistant, helped to lay out and to sharpen issues and departmental positions. The Bundy–Rostow staffs, although they did not regularly focus on council proceedings as such, examined recommendations coming from the bureaucracies to the President and sought to assure the exploration of alternatives. They also provided the President with analyses and commentaries on recommendations in terms of their institutional origins, interagency implications, and intra-Cabinet politics.

Any system that employs the council as an active body for policy deliberations and uses "policy" as a managerial tool would require arrangements for translating policy guidance into more specific operational guidelines and integrated plans. Something designed to do what the Operations Coordinating Board was intended to do could easily be established, although the deficiencies of the OCB, discussed earlier, suggest the need for modified arrangements. The SIG/IRG system, or a variation, could also be charged with this task, provided there were stronger staff support at all levels. Either way, there would be a potential role for the White House national-security staff, ranging from that of monitor to arbiter—depending upon the President's wishes.

This discussion of the council's staff requirements implies a relatively "neutral" role for the staff appropriate either to a State Department–centered or an intermediate system. If the President chose to use the council and a supporting NSC system as instruments of direct and intensive control, the special assistant and NSC staff officers would presumably be expected to exercise a more active and assertive role on behalf of the President.

IMPLICATIONS OF A STATE DEPARTMENT–CENTERED SYSTEM

A State Department–centered system would require a fresh attempt to give effect to the principle of State Department leadership, as stated by President Kennedy and explicitly strengthened by President Johnson in establishing the SIG/IRG system. This approach would seek to make possible the President's relative detachment from day-to-day national-security operations by vesting directive authority in the secretary of state across a broad range of national-security activities, subject to Presidential policy guidance.

The critical requirements for the success of such a system would be: (a) the ability of the secretary of state and his principal subordinates to share the President's perspectives and to command his confidence and support, and (b) effective management arrangements for exercising the secretary's authority. A close working relationship between the secretary of state and the secretary of defense, as well as the director of Central Intelligence and the chairman of the Joint Chiefs of Staff, would also be crucial—as indeed it would be in any system.

If the above requirements could be met, the national-security burden of the President would be significantly reduced. Fewer operational decisions would have come to the White House, and more of the President's time could be devoted to policy matters. Similarly, the President's staff requirements could be kept to a minimum. The staff's principal purpose would be to provide the President with an independent means of assuring himself that the State Department–centered system was operating as it should and that Presidential interests were being taken into account in its operation. This could be accomplished through staff review of reports to the President from the departments and agencies and by selective monitoring of the implementation of policies and decisions. In addition, the staff would provide the President with a source of objective analyses when he wanted it, as well as an independent means of interve;.ing in normal procedures when the circumstances required more direct Presidential control, or when the secretary of state could not or did not resolve differences among—or with—his colleagues. Such a precaution might contribute greatly to the President's confidence in the system and to his willingness to let the departments run their own affairs.

Because of the importance of Presidential policy guidance, national-security staff representatives could follow policy-planning activities in somewhat the same way the Eisenhower Special Staff related to the Planning Board. If the secretary of state were to employ something similar to the SIG/IRG system as a means of exercising a broad interagency responsibility, the same system might also be the primary—not necessarily exclusive—source of policy planning. While refraining from imposing "White House" views, the staff might nevertheless assist in identifying issues and exploring alternatives, particularly by introducing a feeling for special Presidential constraints and domestic political considerations.

Many observers believe that one of the serious shortcomings of the national-security process is the inadequacy of procedures for examining the resource implications of policy proposals. This applies both to allocations for national security as a part of over-all expenditures and to allocations for different purposes within the national-security field. Although the director of the budget and officers of the bureau work closely with the President and the Cabinet members, many believe that little progress has been made toward realizing the Jackson Subcommittee staff recommendation of 1961 that NSC deliberations should be related more closely to the budget process and in particular "that the perspectives of the secretaries of state and defense are brought to bear on an ordering of national priorities at the target-setting stage of the annual budget preparation." [1]

In order more closely to relate policy and resource allocation, and particularly to assist the President in dealing with differences in the State and Defense departments, the White House national-security staff and the Budget Bureau staff—or some group representing the two—might analyze policy proposals and other recommendations before they reached the President or the council. This process could be directly related to the activities of a foreign-affairs program budgeting system if one is ever established. These analyses might be made available to the President either for his exclusive use or for council participants as well.

In a State Department–centered system, the limited size and responsibilities of a White House national-security staff might permit its direction by a single special assistant, assisted by the executive secretary of the NSC. Additional staff requirements would be determined primarily by the extent and nature of the staff's role in policy formulation and by the use made of the National Security Council. Other than the special assistant, none of the staff need have direct access to the President. Lesser staff positions could be filled with qualified but relatively "low visibility" individuals. Senior appointees who might otherwise be considered for the staff could be assigned to the State and Defense departments, where their talents and energies would be more needed.

---

[1] U.S. Congress, Senate, Report of the Jackson Subcommittee, *Inquiry on National Policy Machinery*, III, "Staff Reports and Recommendations" (Washington, D.C.: U.S. Government Printing Office, 1961), p. 40.

IMPLICATIONS OF A WHITE HOUSE–CENTERED SYSTEM

A decision to place the operation of the national-security process more directly under the President's personal control would not necessarily require the jettisoning of existing interagency arrangements. For example, certain elements of the SIG/IRG system (sometimes criticized because of its ambiguous relationship with the President) could be retained, but they could be headed up by a Presidentially designated officer of the White House staff—perhaps the special assistant for national security affairs. In this event, these elements could either report directly to the President, or they could report to him through the National Security Council.

There is no historical precedent for a truly White House–centered national-security system, although various versions have been proposed from time to time, notably by President Eisenhower, and more recently, by Governor Nelson Rockefeller in June, 1968. Such proposals generally fall into two categories: those which would create a super-Cabinet official to exercise over-all direction on behalf of the President, and those which would involve a powerful and comprehensive national-security staff arm—a "super-staff" for the President himself. Both variants emphasize the desirability of focusing planning and operational coordination at the level of the President. Many of those who advocate these approaches reject the central premise of the State-centered system— that one Cabinet officer can effectively exercise authority over his colleagues across a broad range of national-security affairs.

Proposals for a super-Cabinet official have generally been criticized on constitutional, statutory, or political grounds, because of the difficulty of finding someone suitably qualified for the job, and because of the problems that could arise in relations between the President and his secretaries of state and defense. Whatever the merits of the proposal, and despite the title given to him, a super-Cabinet official would require the support of a sizable staff with major responsibilities in all the functional areas. The superstaff proposal would involve essentially the same thing, but would seek to avoid complications arising from placing a new figure of authority between the President and the Cabinet. Advocates of a superstaff argue for it on the grounds of its insulation from departmental influences and its Presidential orientation, and they believe that it would help to correct what they consider to have been weaknesses in procedures in recent years—the lack of structure in agency coordination and the insufficient means of assessing ongoing programs.

A superstaff would necessarily be quite large and complex. It might be broken into several components charged with policy planning, coordination of operations, and evaluation, and these new elements might, to some extent, integrate relevant assets of the Budget Bureau, the Office of Science and Technology, and other executive-office entities.

The policy-planning element of the staff would be primarily concerned with identifying problems and alternatives and suggesting priorities and objectives. It would not only supervise the preparation and presentation of policy proposals to the President to assure adequate examination and interagency discussion, but it would also be an important source of initiatives. Through its linkage to the budget process, it could assume major responsibility for relating policy to available resources.

The coordinating element would logically seek to facilitate interagency communication and programing as well as systematic reporting and monitoring, such as that attempted but never fully realized by the Operations Coordinating Board. In order to avoid some of the acknowledged weaknesses of the OCB, the new body would need to have its own staff—not a borrowed one—and independent sources of information; its chairman would need to be a Presidential representative with the power to direct corrective action and a clearly understood duty to bring deficiencies to the President's attention if necessary.

A program-evaluating element would constitute the most novel departure from past White House staff functions. The nearest current equivalent is the effort of the Bureau of the Budget to evaluate the effectiveness of foreign-aid programs. The extent to which such evaluations can be applied in other areas of national-security affairs is uncertain, but a policy-planning process which introduced more precision into defining goals and operating guidelines might facilitate systematic evaluation. Any staff engaged in similar activity would need to work closely with the departments and agencies engaged in the evaluation—perhaps in the context of a program-budgeting system—but obviously should neither be dependent upon them for information nor susceptible to their pressures.

The principal *advantage* of a White House–centered system would be the close control it would afford the President. If strongly led by a few assistants exercising very substantial authority on his behalf, it would make for a degree of centralization and perhaps of sensitivity to Presidential direction never before attempted nor achieved. The principal staff officers would become, in fact if not in name, super-Cabinet officials. Such a large and complex staff organization might well assume a character and momentum of its own, however, and constitute a layer between the President and the operators. In order to avoid this and to lead, rather than being led, the President would probably have to take close and continuous interest in its operations. Thus, the principal *disadvantages* of such an approach might be to add to the President's burdens rather than subtract from them and to impose an added (and competing) bureaucratic element between him and the departments and agencies.

IMPLICATIONS OF AN INTERMEDIATE SYSTEM

The President may choose to arrange for an intermediate system, to strike a balance between the dependence upon subordinate officials implied by heavy delegation of authority and the centralization and added burdens involved in a White House–centered system. There are several ways of conceiving of such a system, the chief questions being where to draw the lines of responsibility for which purposes. One way of dividing responsibility involves a more or less deliberate division of labor along functional lines—for example, assigning major control over policy planning or resource allocation to the White House and coordination of operations to the Department of State. Another less deliberate way of dividing it would be simply to appoint a strong and aggressive White House national-security staff and to encourage or permit it to engage actively in leading or overseeing the process—even where, in theory, responsibility might lie with the Department of State or another department.

However responsibilities were assigned in an intermediate system, one particularly difficult problem would be to arrange for the White House staff to function without impairing the effectiveness and authority of those having actual responsibility for implementation of policy. Mixed 'or shared responsibilities tend to assume a reciprocal nature: Weakness on either side invites accretion of power by the other, and the resulting imbalance may not, in the long run, work in the President's interest. Obviously, a White House staff starts with an initial advantage in such situations. As one White House observer phrased it: "Power is lying around all over this place waiting to be picked up." Therefore, in any intermediate system, the degree of activity of the White House staff and the personal style of its members may well determine the balance.

During the Kennedy–Johnson administrations, responsibility in many areas was shared between the White House staff and the departments and varied with the issues from department to department and within departments from bureau to bureau. By and large, the intervention of the White House staff was on a selective basis—with the understanding that although the department was primarily responsible, it should not move too far without ascertaining or verifying the President's desires. This was often done through continuous, informal exchanges.

The history of the SIG/IRG mechanism is not conclusive on this score. If the directive authority vested in the secretary of state had been fully exercised, and the IRG's had been uniformly active and effective, much of the existing ambiguity concerning White House staff responsibility might have been reduced. The SIG/IRG structure could easily lend itself to either more or less participation by the national-security staff than has been the case in practice. In the State Department–centered approach discussed earlier, that staff would presumably play a limited role and would function chiefly as the President's eyes and ears and perhaps as his spokesman on selected issues only.

But in an intermediate system, the staff could participate much more aggressively. For example, staff members might be active in developing policy proposals within an interagency coordinating system. They could focus attention on issues which, in their opinion, were not receiving adequate attention from the departments and advance their own initiatives based upon their feel for Presidential thinking. They could also seek to stimulate examination of alternative solutions which might not coincide with prevailing thinking in the bureaucracies.

Through active involvement in a SIG/IRG type of arrangement, even though the system was chaired by the State Department, the White House staff could call attention to particular issues that, because of their specialized nature or the bureaucratic policies involved, needed to be lifted out of normal channels (e.g., removed from an IRG agenda) and addressed by an *ad hoc* group. One of the principal advantages the President could derive from an intermediate system would be a ready ability to move in on a situation of this sort—through his staff—in order to protect himself from bureaucratic inertia or impasses which commonly afflict fixed-membership committees.

Much of what has just been said with regard to identifying issues and developing policy proposals applies equally to interagency coordination of major operations. When the President wished to assure centralized control of implementation, or if he saw a need for specialized handling of an issue by a select group, a national-security staff officer might provide a direct link between the President and that group.

One function in which the national-security staff should probably exercise a clear and independent responsibility within an intermediate system would be monitoring the implementation of specific Presidential policies, programs, and decisions. A distinction should be drawn between routine monitoring by each department and agency as part of its own internal management and selective monitoring in areas of particular importance or interest to the President. If the national-security staff continues to have unfettered access to information concerning departmental operations, selective monitoring could be conducted with a minimum of formal reporting.

Selective monitoring is a particularly important and logical White House function on issues which cut across the interests of several agencies and which call for perspectives that only the President or his innermost circle of advisers possess. To place exclusive responsibility on the State Department might invite unproductive conflict and resentment on the part of other departments. Furthermore, as various veterans of the Eisenhower, Kennedy, and Johnson staffs have pointed out, on some issues it is much better for the White House assistant to "blow the whistle" than for the secretary of state to "use up his capital" with other Cabinet members.

A national-security staff performing these functions in an active manner probably could not be directed by a single Presidential aide. Some of those who worked with both the Bundy and Rostow staffs believe that under such circumstances it would be desirable to include in the staff two or three subordinate deputy assistants who hold Presidential appointments. They need not necessarily be in the line of command, but each should enjoy sufficient access to the President so that between them the President would be guaranteed exposure to all aspects of important issues, and he would have at his elbow a greater depth of specialized expertise than a single individual could offer.

Thus, one of the deputy Presidential assistants might devote his full time to the policy-planning process, assume more or less direct leadership of such of it as was not done in the departments, and keep fully abreast of what was done below. It is conceivable that the special assistant himself could assume this task and thus avoid an undesirable separation of responsibility. Most of those interviewed, however, felt that the burden of the special assistant's other responsibilities would preclude his assuming the extra work. If policy planning were the responsibility of a deputy assistant, it would be imperative that he nevertheless maintain close contact with day-to-day operations while remaining outside the related pressures and responsibilities.

If the White House national-security staff were organized along rough geographical and functional lines, one of the deputy assistants might be charged with responsibility for international economic and financial matters. This family of issues is often

closely related to domestic interests, as reflected in the involvement of the Treasury, Agriculture, and Commerce departments in
national-security affairs.

The specialties of the other deputies would depend upon the
nature of the President's particular concerns and objectives. One or
more might concentrate on defense matters, particularly the relationship between national-security policy and the budget, or the
mutual security–foreign assistance field. Whatever the portfolios
of the senior deputies, the deputies should have a personal relationship with—and access to—the President, yet their activities
should be subject to the over-all purview of the special assistant.

VI

The Department of State:
Its Structure and Role in 1968

When he assumes office, the new secretary of state moves into a large, rather gloomy, paneled office on the seventh floor of the New State Building and assumes charge of the oldest, and possibly the most complicated, department of the federal government. Like the new President whom he is to serve, the new secretary presumably has well-formed views of what he wants to achieve. He is sure, however, to encounter important managerial problems in making the best use of the resources of his department.

No document can serve as an "operator's manual" for the new secretary. This chapter and the chapter following attempt only to describe the State Department as it exists today, highlight some major problems, and suggest varying arrangements that might be considered in fitting the department into an effective system for formulating and executing national-security policy. The choice among possibilities must, of course, be made by the President and the secretary of state.

THE NATURE OF THE PROBLEM

If a cross section of informed Washington observers were asked which government agency most needed fundamental reform, a substantial number would probably name the State Department. But here their agreement would end. Some would criticize the alleged standpatism and old-fashioned ways of the Foreign Service. Others would deplore the subordination of the Foreign Service to political appointees. Still others would see serious shortcomings in the State Department's leadership of other agencies, but they would differ on whether to blame these shortcomings on the department's top management or on its staff.

A full catalog of complaints against the State Department would require several pages but would not greatly advance the present inquiry. The truth is that foreign ministries are rarely popular, particularly in periods when the inability of diplomats to discipline an intractable world is painfully apparent. Hence, much of the criticism of the State Department amounts to discontent with specific foreign policies or, more fundamentally, with the state of the world itself.

It is nonetheless significant that such criticism is frequently cast in organizational or procedural terms. State does pose managerial problems of unusual complexity, and disagreements over how to solve these problems are inevitable. Their nature can be brought out fully only by describing in some detail how the department functions. It may be useful first to set down some fundamental problems which confront a modern secretary of state in administering his department and giving it an appropriate role in the government at large.

Scope. What is the proper sphere of the secretary of state and his department? In what areas should he direct policy, in what areas should he seek merely to influence policy, and in what areas should he simply be generally informed? To what extent must he concern himself with defense policy? With foreign economic and monetary policy? With science and technology? With domestic policy?

Priorities. Whatever his sphere of responsibility, how can the secretary help the President to strike the best balance among competing interests and objectives, foreign and domestic? How can he ensure that all alternatives are weighed, that all relevant considerations are taken into account?

Resources. To what extent should the secretary control or influence allocation of public resources to various overseas programs, both civilian and military?

Initiative. How can the secretary steer a constructive and reasonably consistent long-term course in international affairs and avoid merely reacting to events? Can foreign policy be planned? How can the gap between planning and action be bridged?

Coordination. How can the secretary ensure that the actions of his department and other agencies will be timely, mutually supporting, and consistent with the policy of the President and Congress? How can he best provide political guidance to the Department of Defense and other agencies operating overseas?

No organizational arrangements or procedural devices can ensure satisfactory answers to these questions, but some will be more likely to help than others. These questions will therefore be kept in mind in the following discussions of the present and possible future role of the State Department.

Any new administration will doubtless make changes, large or small, in the role of the secretary and his department in the formulation and execution of national-security policy. Each must, however, begin with what is already in place. The problem, in the words of a curmudgeonly foreign-service officer, will be: "How to build a brave new world with most of the same old people in it." The present role of the State Department is therefore directly relevant to the tasks a new administration will face.

The modern secretary of state must be many things. He is the President's deputy in coordinating most overseas activities as well as the chief administrator of his own department and U.S. diplomatic missions around the world. By custom, he is the President's principal adviser on international affairs. Second only to the President, he is also chief diplomat and negotiator in dealing with foreign governments, chief advocate and defender of the President's foreign policy before Congress and the people, and chief U.S. representative on the all-too-many occasions set by the rigid standards of traditional protocol.

The combined burden of these roles is crushing. It is also increasing, with the growth in complexity of international problems and the consequent proliferation of governmental organizations and programs. Secretary of State Dean Rusk was able to adjust to these burdens gradually, over an eight-year period. A new secretary encounters the full weight of his many roles all at once.

Setting priorities in the use of his own time and finding a way to delegate some of his burdens to his principal assistants are among his most urgent problems.

The Recent Internal Organization of the State Department

All organization charts are inadequate, and the one put out by the State Department in 1968 is no exception. Nevertheless, it provides a starting point, and is reproduced in slightly simplified form in Figure 1.

State's top command consists of the secretary, the under secretary, the under secretary for political affairs (who by law could alternatively be designated "for economic affairs"), a deputy under secretary for political affairs, and a deputy under secretary for administration.

The under secretary is, in theory, the secretary's alter ego, although in practice there is a rough and shifting division of labor between these two officials, with some tasks or problems delegated from the secretary to the under secretary.

No clear concept defines the responsibilities of the under secretary for political affairs, and his assignments are largely determined on an *ad hoc* basis. The line between the functions of the second- and third-ranking officers of the department is much less clear today than it was when the latter bore an economic rather than a political designation. (There is a comparable lack of clear definition between the functions of the counselor and at least one of the two ambassadors at large.)

Contrary to what his title suggests, the deputy under secretary for political affairs does not normally report to the under secretary for political affairs, but to the secretary and the under secretary. The deputy under secretary is usually one of the most senior officers in the Foreign Service. He has the well-defined function of speaking for the State Department on political-military problems and in monitoring operations of the intelligence agencies. A small staff of political-military specialists reports directly to him, but in the intelligence field he relies on a staff subordinate to the director of the Bureau of Intelligence and Research.

The role of the deputy under secretary for administration is

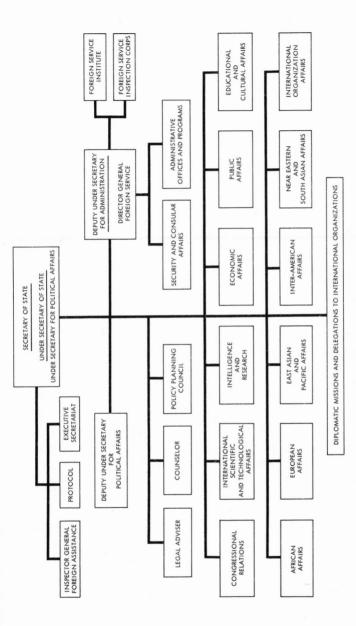

FIGURE 1. Organizational Structure of the Department of State in 1968

roughly what his title implies. Some Foreign Service officers believe that two of his functions might more appropriately be located directly under the secretary. Subordination of both the inspector general and the director general of the Foreign Service to the department's chief administrative officer is seen by these officers as evidence of the low state to which the service has fallen.

Over the years, designation of a general manager has often been proposed as a means of tightening the Department of State's internal administration and easing the secretary's burdens. The merits of this proposal are discussed below, but it should be noted that, at least in recent years, none of the State Department's senior officers (including the deputy under secretary for administration) has functioned as a general manager.

In terms of the classic distinction between staff and line, the State Department today is a line-oriented organization. Given their broad responsibilities, the immediate staffs of the top command are remarkably small. The secretary traditionally regards the senior line officers of the department as *his* staff and takes care that no substantive staff units stand between him and them.[1]

The executive secretariat is staffed by carefully selected substantive officers, but it does not attempt to impose its own substantive views on proposals passing through it en route to the secretary or one of his principal assistants. Its primary mission is to oversee the flow of paper among the top command, the assistant secretaries, the White House, other executive agencies in Washington, and the missions overseas. The executive secretariat also provides administrative services for the Seventh Floor [2] and runs the department's Operations Center—a round-the-clock office for helping to handle crises, large and small.

The small, high-quality substantive staff recently created to support the under secretary in his capacity as executive chairman of

---

[1] As used in the State Department and other agencies concerned with national-security policy, "substantive" refers to the content of policy, as contrasted with the procedures and organizational arrangements for conducting it.

[2] In the State Department, "Seventh Floor" is shorthand for the top officers and their immediate staffs, which are located on that floor. The prestigious connotations of the term are similar to those of the Pentagon's "E Ring."

the Senior Interdepartmental Group represents a new departure. This could mark the beginning of a new approach to the question of staff support for the department's top command.

The five regional bureaus constitute the core of the State Department and largely dominate day-to-day operations. Their scope is virtually unlimited within their areas of responsibility. Much of the liaison with other departments is in their hands. Generally speaking, the functional bureaus and staffs are at a disadvantage in seeking to influence the operational decisions of the regional bureaus.

The regional bureaus, staffed largely by career officers, are also the heartland of the Foreign Service. Each bureau has its own tribal characteristics and traditions. If policy inertia is a problem in the State Department, it is mainly encountered here.

Advice to the President on the selection of the regional assistant secretaries of state is among the most important early actions of any new secretary. If he is to grasp his department quickly and use it to carry out the President's policies, the secretary must be sure that the five regional men share his outlook on international problems and are capable of working smoothly with him as a team.

For many years, the five regional bureaus were subdivided into geographical offices, each composed of several country desks. In 1966, most of the geographical offices were abolished and the desk officers redesignated "country directors." The change in title was intended to underline a change in function. The country directors were to be more senior than the former desk officers and were to be given greater responsibility. They were to report directly to an assistant secretary, to deal with officials of comparable or only slightly lower rank in other agencies, and to exercise much of the same kind of interagency leadership in Washington as an ambassador does overseas. Unfortunately, this promising concept has not been fully realized, and few country directors have performed the role envisioned for them. Most are desk officers with a new title.

Several things went wrong. Some countries were not considered important enough to elevate each desk officer to the new dignity of country director. In such cases, one man was made country director for several countries, an arrangement not greatly different from the old geographical offices. A tendency also developed toward increasing the number of deputy assistant secretaries, some of whom were given geographical responsibilities very much like those of the former office directors. Where the new concept was applied, country directors often found it difficult to live up to their intended responsibilities. This may have reflected the fact that many Foreign Service officers advance to senior grades without acquiring much executive experience. Some blame must, however, be attributed to the failure of those higher in the chain of command to adjust their own ways of doing business. A country director whose superiors treat him like a junior desk officer cannot easily deal with relatively senior officials in other agencies.

As the organizational chart (Figure 1) indicates, five functional bureaus and five functional staffs report directly to the secretary and the two under secretaries. Two ambassadors at large, the chief of protocol, the inspector general of foreign assistance, and at least eight special assistants (some with staffs) enjoy similar direct access to the top. Only one bureau, that of security and consular affairs, reports to a deputy under secretary.

The large number of units that report directly to the top is workable or not depending on the preferences and working style of the secretary. A new secretary will at least want to consider, however, whether a somewhat more pyramidal structure would not be more manageable and impose less of a burden on him and his under secretaries. (Possible ways of grouping some of the functional units, or of modifying their relationships with the top command and the regional bureaus, are discussed later.)

The Foreign Service is a carefully selected, highly motivated elite group, but discontent with its role and performance is widespread, both in its own ranks and among outsiders familiar with the State Department. A book could easily be written on the current state of the Foreign Service (and in fact several have), but here it is sufficient to point out two of the more important continuing problems—morale and skills.

The morale of the Foreign Service has been low. Changing personnel policies and an apparent excess of senior officers have caused individual officers to be concerned about their personal career prospects. Morale has also suffered from uncertainty about the future role of the Foreign Service and from the feeling within the service that the political leadership held it in low regard. Shrinking career prospects in Washington have been particularly disturbing. In recent years, fewer assistant secretaries than formerly have been career officers, and the abolition of offices in the regional bureaus has eliminated a number of attractive senior positions once filled by Foreign Service officers.

Adding to the morale problem, and a serious problem in itself, has been the clear gap between available talent and the skills needed to formulate and carry out U.S. foreign policy in the late twentieth century. The Foreign Service is short of good executives, well-trained economists, specialists in political-military affairs, and officers able to bridge the fields of foreign policy, science, and technology. An intensive and sustained training and recruitment effort is needed to enable the Foreign Service to meet the requirements of the modern world.

STATE–WHITE HOUSE RELATIONS

The relationship between the White House and the State Department is both personal and institutional. Rapport between the President and the secretary of state is crucial. Good rapport at the top does not, however, ensure effective working relations between the White House staff and subordinate levels of the State Department. Nor does the President's regard for the secretary necessarily extend to the department. Thus, President Johnson clearly had full confidence in Secretary Rusk, even though he (like some of his predecessors) was reliably reported as having a "dark view" of the State Department.

During the Johnson Administration, the President and the secretary of state met several times each week and talked frequently on the telephone. The Tuesday lunch meeting, however, was the only regularly scheduled occasion on which the secretary saw the President, and he did so in the company of other officials. The National Security Council, meeting only irregularly during the Johnson and Kennedy administrations, ceased to be the major arena for decision-making it once was.

The under secretary of state must often substitute for the secretary in responding to Presidential requests for information or advice. He therefore needs the personal confidence of the President almost as much as does the secretary. More than a score of other senior officers of the State Department are usually also Presidential appointees and at least in a formal sense may be said to enjoy his confidence. Few, however, have a personal relationship with him, and some do not see him from one annual diplomatic reception to the next. The lack of a visible and constantly renewed Presidential mandate reduces their ability to exert effective leadership over their counterparts in other agencies.

At its best, the network of informal contacts between White House staff members and State Department officers at all levels gives the latter a "feel" for Presidential thinking which would otherwise be largely absent. And in turn this network helps the White House staff keep the President informed of developments and permits him to intervene before his options have been foreclosed. At its worst, the State Department–White House network can breed confusion by transmitting wrong information about the President's views. Moreover, the network can decrease the sense of real responsibility within the State Department.

The flow of paper between the State Department and the White House is much less important than the variety of personal relations described above. President Johnson was known as a "reader," but some State Department memorandums ranked fairly low on his list of preferred reading. Possibly as a consequence, many such memorandums went no farther than the White House staff; others reached the President under cover of summaries prepared by that staff.

Nevertheless, a considerable volume of paper does move from the State Department to the White House, and a much smaller volume flows in the reverse direction. The most important policy papers requesting Presidential approval, or responding to Presidential inquiries, are signed by the secretary or the under secretary. Other official communciations to the White House on less important matters generally go from the executive secretary of the department to the special assistant for national security affairs.

A more extensive flow of informal, unofficial communications (draft cables, internal memorandums, and talking papers) goes from State Department officers to members of the White House staff and is a manifestation of the informal network discussed above. Much of this unofficial documentation is entirely "legal," but some of it can only be described as "bootleg." No one is ever likely to learn the true volume of the "bootleg copies" and unsigned "pieces of paper" passing from the State Department to the White House in a given week, but it is certainly substantial.

THE STATE DEPARTMENT'S RELATIONS WITH OTHER AGENCIES

The emphasis below on formal procedures should not obscure the fact that most of the State Department's interagency business is conducted through an informal network of personal relationships which extend from the secretary of state and his Cabinet colleagues to the most junior officer on a country desk and his counterparts in other agencies. In fact, the more formal arrangements for interagency coordination could not function in the absence of this informal network.

A distinction must also be drawn at the outset between formal doctrine and the actual interagency role of the secretary of state. The most recent formal pronouncement concerning the secretary's role was enunciated by President Johnson on March 2, 1966, in National Security Action Memorandum (NSAM) 341, which set up the system of a Senior Interdepartmental Group (SIG) and subordinate Interdepartmental Regional Groups (IRG's). The key sentence of a White House announcement on the subject follows:

> In order to assist him in discharging his responsibility for the conduct of foreign affairs, the President has directed the secretary of state, as his agent, to assume responsibility to the full extent permitted by law for the over-all direction, coordination, and supervision of interdepartmental activities of the United States Government overseas (less exempted military activities).

Despite the sweeping terms of NSAM 341, the move did not bring about a drastic change in the secretary of state's interagency role, nor would it have been realistic to expect it to do so. The new delegation of authority to the secretary did not represent a sharp break with the past but was an extension of his existing responsibility for coordinating interdepartmental matters overseas. In any case, no verbal formula, however authoritative, can swiftly revolutionize well-established working relationships.

The SIG/IRG System

President Johnson clearly recognized the need to go beyond a verbal delegation of authority to the secretary of state. NSAM 341 also created a new system of interagency committees to assist the secretary in exercising his expanded responsibility.

The SIG, which is the capstone of the system, unfortunately got off to a slow start, because its executive chairman, the under secretary of state, was about to leave office and his successor (partly because he was given a number of special assignments outside the field of foreign policy) was not able to focus on this aspect of his duties for several months. The SIG has consequently been continuously active only since about the middle of 1967.

The regional assistant secretaries of state approached their new tasks as executive chairmen of the IRG's in different ways. Some took the new institution seriously; others, less so. The executive chairman of the Latin American IRG quickly engaged his group in an experimental planning, programing, and budgeting system. The other IRG's did not follow this example, although the IRG for the Near East and South Asia has taken some steps in the same direction.

Much valuable experience has been gained with the SIG/IRG system, but, owing to its slow start and to the pragmatic, experimental approach of the officials charged with its management, it remains in a malleable state. If the system is to continue in some form, the new administration must address several important questions, including the following:

What kinds of business should be handled by the SIG and the IRG's? The agendas of these groups have generally been a mixture of operational, planning, and administrative items, with no clear emphasis in any particular direction.

What should be the relation between the SIG and the White

House? A senior member of the White House staff sits on the SIG, and the President is informed of all SIG actions. Some SIG actions are submitted to the President by the secretary of state (or by the under secretary with the knowledge and approval of the secretary) for final approval. Only rarely are items discussed by the National Security Council after the SIG has considered them.

What is the proper division of labor between the SIG and the IRG's? The SIG thus far has not hesitated to take up problems falling within the jurisdiction of a single IRG, although in such cases it may ask the IRG for its advice. The SIG has only in a few instances functioned as a court of appeals from IRG decisions.

Should the IRG's be supported by subordinate country or functional committees? This arrangement exists in the Latin American area and partially in some other areas.

Operations

Before discussing the Department of State's relations with particular agencies or groups of agencies, it may be useful to consider the department's current interagency role in broad, functional terms.

An ideal national-security process would move in stately and orderly progression from policy planning, through programing and resource allocation, to specific operational decisions and actions. For better or worse, the government does not operate that way. Making operational decisions is the heart of the national-security process. Coordination of operational decisions between agencies is at least as important as are the interagency arrangements for policy planning. More policy is made through operational decisions than through policy-planning papers.

Most operational coordination in Washington is done through an informal network of consultation, based on established ground rules about which agency should take action on a given piece of business and which agencies should clear it. The action agency of course has the initiative, and the State Department enjoys this advantage in the coordination of action on virtually all political problems and on some economic and political-military problems (notably many of those involving government-to-government negotiations).

In borderline cases, the State Department can more easily assume action if it has handled closely related business in the recent past, if the problem at hand was first raised in an embassy message, or if the issue clearly bears significantly on U.S. relations with a particular country. State can claim clearance rights on a fairly wide range of operational problems in which another agency has action. Here again, precedent and the extent to which a problem bears on our international relations are major determinants of the department's rights.

The process of clearance varies greatly and ranges from clearances "in substance" obtained in telephone conversations between relatively junior officers to clearances obtained in face-to-face meetings among senior representatives of the agencies concerned. SIG and IRG meetings are of course institutionalized versions of such meetings when operational matters are discussed.

In their coordinating roles, the secretary of state and his subordinates usually rely much more on persuasion and on specialized knowledge and experience than on authority, whether statutory or Presidential. This is true whether the State Department is the action agency or is seeking to influence action by another agency.

No system for coordinating routine operations can be relied on to work well in crises, when decisions must be made rapidly and senior officials up to and often including the President must be involved in matters of relatively small detail. The Kennedy Administration instituted two useful innovations, developed further under President Johnson, which increased the State Department's ability to deal with crises—the State Department Operations Center and the crisis working groups and task forces.

For the first time, the Operations Center gave the State Department a true, twenty-four-hour "watch" capability and a continuing point of contact with the White House Situation Room, the Pentagon's National Military Command Center, and the CIA Operations Center. The crisis working groups, housed in the State Department's Operations Center, are a means of rapidly expanding the personnel and capabilities of an ordinary country desk and elevating it organizationally, thus reducing the number of clearances required for action and increasing the control of the secretary or under secretary. These working groups typically consist of the desk officers normally concerned with the crisis area, reinforced by other State Department officers and in some cases also by officers from other agencies. Interagency coordination in crises is accomplished either through the IRG or, more frequently, through a special interagency task force, which is a committee drawn from the agencies represented on the IRG. The chairman of the task force is usually also director of the working group.

Creation of working groups and task forces is the responsibility of the executive chairman of the IRG. Policy recommendations from task forces (or conceivably, directly from working groups) could in principle go to the IRG or the SIG. In the interests of speed, however, they are more likely to be handled informally at whatever level appears to be appropriate.

The system appears to function quite well in most crisis situations. Major crises (such as the 1967 Arab–Israeli war) have, however, been handled by special arrangements centered in the White House. Crises at the lower end of the scale are often dealt with by normal procedures.

Despite its name, the Vietnam Working Group has usually functioned more like a country desk than a crisis working group. It is not housed in the Operations Center, and its director reports to a deputy assistant secretary of state, rather than to the secretary or under secretary. During and immediately after the Tet Offensive of February, 1968, however, part of the Vietnam Working Group did move into the Operations Center and functioned as a true crisis working group. The Vietnam Task Force, it might be noted, is a continuing interagency committee chaired by the assistant secretary of state for East Asian and Pacific affairs.

Monitoring

In a perfect world, a decision by the President or by subordinate officials acting in his behalf would always be followed promptly by appropriate action. Several Presidents have commented on how far this ideal is from reality. Clearly, some system of follow-through or monitoring is needed to check into the timeliness and effectiveness with which operational decisions are carried out. A major purpose of any monitoring system should be to reveal deficiencies in interagency coordination and recommend means of curing them.

Within the State Department, the executive secretariat monitors day-to-day actions on problems of major concern to the secretary and his principal assistants. The Foreign Service Inspection Corps is also essentially a monitoring device, but it is concerned with the general thrust of actions taken by field missions pursuant to directives from Washington rather than with individual actions. The Inspection Corps examines embassy relations with other U.S. Government agencies in a given country, but it does not directly inspect the work of those agencies. The Foreign Service Inspection Corps does, however, collaborate informally with the separate inspection systems of both the U.S. Information Agency (USIA) and the Agency for International Development (AID).

Planning

Planning is not part of the State Department's tradition. Mention of the word in some circles there produces a glazing of eyeballs or uncomprehending remarks, such as: "Planning? Why I plan every day of the year." It is not surprising that the State Department's leadership of interagency planning has been less than fully successful.

Two types of planning must be distinguished here. There is policy planning, which analyzes long-range problems on the assumption that discernible trends continue, and there is contingency planning, which considers what to do if something happens which is contrary to normal expectations and which may require the United States to take urgent action. Even though policy planning does not normally concern itself with contingencies directly, it must at least implicitly take them into account. Similarly, contingency planning must reflect the broad objectives laid down in policy planning.

Policy planning in the State Department is in theory the responsibility of both the operating bureaus and the Policy Planning Council. In practice, the bureaus have until recently done little work of this sort, except implicitly in connection with operational decisions. It has, however, always been possible to find a staff officer in each regional bureau who would admit to having some planning as part of his job. The creation of the IRG's has increased policy-planning activity in some bureaus to some extent.

Much of the work of the Policy Planning Council (designated S/P in State Department terminology) involves the participation of other agencies. Interagency working groups help S/P in the preparation of National Policy Papers (NPP's) [3] and on a few other selected projects. More frequently, specialists in other agencies are brought in on an individual, informal basis.

Most major S/P papers and a smaller number of papers prepared in other agencies are discussed in the Interagency Planning Group, which meets weekly under the chairmanship of the head of the Policy Planning Council. This group, formed in 1961 to fill part of the vacuum created by abolition of the NSC Planning Board, rarely expresses collective judgments, but exists almost entirely for the self-education of its membership, a group of senior officers drawn from the State and Defense departments, the CIA, and the White House staff. The Interagency Planning Group has not established any special or continuing relationship with either the National Security Council or the SIG/IRG system.

The final stage in the processing of S/P papers is discussion of the papers' analyses and recommendations at a meeting chaired by the secretary. Senior State Department officials with an interest in the subject of a given paper attend these meetings, and officials of other agencies are sometimes invited. The meetings serve principally as an occasion for the exchange of views on long-range problems. They may, however, result in action decisions by the

[3] National Policy Papers (NPP's) are comprehensive and authoritative statements of U.S. policy promulgated by the secretary of state under authority of National Security Action Memorandum 281, February 11, 1964. Almost all NPP's (only about twenty have been approved) deal with policy toward single countries. Secretary Rusk assigned general responsibility for the preparation of NPP's to the chairman of the Policy Planning Council and also issued detailed regulations governing their interagency coordination and clearance.

secretary, particularly if the S/P paper under discussion contains action recommendations.

Policy planning in the political-military field constitutes a special problem for the State Department. Both the Policy Planning Council and the Office of Political-Military Affairs have responsibilities in this field, but the real center of political-military planning is in the Pentagon, particularly in the offices of the assistant secretaries of defense for systems analysis and for international security affairs. The most important and influential political-military policy-planning papers are the Draft Presidential Memorandums (DPM's) on important security problems, which the secretary of defense sends the President each year as part of the annual budgetary cycle. The DPM's, in turn, strongly influence the posture statements which the secretary presents annually to Congress. State submits comments on both the DPM's and the posture statements, but these comments come fairly late in the process and are not always reflected in the documents that go forward to the President or the Congress. State has not made a general practice of providing policy guidance to the Defense Department on the problems treated in the DPM's and the posture statements before work on those documents has gotten under way.

In recent years, an informal exchange of views has developed between planning officers in the State Department and in the joint staff of the Joint Chiefs of Staff. State is now consulted informally on annual revisions of the Joint Long-Range Strategic Survey and on parts of the Joint Strategic Objectives Plan.[4] State also collaborates with the joint staff and the Office of the Secretary of Defense in the Special State-Defense Study Group, which undertakes major long-range studies in the political-military field.

Contingency planning in the State Department has been principally the responsibility of the operating bureaus, with the Policy Planning Council acting theoretically in a monitoring and coordinating role. Neither the bureaus nor S/P did much about contin-

---

[4] The first of these papers deals with the period five to eight years from now and is used in projecting future force goals. The second is concerned with the period ten to twenty years in the future and is designed to assist in research and development decisions.

gency planning, however, until 1965, when the Contingency
Coordinating Committee (CCC) was established with representation from the State and Defense departments and the CIA. The
CCC, under the chairmanship of the State Department's deputy
assistant secretary for political-military affairs, set priorities for
political-military contingency planning, established *ad hoc* interagency working groups to prepare draft contingency studies, and
took part in the review of such studies.

The Contingency Coordinating Committee was abolished in
1968 and its responsibilities turned over to the IRG's. The IRG's
were also specifically charged with studying political and economic
contingencies which had been outside the purview of the CCC,
and had, as a consequence, been relatively neglected. The newly
established Political-Military Group [5] was assigned a special monitoring role over political-military contingency planning.

This arrangement is too new to permit any judgment concerning
its adequacy. One basic problem, however, remains largely un-
solved. Most military plans (by their nature, military plans are
normally contingency plans) are prepared outside Washington in
the unified commands and, for entirely defensible reasons, are very
closely held. In the State Department, most contingency thinking
(planning would be too formal a term) is in the heads of operating
officers and not recorded fully on paper. In this situation, the
obstacles to ensuring that responsible civilians are fully aware of
relevant military considerations and that military plans proceed
from proper political assumptions are truly formidable. Interagency
collaboration in a few selected, contingency studies can only begin
to chip away at this problem.

Resource Allocation

No Cabinet officer can be sure that he will be given the resources
needed to carry out the programs for which he is responsible. The
secretary of state is further handicapped by a wide disparity between the extent of his responsibility for interdepartmental oper-

[5] The Political-Military Group is in effect a functional IRG which deals
with political-military problems not easily handled by a single IRG with a
geographically limited jurisdiction. The group is chaired by the deputy assistant secretary of state for political-military affairs.

ations and policy planning and the extent of his ability to influence relevant decisions about resource allocation.

The only budget submission over which the secretary exercises full and direct control is that of the State Department proper, not including AID, USIA, the Arms Control and Disarmament Agency (ACDA), or the Peace Corps. The resource problems posed by this budget (Shall Consulate A be closed? Should Embassy B have an assistant general services officer?) rarely have major policy implications. The only operational programs included in the budget of the State Department proper are some small cultural and educational programs. (In fiscal year 1968, Congress appropriated $46 million for educational exchange programs. The appropriation for fiscal year 1969 was only $31 million.)

The secretary of state or his designated subordinates approve the requests for economic and military aid appropriations prepared in AID, the Defense Department, and the Agriculture Department. State's role in this process, however, is largely reactive and, owing to staff limitations, rarely intensive. Procedures and staff capabilities for relating aid and other resource decisions to policy goals do not yet exist in the State Department, except possibly for Latin America. This deficiency is particularly glaring in the case of Defense Department expenditures, which inevitably have a major impact upon U.S. interests and objectives overseas.

For several years, the State Department, with some support from the Bureau of the Budget, has been groping toward creating a planning, programing, and budgeting system (PPBS), which would embrace all of the major agencies operating overseas (excluding military activities, except military attachés and military-assistance programs). Such a system would facilitate a more rational weighing of alternative means of achieving foreign-policy goals and would, in particular, bring to light interagency budgetary trade-offs, such as AID v. CIA counterinsurgency programs, or AID public-safety programs v. internal, security-oriented military-assistance programs. A foreign-affairs PPBS under State Department management would also automatically give the secretary of state considerably more control over the budgets of the agencies included in the system. It would not, however, solve his problem of gaining greater influence over the Defense Department budget. For such influence, the secretary must rely principally upon providing timely political guidance to the secretary of defense on military-budgetary decisions with major implications for U.S. foreign policy.

Earlier work on the now moribund comprehensive country-programing system will be useful, if and when a full-fledged foreign-affairs PPBS is created. The Country Analysis and Strategy Papers (CASP's) on Latin American countries amount to an experimental PPBS. Also, the SIG staff has worked with the Budget Bureau in an experimental joint review of all budget proposals for three selected countries. The director of the SIG staff and a senior Budget Bureau official met in turn with the regional assistant secretaries of state to discuss the fiscal year 1969 budget submissions by operating agencies in their areas of responsibility.

The State Family

The secretary of state and his department have special relationships with AID, USIA, and ACDA. Some might include the Peace Corps in this group, because it was established as an agency of the Department of State. The secretary of state has, however, delegated most of his largely administrative authority over the corps to its director; the corps, concerned with avoiding identification with official U.S. policy overseas, would probably decline any offer of full-fledged family membership. The heads of AID, ACDA, and USIA attended Secretary Rusk's small staff meetings; the director of the Peace Corps did not.[6]

The secretary of state has direct-line authority over AID and ACDA. His authority over USIA is limited to policy direction. It does not follow, however, that the State Department has less influence over USIA than over AID or ACDA. By well-established tradition, USIA has tended to limit itself to operations. For its

_____

[6] Legal niceties aside, perhaps the best indication of who belongs to the State Department family is in telephone arrangements. State, AID, and ACDA share the same government code (182), and all of their employees are listed in the same telephone directory. Part of USIA is on code 182, but only USIA personnel with titles appear at the back of the State–AID–ACDA directory. The top Peace Corps officers are also in the back of this directory, but their telephones are on code 128.

part, the State Department has developed a flexible but effective system for quickly providing policy guidance to USIA.

The secretary of state's authority over ACDA is diluted by the fact that the director of ACDA is by law an adviser of the President as well as of the secretary. Moreover, both the State Department and ACDA are policy-making and negotiating agencies, so no opportunity has existed for the kind of division of labor which has long characterized State Department–USIA relations. Despite this, working relations between the department and ACDA are generally good. The director of ACDA works with and through the secretary of state, rather than directly with the President. Possibly because of the State Department's limited staff capabilities in the field, staff work on disarmament and arms-control problems is generally done in ACDA. Formal interagency coordination in this field is entrusted to the Committee of Principals, chaired by the secretary. This committee also includes the secretary of defense, the chairman of the Joint Chiefs of Staff, the director of Central Intelligence, the chairman of the Atomic Energy Commission, the director of ACDA, and senior White House staff officers in the fields of science and national security.

State's relations with AID are much more complicated than are its relations with USIA or ACDA. In the case of AID, the operations–policy guidance division of responsibility would appear to make sense, but it has somehow not come off. State has not maintained an adequate capability to guide foreign-aid policy in the same comprehensive way that it guides information policy.[7] AID, on the other hand, has developed a substantial policy-planning capability of its own.

Generalizations about State Department–AID relations are, however, difficult. Special arrangements have been established

[7] During the Eisenhower Administration, the head of AID's predecessor agency, the International Cooperation Administration, reported to Douglas Dillon, who first was under secretary of state for economic affairs, and later, under secretary. Dillon was assisted in supervising aid operations by a special staff in his own office. At this time, the Department of State's Economic Bureau also included an Economic Development Division. Both the special Dillon staff and the Economic Development Division were dismantled early in the Kennedy Administration.

between the State Department and AID in two of the four regions in which AID operates. State and AID's Latin American bureaus were merged several years ago and placed under the assistant secretary of state for inter-American affairs. Somewhat more recently, the State Department and AID bureaus for East Asia and the Pacific were physically collocated (placed "back to back" in the bureaucratic vernacular), but they were not combined organizationally.

The latter of these two arrangements is generally credited with improving working relations between the staffs concerned. The former may well have gone too far. Critics argue that State Department–AID integration in the Latin American field has confused lines of authority, suppressed a useful adversary relationship between the two agencies, and imposed an impossible administrative burden on the head of the combined staffs.

State–Defense Relations

Less than two decades ago, Secretary of Defense Louis Johnson obtained a Presidential directive that there should be no contacts between officials of the State and Defense departments except through his own office. This restriction has long since broken down, and relations between the two departments at all levels have grown enormously in volume, range, and complexity. On any given day, hundreds of civilian and military officers on both sides of the Potomac are engaged in scores of collaborative or competitive endeavors which range from matters as routine as trip plans for a Congressman to the most profound strategic questions. The current extent of State and Defense department relations is, of course, an accurate reflection of both the magnitude and the interlocking nature of the security and other foreign problems which confront the United States today. Both departments are increasingly in one another's business.[8]

[8] It is interesting to note that the staff of the assistant secretary of defense for international security affairs (ISA) is often (and with some reason) referred to as "Defense's State Department." ISA's much smaller counterpart in the State Department, the Office of Political-Military Affairs, has yet to earn the parallel back-handed compliment of being called "State's Defense Department."

Over the years, the tone of the State Department–Defense Department relationship has greatly improved. More and more officers from both departments have been classmates at one of the war colleges. The successful State-Defense exchange program has given further impetus to the growth of mutual trust and cooperation. Close and friendly personal relations between successive secretaries of state and defense must also be given a share of the credit.

Problems traceable to the different missions and points of view of the two departments nevertheless persist. But this does not mean that Defense always gives more weight to "military" considerations and State to "political." The civilians in the Department of Defense, who must battle daily with the joint staff, are in fact often less "military" than are their colleagues in the State Department. Also, foreign-policy considerations can as easily favor carrying a big stick as walking softly. Economic considerations, too, bear unevenly on the two departments, with the Defense Department understandably much more conscious than the State Department of the budgetary and foreign-exchange costs of military deployments.

The division of the Defense Department along civilian-military lines inevitably influences State and Defense department relations. The Joint Chiefs of Staff and the joint staff under them welcome, and on occasion actively seek, opportunities for a direct exchange of views with the State Department. The Defense Department civilians, on the other hand, try to ensure that the department speaks with one voice and would probably prefer to hold State Department–Joint Chiefs of Staff contacts as much as possible to civilian-controlled channels. In this situation, subordinate State Department officers sometimes yield to the temptation to play one side of the Defense Department against the other. Representation of both sides of the Defense Department on the SIG and the IRG's would appear at first sight to be a sure cause of complications in State–Defense relations. The fact that, at least at the SIG level, such complications have not been serious must probably be credited to good coordination within the Defense Department and forbearance on the part of the State Department.

The Intelligence Community

State's relations with the intelligence agencies fall under two headings—monitoring clandestine operations overseas and analyzing and interpreting foreign developments.

The first of these functions is managed in two ways: Major decisions are handled by a State–Defense–CIA–White House committee chaired by its White House member. Lesser proposals are cleared by the State Department at the assistant secretary level. Staff work within the State Department on clandestine operations is performed by a small staff reporting to the director of intelligence and research. Day-to-day liaison on such operations, however, is primarily the responsibility of the deputy under secretary for political affairs, who also represents the State Department on the interagency committee mentioned above.

State's role in the analysis of foreign developments is much greater. State suffers, however, from an almost complete lack of a basic intelligence-research capability which dates from its voluntary relinquishment to the CIA in the early 1960's of the staff engaged in contributing to National Intelligence Surveys.[9] State also has chosen not to compete across the board with the CIA and the Defense Intelligence Agency in the current intelligence field and limits its current intelligence output to memorandums on selected subjects.

In the field of intelligence estimates, however, the State Department plays a major role, especially in political matters. The director of intelligence and research sits on the U.S. Intelligence Board, which approves National Intelligence Estimates (NIE's) and also deals with other interagency intelligence problems. State submits written or oral contributions to virtually all NIE's, and State Department intelligence analysts participate actively in NIE working groups.

The quality of the State Department's political contributions to the NIE process is generally very good, although other agencies

[9] The National Intelligence Surveys are encyclopedic descriptions of conditions and trends in foreign countries. The State Department formerly made major political, economic, and sociological contributions to the program.

sometimes harbor the suspicion that the positions taken by the State Department are unduly influenced by the policy views of its operating bureaus. State's economic, scientific, and political-military contributions are spottier, and a modest effort is under way to improve the department's intelligence-research capabilities in these fields.

STATE AND THE ECONOMIC DEPARTMENTS

In the world today, it is a poor agency indeed that does not see its proper role in global terms. State must therefore cope with the sometimes conflicting interests and aspirations of a large number of agencies whose primary missions are domestic. Most of the resulting problems, however, impinge upon only a narrow range of the State Department's responsibilities. For present purposes, we will concentrate on the State Department's relations with three powerful economic departments: Treasury, Commerce, and Agriculture.

The Treasury Department (along with the Federal Reserve Board) has successfully claimed a leading role in international monetary policy. In this field of foreign policy, the secretary of the treasury rather than the secretary of state is responsible for coordinating the views of other agencies and recommending courses of action to the President. State, however, has a strong voice in interagency deliberations, and broader considerations concerning U.S. international relations are given considerable weight.

Treasury has the unpopular task of reminding the departments of State and Defense, as well as the other national-security agencies, that many otherwise desirable actions abroad would have unacceptable consequences on our balance of payments. To the Treasury Department's credit, it has not generally taken sides in interagency disputes (as, for example, on the question of troop levels in Europe), but has merely insisted that the balance-of-payments implications of alternative courses of action be faced and that necessary compensatory measures be taken.

The informal interagency committee on international monetary problems, chaired by the under secretary for monetary affairs of the treasury, has been cited as an outstanding example of an effective instrument for interagency coordination. The success of this committee can apparently be attributed to its small size (Treasury, State, the White House, and the Council of Economic Advisers) the high level of its membership, and its informal procedures. Some credit is due to the happy accident that its members have been unusually compatible, both intellectually and psychologically. Treasury (in these cases the secretary himself) also chairs the National Advisory Council on International Monetary and Financial Policies (NAC) and the Cabinet's Balance of Payments Committee. Some observers believe that both of these bodies should be chaired by the secretary of state; others see nothing wrong in Treasury's chairmanship.

The Commerce Department understandably gives greater weight than does the State Department to the expansion of exports and the protection of domestic producers from "disruptive" foreign competition. One might therefore expect to find a considerable element of controversy in State–Commerce relations. This is indeed the case with textile-import policy, but the fact that controversy is not more widespread may probably be attributed to several circumstances. First, the Commerce Department is not as narrow in its outlook as is sometimes alleged, nor the State Department as unresponsive to domestic economic interests. Second, the entire government has been committed to a policy of trade liberalization, which has helped to reconcile the differing emphases of the State and Commerce departments. And finally, during the past few years, the center of trade-policy formulation has been moved out of the Commerce Department to the Office of the President's Special Trade Representative.

As for the Agriculture Department, the secretary of agriculture, rather than the secretary of state or the administrator of AID, has the leading role in one major component of our economic-aid effort. As appropriations for AID have been decreased, the grant or sale of agricultural commodities on concessional terms under Public Law 480 has assumed greater importance as a means of relieving economic distress and assisting in the development programs of many poor nations. The secretary of state does not possess direct-line authority over these programs (as he does over aid programs administered by AID). State must seek to influence them indirectly through AID's member on the Interagency Staff Committee (ISC) chaired by Agriculture and through AID's staff on Food for Peace. Coordination between AID and the Department of Agriculture, it might be noted, has been improved by a joint programing arrangement, although there is room for still further improvement.

The great deficiency in Public Law 480 programs is in the excessively involved clearance procedures to which they are subjected. Proposals, which are usually initiated in the field, are referred first to the ISC, which operates under a rule of unanimity. After agreement has been reached among the representatives of the departments of Agriculture, Defense, Treasury, and Commerce, as well as AID and the Bureau of the Budget on the ISC, a joint memorandum to the President is drafted for the signature of the secretary of agriculture and the administrator of AID. Before it reaches the President's desk, however, this memorandum must be passed on by the NAC and personally approved by the secretary of the treasury and the director of the Budget Bureau.

The establishment of the SIG and the IRG's has had no effect thus far on the handling or substance of Public Law 480 programs. The White House announcement concerning NSAM 341 and the SIG/IRG system expressly stated that these programs "will remain the responsibility of the Department of Agriculture," thereby exempting them from the delegation of Presidential authority to the secretary of state.

Science, Technology, and Foreign Policy

There is growing consciousness of the importance of science and technology in the State Department, but, outside of a few specialists, the ability to act upon this emerging awareness is still largely lacking. Nonetheless, several recent developments reflect the Department of State's growing interest in science and technology:

1. The director of the department's Office of International Scientific and Technological Affairs (SCI) was raised to the rank (but without the title) of assistant secretary.

2. The secretary has attended occasional luncheons with leading scientists, organized by the director of SCI.
3. In the spring of 1968, SCI, the State Department's Policy Planning Council, and the National Academy of Sciences jointly sponsored a meeting of scientists and State Department officers to identify possible future developments in science and technology which might have important implications for foreign policy.

The SCI maintains active liaison with the White House Office of Science and Technology, NASA, the AEC, and a number of other agencies with responsibilities for nonmilitary aspects of science and technology. The purpose of this liaison is, on the one hand, to assist these agencies with problems which they encounter with foreign governments and, on the other hand, to try to ensure that they give proper weight to foreign-policy considerations in their own planning and operations. The secretary and his principal assistants are inevitably drawn into some of the more difficult of these problems. The secretary is, in addition, a member of the National Aeronautics and Space Council and the National Marine Sciences Council, both of which are chaired by the vice president.

Military science and technology (principally space and nuclear weapons) are the responsibilities within the State Department of the Office of Political-Military Affairs, rather than of SCI.

OVERSEAS OPERATIONS

The Ambassador and the Country Team

The authority of the ambassador over the various agencies represented in his mission was sharply defined in a letter that President Kennedy sent to all ambassadors on May 29, 1961. The key portion of this letter reads:

> You are in charge of the entire United States Diplomatic Mission and I shall expect you to supervise all of its operations. The Mission includes not only the personnel of the Department of State and the Foreign Service, but also the representatives of all other United States agencies which have programs or activities. . . . I shall give you full support and backing in carrying out your assignment.
>
> Needless to say, the representatives of other agencies are expected to communicate directly with their offices here in Washington, and

in the event of a decision by you in which they do not concur, they
may ask to have the decision reviewed by a higher authority in Washington.

However, it is their responsibility to keep you fully informed of
their views and activities and to abide by your decisions unless in
some particular instance you and they are notified to the contrary.[10]

Individual ambassadors vary in their ability and desire to convert
this broad grant of authority into effective control. Like the President himself, ambassadors must persuade as much as command.
If nothing else does so, the right of other agency heads to appeal
from an ambassador's decisions inhibits his adoption of an excessively authoritarian style.

Many ambassadors rely heavily on a committee of local agency
heads known as the country team. In both its composition and
method of operation, the country team varies from country to
country. For example, the military attachés are included in some
and excluded from others. Some operate like an executive council
with a formal agenda and recorded actions. Others are purely advisory, with all important decisions remaining the exclusive prerogative of the ambassador. A few ambassadors go so far as to reject
the idea that there is such a thing as a country team, on the ground
that the very concept subverts their authority as personal representatives of the President.

Planning and Programing in the Field

Overseas missions are properly operational in their orientation.
With occasional exceptions, they do not undertake policy planning
on their own initiative. They correctly expect policy to be formulated in Washington.

Since 1961, however, when President Kennedy dismantled the
elaborate NSC–OCB system, most missions have not been provided with authoritative and comprehensive statements of U.S.

---

[10] This grant of authority, it will be noted, is somewhat less sweeping than
President Johnson's delegation to the secretary of state in 1966 of "responsibility to the full extent permitted by law for the over-all *direction*, coordination, and supervision of interdepartmental activities of the United States
Government overseas (less exempted military activities)." [Emphasis added.]

policy toward their countries of responsibility.[11] Some missions have complained about this, while others have welcomed the lack of constraining policy guidance. Almost all (except those few enjoying the mixed blessing of a National Policy Paper) have had to derive relevant policy objectives from speeches by Washington officials, operational cables, directives applicable to specific agency programs, and their own sense of what objectives ought to be.

Even when no doubt exists concerning objectives, an ambassador faces a difficult task in trying to weave the various programs of his mission into a coordinated whole. The programing cycles of the various agencies do not match, and embassy staffs are not yet accustomed to identifying and assessing possible interagency trade-offs. Establishment of a foreign-affairs PPBS would, of course, have a revolutionary impact upon programing in the field as well as in Washington.

Embassy-Military Relations

The 1961 Kennedy letter cited above also outlined the relations of ambassadors with the U.S. military in the following terms:

> Now one word about your relations to the military. As you know, the United States Diplomatic Mission includes Service Attachés, Military Assistance Advisory Groups and other Military components attached to the Mission. It does not, however, include United States military forces operating in the field where such forces are under the command of a United States area military commander. The line of authority to these forces runs from me, to the Secretary of Defense, to the Joint Chiefs of Staff in Washington, and to the area commander in the field.
>
> Although this means that the chief of the American Diplomatic Mission is not in the line of military command, nevertheless, as Chief of Mission, you should work closely with the appropriate area military commander to assure the full exchange of information. If it is your opinion that activities by the United States military forces may adversely affect our over-all relations with the people or government

[11] The Country Guideline Papers prepared in the State Department in the early 1960's had no standing with other agencies. They have, in any case, not been kept up to date.

of . . . you should promptly discuss the matter with the military commander and, if necessary, request a decision by higher authority.

This arrangement has worked reasonably well when the ambassador and the military commander have been stationed close together and have had roughly identical areas of responsibility. In this situation, the ambassador still must establish his dominant authority in matters affecting relations with the host government, but once this is clear, a good basis for cooperation exists. In some instances, the military commander has in effect become a member of the local country team.

Backstopping in State

No matter how well an ambassador may manage his mission on the spot, his authority can rapidly be undercut if his more important recommendations are lost in a tangle of interagency discord in Washington or simply ignored. Because very few issues can be carried to the President, the ambassador is ultimately dependent upon the support of the secretary of state and his subordinates, especially the appropriate regional assistant secretary and the country director.

The danger of course exists that an overly responsive country director will become little more than the Washington representative of the ambassador to the country on which he works. Few ambassadors, however, are likely to concede that this danger is serious at this time. Ambassadorial complaints about inadequate support from the State Department are both numerous and loud.

VII

Prospects and Problems for the Department of State

The purpose of this chapter is to focus on four major problem areas—interdepartmental operations, planning, resource allocation, and internal organization—with emphasis on identifying and assessing alternatives to present arrangements. For the most part, we will assume that the secretary of state retains the responsibilities, delegated to him by the President in NSAM 341, for the over-all direction, coordination, and supervision of interdepartmental activities of the U.S. Government overseas. At the end of the chapter, this assumption will be relaxed in order to examine briefly the effect of alternative national-security systems on the secretary's problems.

INTERDEPARTMENTAL OPERATIONS

Coordination in Washington

As noted earlier, most operational coordination in Washington is effected by an informal network of consultation. This is as it should be. The question is whether *all* coordination should be handled in this way. A loose, unstructured system could conceivably work. The case for formal coordination procedures for the more important operating decisions is nevertheless quite strong. The absence of formal procedures magnifies several defects inherent in large bureaucracies. For example:

1. The action agency, and even the action officer, can gain an unfair advantage over other legitimately concerned government agencies.
2. Many action officers are chronically overwhelmed by day-to-day business and, left to themselves, may take an excessively short-run view.
3. Because it makes life simpler for them, action officers and even

147

their immediate superiors sometimes avoid carrying problems to higher levels as long as possible.

A more formal method of handling selected operational decisions can moderate, if not eliminate, these defects.

The SIG/IRG system, for example, has handled some important interagency operational problems and could probably handle more with a modest increase in supporting staffs and the assistance of interagency country committees. An expansion in SIG/IRG operational capabilities would, however, bring to the fore several problems which are already at least potentially present.

A retired senior official has likened the SIG/IRG system to the Indian rope trick: "It has no top and leads nowhere. You climb up the rope with your problem, and both you and the problem disappear." The implication of this semifacetious remark is that the SIG/IRG system should be tied formally and explicitly to the President. The author of the remark of course ignored the fact that NSAM 341 provided for appeals to higher authority from decisions of SIG's executive chairman, but inherent in the SIG/IRG system is the potential danger that too much will be decided at lower levels and that the President's options will be foreclosed or reduced before he is even aware of a problem. White House staff membership on the SIG and the IRG's and the reporting of important SIG decisions to the President provide him with a considerable amount of protection, however. President Johnson occasionally took the added precaution of pulling major operational problems out of the SIG/IRG system, either before or after SIG or IRG action, and dealt with them directly after hearing debate in an NSC meeting or in an *ad hoc* forum. A new President may wish to continue this practice if he decides to retain the SIG/IRG system. Routine referral of items from the SIG to the National Security Council would appear to be unnecessary and would of course be inconsistent with NSAM 341's delegation of authority to the secretary of state.

Representatives of nonmember agencies are invited to SIG and IRG meetings when items of interest to them are to be discussed. This arrangement does not, however, settle the question of

SIG/IRG jurisdiction over the operations of those agencies. In part, the problem is one of law; for example, the secretary of agriculture's long-standing legal jurisdiction over Public Law 480 matters explicitly was not altered by the SIG/IRG institution when it was established. Nevertheless, even without changing the law, there is probably room for clearer definition and a more effective role for the SIG/IRG in these matters, if that is what the President and secretary desire. The President might, for example, issue a supplement to NSAM 341 which would lay down more precise guidelines on the jurisdiction of the SIG and the IRG's. Or the executive chairmen of the SIG and the IRG's might assert jurisdiction in appropriate borderline cases and let the affected nonmember agency appeal to higher authority if it wished.

An expansion of the operational work of the SIG/IRG system could increase the number of appeals from country committees to the IRG's and from the IRG's to the SIG. The system should be able to accommodate appeals, but its managers could hold down the volume by directing operational problems to the level most likely to settle them and, as at present, by occasionally asking an IRG to advise the SIG on a given problem rather than to take action on it.

The SIG/IRG system could as easily attempt too much as too little. Generally speaking, SIG and the IRG's should deal only with important problems of concern to more than one agency and about which reasonable men might hold differing views. Exceptions might occasionally be made if SIG or IRG consideration of a problem would serve to activate a truculent or lethargic operating agency.

Over-all arrangements for interagency handling of crises work well, according to most informed observers, and only minor improvements appear to be in order. In particular:

1. A special effort should be made to assign to crisis task forces and working groups at least some of the persons who have worked on a relevant contingency study (if one exists).
2. These task forces and working groups should begin work by familiarizing themselves with any relevant contingency study (kept on file in the Department of State's Operations Center). Their

last action before disbanding should be to write a critique of that study.

3. Task forces and working groups should not be created in every crisis but only when normal procedures and staffing are clearly inadequate.

Coordination Overseas

The clear authority of the ambassadors and the flexible use of country teams has reduced most procedural coordination problems overseas to manageable proportions. Nevertheless, if the President retains NSAM 341, he may, in the interests of consistency, wish to address a new letter to U.S. ambassadors which will define their interagency authority in exactly the same terms as that of the secretary of state.

More overseas missions should be provided with authoritative and up-to-date statements of U.S. policy toward their countries of responsibility. The needs of some missions could be met by regional or subregional policy statements.

The guidelines on embassy-military relations provided in the 1961 Kennedy letter have proved generally workable, but improvements should be sought in two areas.

First, relations between ambassadors and military officers in charge of unified commands overseas [1] pose a complex problem of coordination, because these officials usually live and work at considerable distances from one another. Some decisions affecting relations with specific countries are therefore made at military headquarters where the Department of State has no independent voice.[2] A satisfactory solution to this problem may never be found. The creation of regional State Department field offices may be excluded from serious consideration. Such offices would be expen-

[1] A military unified command is an organization of army, navy, and air force units overseas under a single commander who reports through the secretary of defense to the President as Commander in Chief. Examples are the European Command, with headquarters outside Stuttgart, Germany, and the Pacific Command, with headquarters outside Honolulu.

[2] The present political advisers to the unified commanders, it might be noted, are not regional representatives of the State Department but are detailed from the department to serve as members of the staffs of the commanders.

sive and would interpose an unnecessary bureaucratic layer between the secretary of state and the ambassadors overseas. More frequent contact between ambassadors and the unified commanders would probably be helpful. If the necessary money could be found, more frequent regional political-military conferences might prove advantageous in many ways, including improved coordination.

Second, crisis deployments of U.S. forces to foreign countries are not explicitly covered in the Kennedy letter. These deployments typically occur in a setting of rapidly moving political and military events, and in such situations, division of responsibility between the U.S. military commander and the ambassador on the scene can be inefficient and even dangerous. One or the other should be placed in charge of all U.S. operations, both civil and military.

Monitoring

Basic responsibility for monitoring operations probably belongs with the normal chain of command (secretary of state to ambassador), but various supplementary devices could also be used; for example, the SIG and the IRG's could be given a role in monitoring implementation of policies. Closer, perhaps more formal links could be created among such functions as the following: policy planning, agency programs, and budget requests. In theory, this approach would be highly effective, at least in controlling the general content of programs. (This subject is explored below.) Also, the mandate of the Foreign Service Inspection Corps could be broadened to cover the substantive work (but not the internal financial management) of all components of overseas missions. Expansion of the corps to include qualified senior officers from the other agencies concerned would then be necessary. To emphasize the corps' new role, the inspector general might report directly to the under secretary of state in the latter's capacity as executive chairman of the SIG.

PLANNING

Two kinds of policy planning must be distinguished: (1) the analysis of strategic alternatives, and (2) the spelling out of means of carrying out approved strategies. The first kind of policy planning helps officials at higher levels choose among possible strategies and also gives them a strategic framework for operational decisions. The second provides guidance for officials at lower levels.

The secretary of state must be concerned with both kinds of policy planning. In his relations with the President, he must himself be a strategic analyst. And in administering his department and performing his interagency role, he must provide policy guidance for subordinate officials in Washington and overseas. In both connections, the secretary needs staff support and effective procedures for handling the two kinds of policy-planning documents—strategic-analysis papers and policy-guidance papers.

Strategic-analysis papers should be prepared by a staff, such as the Policy Planning Council, which is free from excessive bureaucratic constraints and functionally separate from day-to-day operations. An adversary relationship between policy planners and operators can in fact be very useful to the secretary and his principal assistants as a means of surfacing alternatives to current policies.

Because the chief purpose of strategic-analysis papers is to assist senior officials, formal interagency review is usually unnecessary. It may also be undesirable, if, as often happens, it brings into play the "lowest common-denominator effect," which is the compromising of differences at the expense of meaning. Strategic-analysis papers require only one procedural arrangement—a regular forum at which appropriate officials can discuss the fundamental issues which such papers should raise.

Strategic-analysis papers of direct interest to the President might be discussed in the National Security Council or in smaller White House meetings. Prior discussion of such papers, for example in the SIG, and IRG, or in something like the Interagency Planning Group, which meets frequently under the aegis of State's Policy Planning Council, might often be useful. Moving a strategic-analysis paper to successively higher forums should not, however, be regarded as a review or clearance process, although the differences of view expressed at a lower level might be recorded and circulated to participants in the next higher level discussion. When the SIG meets on a major strategic-analysis paper, the secretary of state, as well as the under secretary, might wish to attend. Alternatively, the secretary might, as at present, convene an *ad hoc* meeting whose composition would be determined by the subject to be discussed.

Many strategic-analysis papers need not be discussed at all three levels. A few might go directly to the National Security Council or another meeting chaired by the President. Others might stop at the SIG or an *ad hoc* meeting chaired by the secretary of state, with or without having first been discussed by subordinate groups with interagency representation. Still others might not go higher than the subordinate groups.

The Interagency Planning Group (IAPG), could be given a key role in the kind of flexible arrangement described above. Subject to the general supervision of the secretary of state, it could set planning priorities and make assignments for the production of strategic analyses. Papers dealing with a single region could be delegated by it to the appropriate IRG by agreement between the chairmen of the two groups. Any disagreements could be settled by the under secretary of state in his capacity as executive chairman of the SIG. The IAPG would then in effect become a "planning" IRG. Staff support for the IAPG would be provided, as at present, by constituent agencies, with State's Policy Planning Council in a leading role.

Whatever arrangement is adopted, all major strategic-planning efforts, including the secretary of defense's draft Presidential memorandums (if they continue to be prepared in the new administration), should be subjected to interagency discussion at an appropriately senior level. Such discussion would give the secretary of state or his representative an opportunity to provide political guidance for the other agencies in their internal planning and programing.

The case for formal, structured procedures is much stronger for policy-guidance planning than for planning as an aid to strategic thinking. Policy guidance must be authoritative, and authority in national-security policy must come from the President or someone empowered to act for him. The President or his representative would probably not wish to approve a comprehensive statement of U.S. policy on a given subject, or toward a particular area, before that statement had been carefully reviewed by all agencies concerned. Such review can best be ensured by clearly defined procedures.

Policy-guidance papers could be produced through special procedures, as in the case of National Policy Papers, or the task could be turned over to the SIG/IRG system. The major justification for the present NPP procedures is the belief that the Policy Planning Council, which is responsible for NPP's, can take a more objective view of policy options than can the regional bureaus, which are committed to current policy. This argument, however, loses much of its weight if policy-guidance papers are no longer viewed as vehicles for presenting strategic alternatives to senior officials. If the SIG/IRG system is retained, there appears to be no good reason why it should not be given responsibility for the preparation of policy-guidance papers. Possible problems in entrusting policy planning to operating officers could be minimized by involving the IRG staffs and other regional staff officers at least in the review of policy-guidance papers. Much of the drafting work, however, would inevitably fall on the country directors, who would find this task an additional reason to organize interagency country committees to share the burden.

Policy-guidance papers should draw on relevant strategic-analysis papers, to the extent that the analytical approach and conclusions of the latter are endorsed by senior policy officials. The discussion of a strategic-analysis paper may in fact lead directly to the preparation of a related policy-guidance paper, but the two processes should probably (as a general rule) not be merged. An overly ambitious attempt to do precisely this may explain both the excessive cost of National Policy Papers and their limited success in raising serious issues to the level of the secretary of state.

Good policy planning must obviously take general account of possible contingencies. But there is also a need for more specialized and detailed planning to focus on specific, usually narrowly defined contingencies, the occurrence of which would precipitate a crisis or something approaching one. The term "contingency planning," as used here, does not deal with broad strategic alternatives, nor does it provide policy guidance for operating officials. Rather, if effective, it does three things: (1) it increases the likelihood that all relevant factors receive proper consideration in a given contingency, if it should actually occur; (2) it educates those who do the planning, making them more useful in the event, and (3) it identifies measures which might be taken in the near term, either to fend off undesirable contingencies or to improve the government's ability to cope with them. The last of these functions is contingency planning's contribution to policy planning.

Normally, policy planning (particularly the analysis of strategic alternatives) is best done by staff officers who are not involved in daily operations. The reverse is true of contingency planning. It should be done by officers who have an acute awareness of practicalities and who are most likely to be charged with meeting a given contingency if it occurs.

The interagency coordination of contingency planning could be handled largely by a special body, such as the recently abolished Contingency Coordinating Committee (CCC), or it could continue to be the responsibility of the IRG's. Centering contingency planning in the White House should be ruled out, as it would tend to remove this function from the operating level where it belongs.

In principle, there is no overriding reason for preferring either a special body or the IRG's. The IRG's might not be able to handle contingency planning if they also assume major responsibility for policy planning and for coordinating operations. Hence, if the IRG's were given a substantial policy-planning role, there would be a case for reconstituting something like the CCC, either as an autonomous body or under the general supervision of the SIG.

Because there are numerous contingencies which might profitably be studied, the interagency machinery for coordinating contingency planning should be able to handle a significant volume of business. In addition, unless action officers in the departments of state, defense, and the CIA are forced to analyze contingencies jointly, there can be little hope of raising their levels of sophistication. From the Department of State's point of view, the problem is to inject political considerations into the joint staff's planning. From the Pentagon's point of view, the problem is to make the State Department more aware of what is and is not militarily possible.

Both jobs are formidable, and one may question whether any

committee operation, however extensive, can produce the desired results. Also, the understandable reluctance of the joint staff to concede that civilians have a need to know military plans poses an obstacle to full communication. It might be desirable, therefore, to create a small, fully cleared, State–Defense–CIA contingency-planning staff to support the Political-Military Group (or a revived CCC). This staff would have access to all relevant planning documents and would have two functions—to comment on interagency planning studies in light of their privileged knowledge of agency plans, and to comment similarly on single-agency contingency plans at the request of the agency concerned.

Resource Allocation

That policies influence resource allocation, or that most policies require resources, is of course beyond dispute. It follows that the more influence the secretary of state has over the allocation of resources to agencies operating overseas, the greater his ability to discharge the kind of responsibilities delegated to him by NSAM 341.

The customary bureaucratic way of achieving this would be for the State Department to devote more staff time and effort, both in Washington and in the field, to reviewing program proposals and budgetary submissions of the operating agencies. In any case, more should probably be done in this direction. Thus, State Department–Budget Bureau cooperation might be expanded to include the following:

1. Joint review of the budget submissions to the President by the other foreign-affairs agencies (AID, USIA, ACDA, and Peace Corps, plus military assistance and Public Law 480 programs)
2. Collaboration in the compilation and review of budgets covering all proposed official expenditures by such agencies in each foreign country in which the United States has major programs (The country directors in the State Department should be given central roles in this kind of review.)

Some knowledgeable observers, both in the State Department and outside, would go considerably beyond such measures. They believe that the secretary of state should be able, in more effective and systematic fashion, to tie in the programs and budgets of the other operating agencies with broad foreign-policy objectives. To this end, they have advocated creation of a planning, programing, and budgeting system (PPBS) covering the State Department proper and at least some of the other foreign-affairs agencies.

Ideally, a foreign-affairs PPBS would enable the secretary of state to apply the optimum "mix" of interagency efforts to the achievement of specified foreign-policy goals. In each foreign country, as well as over all, the "marginal yield" of the last dollar spent on all programs would be equal and no improvement in total results could be realized by shifting funds from one country or program to another. Even if results fell far short of this ideal, it is argued, the effort to relate programs and budgets to objectives would sharpen awareness of choices, quantify some options which are now assessed in qualitative terms, and facilitate trade-offs between programs to increase effectiveness and lower costs. On the whole, however, it seems likely that the principal advantage of a foreign-affairs PPBS would not be in the field of cost effectiveness, but in strengthening the authority of the secretary of state by placing him at the center of the budgetary processes of the agencies covered by the system.

One of the reservations about this kind of PPBS is that, despite some experimental work, no one has a very clear idea of how it would look. Direct borrowing from the successful Defense Department system is not possible. Foreign affairs calls for decisions on much different, less quantifiable problems, and there is as yet no foreign-affairs counterpart to the single defense budget. Serious doubt exists concerning the magnitude and even the feasibility of trade-offs among programs managed by different agencies and financed by different appropriations.

The ability of the State Department, as now staffed, to operate a foreign-affairs PPBS is at least open to question. The State Department has traditionally been almost blind to resource problems. Until recently, efforts by a few administrative specialists to develop a foreign-affairs PPBS were viewed with contempt by most substantive career officers of the department, who, misunderstanding what was proposed, sagely argued that diplomacy cannot be computerized.

The scope of a foreign-affairs PPBS has two dimensions—coverage of subject matter and coverage of agency responsibilities and/or functions. The guiding principle in the first should be to ignore areas of limited pay-off. The system should not cover countries where we have no programs or relatively small ones. Nor should it attempt at first to deal with our participation in international organizations.

Concerning agency coverage, no agency operating overseas (except military commands) should be entirely beyond the system's reach, but all agencies should not be treated the same. The system should deal with all activities in selected countries of the State Department, AID, USIA, and the Peace Corps. Parts of the activities of other agencies should be covered, e.g., military assistance and Public Law 480 programs.

The intelligence agencies pose a difficult security problem. It might be solved by setting up a separate intelligence PPBS which would report to the U.S. Intelligence Board (USIB). Coordination of this PPBS with the foreign-affairs PPBS could be achieved through the State Department's representation on that board, supplemented by informal staff consultation.

The Budget Bureau, of course, would have a central role to play in such a system. At a minimum, it would have to monitor any foreign-affairs PPBS and participate in special studies in the borderland between foreign affairs and defense. Particularly in the early years of such a system, the Budget Bureau could profitably play a much larger role. An informal State–Budget partnership in the management of such a new system would to some degree compensate for deficiencies in the State Department's staff capabilities and help to overcome the predictable resistance of other agencies to unilateral State Department intervention in their budgetary process.

A foreign-affairs PPBS might relate to the SIG and the IRG's in various ways:

1. Program memorandums could be based on policy-guidance papers sponsored by the SIG/IRG system.
2. Major issues surfaced in staff review of country programs and

budget documents could be referred for decision to the appropriate IRG (or occasionally to the SIG).

3. Composite program and budget documents for U.S. programs in entire regions and selected documents for individual countries could be reviewed by the appropriate IRG's, and possibly also by the SIG.

If policy can be planned and operations coordinated across the full range of national-security policy, why should not resource-allocation decisions be made within this broader area, rather than within the smaller field of foreign affairs? The answer is that they should. It does not follow, however, that a national-security PPBS should be created.

To plan a merger of the Defense Department's well-established PPBS with an only vaguely conceived foreign-affairs PPBS is at best premature. At worst, it could result in loss of the ground gained in the Defense Department and jeopardize the new foreign-affairs system before it got well started.

This does not mean that nothing can be done to rationalize expenditures for purposes which cut across the line between defense and foreign affairs. Special studies should seek trade-offs in this border area and refer them for decision to appropriate interagency forums. If the State Department is to play an appropriate role in the conduct of such studies, it will need to develop a systems-analysis capability comparable to that in the Defense Department.

In view of the formidable obstacles to creating a foreign-affairs PPBS, probably the best immediate course for the secretary of state would be to continue the present experimental effort in close cooperation with the Budget Bureau. Pending possible installation of a broader system, the secretary may wish to strengthen the capabilities of his own staff to review the programs and budgets of the operating agencies and to engage in special studies affecting resource allocation in the area where problems of foreign policy and defense overlap.

INTERNAL ORGANIZATION OF THE DEPARTMENT

Like other large organizations, the State Department faces the continuing problem of maintaining the best balance between staff and line components. In addition, it has the special problem of achieving the best adjustment between geographical and functional units. The present dominant position of the five regional bureaus is probably desirable as well as inevitable. Some organizational adjustments may be required to ensure that economic, political-military, and other functional considerations are given appropriate weight. The secretary and his principal assistants may also require greater staff support in connection with their direction of interagency activities overseas.

A possible organizational structure for achieving these results is depicted in Figure 2. The rationale for these suggested modifications is discussed below.

The Under Secretaries

No decisions will be more important to a secretary of state than the choice of the under secretaries and the designation of their functions. Several major questions come to mind: Should the under secretary be the general manager of the department, or the secretary's alter ego? If the latter, should someone else be general manager? What, in any case, should be the function of the third-ranking position? Should there always be an under secretary for economic affairs?

The case for regarding the under secretary as the secretary's alter ego is very strong. The secretary cannot avoid spending considerable time on ceremonial matters, in appearances before Congressional committees, and in conferences outside the country. The under secretary must take over frequently for the secretary and often with little advance notice.

All of this may be granted, but it is still proper to ask why an alter ego cannot also be a general manager. The main reason is that the amount of work would be too much for one man. A good case can be made for increasing the ability of the under secretary to substitute for the secretary by giving him a more prestigious title such as "deputy secretary," or even "minister of foreign affairs." The mere act of changing the title, accompanied by a public declaration of the purpose of the change, would be more important than the precise title chosen. A move of this sort would of course

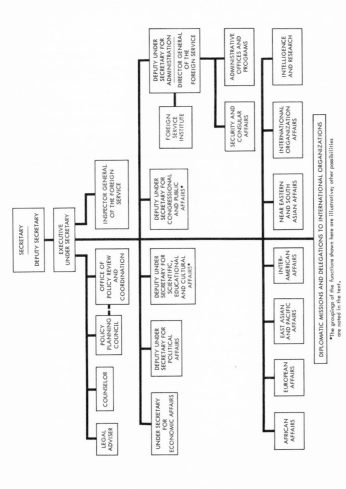

FIGURE 2. Possible Modified Organization of the
Department of State

still further diminish the feasibility of assigning the role of general manager to the under secretary.

Up to this point, we have assumed that the department needs a general manager. But is this true? No categorical answer is possible. The secretary of state may prefer simply to assemble a good top team and to parcel out managerial tasks on an *ad hoc* basis without setting up any single person as a buffer between himself and his department. If so, only the President would be entitled to say that this is wrong.

There are, however, advantages in having a chief of staff who can keep the flow of routine business moving and free the top man and his deputy for consideration of major problems. As the work of the Department of State continues to grow, these advantages may bulk larger in the minds of the secretary. The creation of a general manager would become almost unavoidable if the State Department were to be given central responsibility for operating a foreign-affairs PPBS in addition to the coordination of overseas operations.

To carry sufficient authority both in and out of the department, the general manager should probably have the rank of under secretary, with an appropriate descriptive designation, such as "executive." The executive under secretary would supervise the day-to-day work of the bureaus and would decide operational issues on behalf of the secretary, when he was confident of the latter's views. Only when in doubt would he refer problems to the secretary or the deputy secretary. The executive under secretary would also help the deputy secretary on SIG matters and chair the SIG in the latter's absence.

A good case can also be made for the permanent establishment of the position of under secretary for economic affairs, as either the third- or fourth-ranking job in the department. As we have seen, the State Department faces special problems in asserting foreign-policy considerations against the domestic interests represented by the great economic departments. An able and vigorous assistant secretary for economic affairs can deal effectively with those departments, but his hand would be strengthened if he carried the rank of under secretary. It might in fact be desirable to have both an under secretary for economic affairs and an assistant secretary for economic affairs. The former would concentrate on interagency problems at or near the Cabinet level, and the latter would devote major attention to administering the State Department's Bureau of Economic Affairs.

Under the present law, the under secretary for economic affairs would, of course, have to displace the existing under secretary for political affairs. As was pointed out earlier, the duties of the latter official are largely *ad hoc*. They could easily be parcelled out among the counselor, the ambassadors at large, and (if one were created) the executive under secretary.

A *Strengthened Functional Tier?*

A stronger group of functional units would reduce somewhat the burdens of the secretary and the under secretaries, increase the attention paid to functional (as opposed to geographical) considerations, and raise the probability that the secretary and the President would receive alternative proposals rather than single solutions. The deputy under secretaries for political affairs and for administration form part of such a tier. An under secretary for economic affairs would be a further extension of it; he would carry a higher rank because of his need to deal directly with the heads of the economic departments. The functional tier could be completed by adding a deputy under secretary for scientific, educational, and cultural affairs (who would assume the duties of the present assistant secretary for educational and cultural affairs, plus those of the director of the Office of International Scientific and Technological Affairs) and a deputy under secretary for Congressional and public affairs (who would combine the functions of the present assistant secretaries for Congressional and for public affairs and also be charged with seeing that domestic aspects of foreign-policy problems received appropriate consideration).

This arrangement of functional responsibilities is of course only one of a number of possibilities. Thus, the suggested merger of Congressional and public affairs might on further examination be found to create more problems than it would solve. Or a case might be made for giving the scientific function to the under secretary for economic affairs. The precise arrangement adopted is much less important than the basic purpose, which is to give functional units a stronger mandate to propose alternatives to the recommendations of the regional bureaus.

Whatever its composition, a functional tier should not stand between the secretary and the regional bureaus (or the Bureau of International Organization Affairs, which would continue to occupy a place in the department's structure similar to that of a regional bureau). The senior functional officers would, however, monitor the activities of the regional bureaus and would be empowered to intervene when they believed it necessary. They would also, of course, be given primary responsibility for handling certain predominantly functional problems. Each would engage in day-to-day liaison with other agencies in his functional field, and several would play major roles in helping the secretary discharge his interagency responsibilities.

The under secretary for economic affairs would have direct line authority over the existing Economic Bureau. Other senior functional officers would be supported by smaller staffs already in existence. The new deputy under secretary for scientific, educational, and cultural affairs should probably be relieved of the chore of administering the cultural and educational exchange programs. Having those programs in the State Department has been somewhat of an anomaly, because in the field they are administered by the U.S. Information Service (USIS), and because they are in fact the only operational programs in the State Department. Their transfer to the U.S. Information Agency (USIA) would make good organizational sense and relieve the State Department of an unnecessary burden.

Staff Support of the Top Command

The staff in the State Department should subject the recommendations of the line officers to careful scrutiny to ensure that adequate weight has been given to all relevant considerations. Most importantly, staffs should, whenever appropriate, make sure that the top policy-making officers are presented with all alternative courses of action, rather than with single proposals. The importance of these staff functions has increased with the growing complexity of international affairs.

It is a common complaint in large bureaucracies that proliferation of staff interferes with the line organizations. The implication is: The fewer the staff officers, the better. The State Department is living proof that this proposition is not necessarily true. Whatever its other deficiencies, the State Department does not have too many staff officers.

The role of a stronger functional tier in strengthening staff support for the top command has been discussed above. There are also other, more modest changes which may recommend themselves to the secretary.

The executive secretariat might be given a broader, more substantive mandate and renamed something like the "Office of Policy Review and Coordination." The head of this office would have the rank of assistant secretary. He would report to the executive under secretary, but he would also provide staff support to the other members of the top command. The office would have two divisions —program appraisal and current operations.

Logically, the Office of Policy Review and Coordination should also have a planning division, but this would create problems, because the State Department already has a well-established planning unit, the Policy Planning Council. One solution would be to convert the council into the planning division of the new office, but this would deprive it of its direct access to the secretary and might threaten its important freedom to innovate. It would probably be better to leave the Policy Planning Council where it is organizationally, but physically collocate it with the new office and assign it the task of supporting the new office in commenting on major policy proposals (including the programs of operating agencies) which are en route to the SIG or to the secretary, the deputy secretary, or one of the under secretaries. To ensure close collaboration, the deputy chairman of the Policy Planning Council might be made concurrently a deputy director of the proposed Office of Policy Review and Coordination.

The program-appraisal division of the new office would have primary responsibility for supporting the secretary, the deputy secretary, and the under secretaries in reviewing the programs of various agencies operating overseas and in experimental work looking to the eventual development of a foreign-affairs PPBS. One of its sections might help the under secretary for economic affairs co-ordinate foreign economic policy. In time, the program-appraisal division might also develop a modest systems-analysis capability.

The current-operations division could deal both with operational issues en route to the SIG and with those to be dealt with by the secretary, the deputy secretary, or an under secretary outside the SIG. After decisions had been taken on these issues, the operations division would monitor their execution. This division would be the principal point of contact between the new office and the staffs of the regional bureaus. It might therefore be organized largely along geographical lines. The operations center would be part of the current-operations division.

The staff of the proposed Office of Policy Review and Coordination should be drawn from the other national-security agencies as well as from the State Department. Staff members from other agencies should serve for at least two years and should owe their loyalty to the State Department rather than to their home agencies. They should not represent their home agencies or even be viewed as liaison officers between the State Department and those agencies. The success of the State–Defense exchange programs testifies that officers participating in such programs experience little difficulty in working for new masters.

Great care would have to be taken to keep the proposed office from pulling work into its orbit which might better be done by either the regional bureaus or by one of the new tier of functional offices. The office should be a small, elite organization, dedicated to helping move problems expeditiously toward solutions, while avoiding advocacy of particular solutions. Its main purpose should be to marshal alternatives among which the secretary and other senior officials can choose.

The Regional Bureaus

The regional assistant secretaries probably also require increased staff support, if only because of their extra burden as executive chairmen of the IRG's. One deputy assistant secretary in each regional bureau (preferably *not* an additional deputy) should be charged with program review and coordination.

The country-director concept is sound and should be given a further trial. A fresh start should be made by reviewing the organization and operating methods of the regional bureaus to see if more responsibility could be delegated to the country directors and if the number of both multiple-desk country directorates and deputy assistant secretaries could be reduced. Assignments as country directors should be reserved for officers who have demonstrated executive ability. For many countries, an interagency country committee should be formed under the chairmanship of the country director. Such committees (which already exist for some countries) would both enhance the effectiveness of the country directors and contribute to the effectiveness of the IRG's. They would operate much as do the IRG's, but would be subordinate to the IRG's; and would of course deal with matters relating only to a single country.

State–AID integration at the regional-bureau level, as we have seen, has not been an unmixed success in the one area (Latin America) in which it has been tried. It is doubtful that such integration would work even as well in other regions. Latin America is a very special area in that international cooperation is more advanced there than in any other part of the less-developed world. The AID programs in Latin America are pursuant to the Alliance for Progress, which was set up by the Organization of American States. These factors favoring integration do not exist in other, more diverse areas.

No such doubts can be raised concerning the broader application of State Department–AID collocation. It has been successful in the East Asian bureau, and it should be extended to the State Department and AID bureaus for Africa and for the Near East and South Asia.

A Larger State Department?

One way to deal with interagency problems is to abolish the offending agencies. The argument has often been made (usually by exasperated State Department officers) that AID, or USIA, or

ACDA, or even the Peace Corps should be merged fully into the State Department. Close examination of these proposals, however, suggests that in each instance merger would not on balance be desirable.

It is true that merger would increase the direct-line authority of the secretary of state over these organizations, but the need to do so is highly questionable in view of the secretary's statutory authority, supplemented by the broad delegation of Presidential authority effected by NSAM 341. Merger might facilitate creation of a foreign-affairs budget, but there is no assurance that Congress would agree to such a budget, nor can it be argued that creation of such a budget awaits merger of several related agencies into the State Department.

Against these questionable advantages must be weighed several clear disadvantages of merger:

The managerial burdens of the secretary and his principal assistants would be significantly increased. Staff skills needed to help absorb those burdens are currently in very short supply.

The special points of view pressed by AID and ACDA (and to some degree USIA) would probably be downgraded and might be submerged within the State Department hierarchy. The secretary would be less sure of hearing the case for giving developmental or disarmament goals greater weight in some circumstances than short-run political considerations.

The public-relations value (both at home and abroad) of visibly autonomous aid, disarmament, or information agencies would be sacrificed.

Other Internal Problems

A number of other internal problems deserve at least brief attention here. First, at some point in the decision-making process, proper account must clearly be taken of the domestic consequences of various possible courses of action abroad. The questions are when and how.

Policy-planning documents traditionally do not take domestic considerations into account explicitly nor do most written recommendations for dealing with operational problems. Resource-allocation proposals sometimes do, especially if they deal with large sums of money. In most circumstances, domestic considerations are brought into the picture rather late, and often not very explicitly.

A good case can be made that foreign-policy recommendations submitted to the secretary of state and the President should be "pure," that is, based only on considerations of foreign-policy interests, not on domestic repercussions. By training and experience, few foreign service officers are highly qualified to deal with domestic considerations, and an attempt to make them do so could be disastrous.[3]

At the same time, domestic constraints on our actions abroad are important and may become increasingly so. Arrangements for routinely injecting these constraints into the policy-making process would appear to be very much in order. The secretary and his immediate assistants should not, along with all of their other burdens, have to be their own staff officers in dealing with the domestic side of their duties.

A partial solution to this problem might be found by upgrading and combining the Congressional and public-relations functions. In addition, a close working relationship might be established between the proposed deputy under secretary for Congressional and public affairs and the proposed Office of Program Review and Coordination. Representatives from the deputy under secretary's office might sit in the latter office and refer selected action recommendations or policy-planning papers to their home office for comment.

A second internal problem arises from the intelligence function.

[3] Secretary Rusk made his views on this point quite clear only a month after he assumed office by telling a group of policy-making officers of his department:

> We do not want policy officers below the level of Presidential appointees to concern themselves too much with problems of domestic politics in recommending foreign-policy action. In the first place, our business is foreign policy, and it is the business of the Presidential leadership and his appointees in the department to consider the domestic political aspects of a problem. Mr. Truman emphasized this point by saying, "You fellows in the Department of State don't know much about domestic politics."

The independence of the intelligence-research function from the operating bureaus should be maintained, and the director of intelligence and research should continue to have direct access to the secretary. Like the Policy Planning Council (with which it should continue to have close relations), the Bureau of Intelligence and Research (INR) should be free to dissent from prevailing views and to carry its dissent, if necessary, to the very top of the department. INR's independence is also important to its standing and effectiveness within the Washington intelligence community.

The location in INR of the staff, which follows certain operational intelligence matters, is something of an anomaly. This staff in reality serves the director of intelligence and research much less than it does the deputy under secretary for political affairs, and it should be transferred to the latter's direct supervision.

Finally, at all levels of the State Department, the problem of quickly getting the information needed to deal with the tasks at hand is becoming more acute. The difficulty is not so much lack of the desired information as it is one of separating the relevant from the irrelevant. The department is in danger of drowning in a rising flood of words—cables and airgrams from posts overseas, intelligence reports and studies of various sorts, press reports, and the writings of private scholars.

A thorough staff study of the problem of information management in the State Department was completed in 1968, and preliminary work has begun on designing a modern information system suitable to the needs of the secretary and his department.[4] In his

---

[4] Unfortunately, the secretary is unlikely to be able to solve his information-management problem by recruiting an aide with the intellectual capacity of Mycroft Holmes, whose role in the British Government was described by his brother, Sherlock, in the following terms:

Well, his position is unique. . . . There has never been anything like it before, nor will be again. He has the tidiest and most orderly brain, with the greatest capacity for storing facts, of any man living. . . . The conclusions of every department are passed to him, and he is the central exchange, the clearing-house, which makes out the balance. All other men are specialists, but his specialism is omniscience. We will suppose that a minister needs information as to a point which involves the Navy, India, Canada, and the bimetallic question; he could get his separate advices from various departments upon each, but only Mycroft can focus them all, and

own interest, the new secretary will want to check into the status of this work and see to it that it is given appropriate priority and support.

THE EFFECT ON THE STATE DEPARTMENT OF ALTERNATIVE NATIONAL-SECURITY SYSTEMS

The discussion thus far has proceeded on the assumption that NSAM 341 continues in effect and that recent trends toward a national-security system more clearly centered in the secretary of state accordingly continue. This may of course not prove to be the case. Two broad alternatives to this assumption (a White House–centered system and an intermediate or mixed system) and their relative merits were considered in Chapter II. It remains to discuss the general consequences for the future organization and functioning of the Department of State if either of these alternatives were to be adopted.

A White House–centered system would, by definition, eliminate any significant degree of State Department primacy, and it would place the management of all components of the national-security process (policy planning, coordination of operations, and resource allocation) in the hands of a staff (or staffs) directly under the President. Such a system would have no place for the SIG and the IRG's in their present roles. These organizations (as well as country committees) could, of course, survive as mere interagency discussion groups. Alternatively, the SIG/IRG system might be reoriented by shifting chairmanship of the SIG to a senior member of the White House staff and by having the SIG support the National Security Council in much the same way as did the NSC Planning Board during the Eisenhower Administration. Even though the State Department might under this arrangement retain chairmanship of the IRG's and country committees, the SIG/IRG system as a whole would be White House–centered.

The net effect of any White House–centered system on the State Department's staff requirements is not easy to predict. The secre-

---

say offhand how each factor would affect the other. . . . In that great brain of his everything is pigeon-holed and can be handed out in an instant. Again and again his word has decided the national policy.

tary and his principal assistants would clearly be major participants in such a system and might require about as much staff support as they would in a State Department–centered system.

Somewhat surprisingly, the case for modifications in the State Department's top command which were set forth earlier would be almost as strong in a White House–centered system as in one clearly centered in the secretary of state. The burdens on the secretary and his principal assistants would probably decrease moderately with a reduction in their interagency responsibilities. But such a decrease is by no means a foregone conclusion. Battling for the foreign-policy interest without the advantages of primacy could prove just as burdensome as managing a State Department–centered system.

An intermediate system which centered some components of the national-security process in the White House and others in the State Department would, by definition, make even less difference in terms of the department's functioning and organization. Depending upon which functions were left in the State Department, it would have greater or lesser effect on the SIG, the IRG's, and the country committees. The impact on the State Department's staff requirements and on the need for organizational modifications would also be variable but probably somewhat less than in a White House–centered system.

VIII

A Decade of Changes in the Department of Defense

The life and security of the nation may depend on the President's ability to assert effective control over the Department of Defense. The Defense Department budget amounts to about half of the national budget, and this alone forces close attention on the far-reaching decisions of the President and his secretary of defense about defense expenditures. This will be true if such expenditures continue at present levels or increase; it will be even more true if they are to be cut back.

In earlier times, military forces were organized into armies and navies, depending on whether they fought on land or sea. War was war and peace was peace, and it seemed a simple matter to decide whether a question was purely "military," or "political," or "economic," or whatever. Today there is no simple, widely accepted principle for organizing armed forces, and there are very few problems which are purely military or purely civilian. Nevertheless, those who man the Department of Defense and the armed forces do come from either civilian or military backgrounds, and their instinctive habits of mind often result in different ways of addressing problems. Well-defined professional and vocational backgrounds generate different approaches and perspectives. It is vital that such different approaches and perspectives be brought to bear on national-security affairs, but a President does have to decide on the basic mix between civilians and professional military men in the leadership of the Department of Defense.

"Civilian control" in the narrow sense is not really the issue. We automatically have civilian control by the very fact that the President is a civilian, and the secretary of defense is his personal

173

appointee. The real issue is: What kinds of questions can best be decided by civilian executives? What kinds of questions can best be decided by professional military leaders? And what kinds of questions require combined judgments? The essential problem is: How can political authorities establish and maintain appropriate control without jeopardizing or inhibiting the expression of professional military judgment?

At the top of the civilian and military sides of the Department of Defense are the Office of the Secretary of Defense (OSD) and the Office of the Joint Chiefs of Staff (OJCS), respectively. There has been a steady growth in the authority and power of both, but the growth has not been even or in all respects parallel. Moreover, the civilian and the military officials have not always had a clear conception of the roles and contributions of their respective opposite numbers. Misunderstandings have sometimes produced confusion, and men of talent and good will on both sides of the line have often appeared to be in conflict, when actually they merely failed to appreciate the roles of the other side. Moreover, statutes and directives have often contributed to these misunderstandings because they were not precise in delineating roles and relationships.

THE "McNAMARA REVOLUTION"

What is now called the "McNamara Revolution" in the Department of Defense is in part the continuation of an evolutionary process started in the 1940's and accelerated in the 1950's. Centralization in national-security affairs began with the National Security Act of 1947, which created the position of secretary of defense but failed to provide him with staff or a department. The 1949 legislative amendments carried the process further by creating the Department of Defense. President Eisenhower's 1953 and 1958 Defense Department reorganizations shifted the balance of authority and responsibility in the military establishment away from the separate services, toward the secretary of defense and the collective Joint Chiefs of Staff. The 1958 reorganization was particularly significant because it put the secretary squarely in the military chain of command, just under the President, and directly over the unified and specified operating commands.[1] Before that, the service departments had acted as "executive agents" for operational matters affecting particular unified and specified military commands—for example, army for Europe, navy for the Pacific, and air force for the Strategic Air Command. The 1958 legislation confined the service departments to administrative, training, and logistical functions.

The reorganizations of 1953 and especially of 1958 created the base for what was to follow, but for the most part it did not follow until after 1960. Probably the main reason why it did not was the extraordinary status of President Eisenhower in the eyes of almost all Americans. He was regarded by virtually everyone as the nation's foremost military hero and military expert, and the defense secretaries who served under him shared this widespread attitude. Those who say that Eisenhower was served by "weak" defense secretaries have not perceived the true nature of the situation. His defense secretaries were able executives, but they worked for a President who had relatively little need for a "strong" secretary in either the military-adviser or command role. President Eisenhower was almost unavoidably his own secretary of defense. Where he felt the need for a "strong" Cabinet member was in coping with the other aspects of foreign affairs; hence, Secretary of State John Foster Dulles emerged in this role.

Whether or not Secretary Robert S. McNamara's innovations amounted to a "revolution," it was he who fully exploited the implications of the 1958 legislation. He moved decisively from the moment he took office, and he was apparently convinced that new legislation was not required for him to carry out his duties with aggressive vigor. More importantly, he was imbued with the philosophy that industrial management required strong executive leadership, and he conceived of the job of being secretary of defense somewhat along the industry-manager model. He was determined to be an activist leader and not merely the judge of competing alternatives or a negotiator among competing interests.

[1] For an explanation of "unified command," see note 1 on page 150. A specified command is one that is not geographically delineated, the best example being the Strategic Air Command.

Asserting this role from the outset, McNamara prepared a list of subjects for extensive review, including existing defense policies, strategies, and programs. The review tasks were assigned to appropriate offices in the Department of Defense, within the Joint Chiefs of Staff arena, to the separate services, and elsewhere. The results of the reviews generally displeased the secretary for at least two reasons. First, each document tended to reflect the institutional perspective of the office drafting it, and second, most seemed to rely on verbal, conventional wisdom instead of hard, fresh analysis.

McNamara quickly determined the need for two courses of action. First, he wanted to introduce new analytical techniques to replace the traditional, mainly verbal-philosophical methods of the past. Second, he wanted a strong staff capability within OSD, which, sharing his departmentwide perspective, could exercise those techniques. The first of these two concerns led to PPBS, which was initially centered in the Office of the Comptroller of the Department of Defense, at first Charles Hitch and later Robert Anthony. The second resulted in creation of the Office of Systems Analysis (SA), initially a part of the Defense Department Comptroller's Office but later established at assistant secretary level in 1965, with Alain Enthoven heading it throughout. Other key individuals and offices in OSD that worked closely with Secretary McNamara in the early years of the Kennedy Administration were Paul Nitze, assistant secretary of defense for international security affairs (ASD/ISA), and Harold Brown, director of defense research and engineering (DDR & E).

Reinforcing McNamara's disenchantment with the many organizations he inherited were particular reservations concerning the Joint Chiefs of Staff. In connection with the deteriorating situation in Laos during the spring of 1961, the President had invited McNamara and the five members of the JCS to the White House to discuss the matter. On that occasion, the President found himself exposed to five divergent but vigorously defended military points of view. This unsettling experience followed shortly after the Bay of Pigs episode, which had begun to engender some loss of confidence in the JCS on the part of the President and his defense secretary. After this meeting, McNamara sought and quickly obtained the President's permission to use the JCS chairman as principal spokesman for the chiefs as a whole. However, the incumbent chairman had been associated with the Bay of Pigs debacle, and, in addition, the President found it generally difficult to communicate easily with him. In late June, 1961, therefore, the President appointed retired General Maxwell Taylor (Army Chief of Staff, 1955–59) as his "Military Representative" in the White House, a post the general held until he was appointed chairman of the joint chiefs in October, 1962.

These, then, are the basic dimensions of the "McNamara Revolution," but in a way it should perhaps be called the "Kennedy Revolution." The relationship between the President and any Cabinet officer is both institutional and personal, and the rapport and mutual confidence emerging between the two men is always a major factor in determining the institutional relationship. Rapport and confidence developed very quickly between President Kennedy and McNamara, partly because their temperaments were similar in many respects. Both were impatient for quick but carefully researched solutions, and both were more than willing to experiment with new leadership and new organizational arrangements. Finally, when confronted with a deficient organizational component, both were inclined to bypass or overlook it, rather than overhaul it for the long pull. In dealing with the White House, McNamara took care to keep the President fully informed at the outset, including the registering of dissenting opinions in the JCS or elsewhere, but he proceeded on the assumption that it was basically his responsibility as secretary to settle Pentagon disagreements. This left the President the option of reversing any decision, but it relieved him of the need to dig repeatedly into complex Pentagon issues.

McNamara was a blessing to Kennedy because the new President needed the kind of detailed, systematic evidence that McNamara's procedures provided before he ran the risk of overruling the professional military. By contrast, President Eisenhower's status as the nation's leading military expert had allowed him to do so with relative impunity. Moreover, McNamara's systematic methods in the Pentagon enabled the President to be somewhat less formal and systematic at the White House level when considering national-security matters. During the first weeks and months of his administration, President Kennedy occasionally doublechecked some of McNamara's decisions with various officials of the separate armed services, but, as he developed more and more confidence in his defense secretary, the President was increasingly willing to let McNamara really run his department. McNamara, of course, continued to keep the President informed of major problems. The close relationship between the President and the secretary became, if anything, even closer in the Johnson Administration than in the Kennedy Administration, the most notable difference being a tendency on President Johnson's part to meet longer and more frequently with his secretary and other defense advisers than President Kennedy had (in part this resulted from President Johnson's preoccupation with the Vietnam War).

ROLES OF THE SECRETARY OF DEFENSE

The trends discussed above, which enlarged the authority of the secretary of defense, highlighted a number of his roles or functions, which, for purposes of analysis, should be distinguished from each other. In short, the secretary of defense wears several hats, and those who work with and for him can become confused not only about which hat he may be wearing at any given time, but also by the particular requirements of any one of the hats. And these functional distinctions are only part of the story, because so much depends on the personalities of key individuals—especially the President and the secretary of defense—and the nature of the relationship that emerges between them. In any case, at least three critical roles can be identified for the secretary of defense.

First, the secretary is a personal adviser to the President. He is "the President's man," chosen to lead and direct the Department of Defense, a member of the Cabinet, and in recent years one of the closest members of the President's inner circle. Ideally, the secretary ought to be the most knowledgeable man in government concerning any subject pertaining to the role of military force in the attainment of national objectives. In practice, however, this is difficult to achieve because he is seldom a man of military background. He is therefore provided with elaborate staff assistance, including the Joint Chiefs of Staff themselves—the nation's top professional military men.

Any President will no doubt reach out for a variety of advice on most national-security issues, but if the secretary of defense has gained the President's confidence, the President will want to rely primarily on him for advice on the defense aspects of national-security matters.

The second role of the secretary of defense, that of military commander, is more formal and structured than the first, which is a highly personal and perhaps even intimate relationship. The second role derives from the Defense Reorganization Act of 1958, which designates the secretary as first in the chain of command under the President.

The secretary's third role is that of "manager" or chief executive officer of the Department of Defense. While it is misleading to push too far the analogy between a major governmental department and a large industrial corporation, there are some evident parallels—the receipt and disbursement of money, the maintenance of plant and equipment, procurement and distribution, and the support of personnel. The Department of Defense in all of these respects is larger by far than any other governmental department (as well as larger than any industrial corporation), and hence the secretary of defense as the "big boss" of this enterprise has enormous managerial responsibilities. If the President is likened to a chairman of the board, then the secretary of defense is clearly the chief executive officer and general manager of that part of the over-all governmental corporation which is the Department of Defense. One can take issue with any particular managerial decision by the secretary of defense—for example, the decision to purchase the TFX aircraft—on the grounds that the decision was poorly staffed, or that the wrong or inappropriate sources of advice were heeded, or on other grounds, but one can scarcely argue that the secretary was not the final and appropriate locus of authority for this kind of decision.

ROLES OF THE JOINT CHIEFS OF STAFF

The JCS, considered as a collective entity, also plays several roles, and in some respects these are parallel to those of the secretary of defense.[2] By law, it has a responsibility to serve corporately, as principal military adviser to the President, the secretary of defense, and the National Security Council (or presumably to such other comparable organization as the President may prefer to use). The particular relationship between the JCS on the one hand, and the President and the NSC on the other, is one of the sources of confusion and occasional dismay in the policy-making process because, on those occasions when the secretary and the chiefs may disagree, it can appear that the secretary of defense and the JCS are rival and competitive military advisers to the President.

Recent Presidents have seldom wanted to create the impression of having cut themselves off from direct consultation with the military chiefs, especially during shooting wars or other situations when the American people expect the President to listen to his professional military men. But while the members of the JCS are certainly distinguished military men, they come from different military backgrounds and often have diverging perspectives. It is therefore easier for the President to turn to a single man for his military advice (for example his secretary of defense) than to solicit the views of the chiefs—who may differ among each other or with the secretary. The President may face the dilemma that if he heeds only his secretary, he may undermine the morale and the usefulness of the chiefs and of the armed forces as a whole; whereas, if he heeds the chiefs too often, he may undermine the secretary's position. Equally important, to listen to one to the exclusion of the other can deprive the President of alternative sources of well-informed advice.

---

[2] The Joint Chiefs of Staff (JCS) evolved early in World War II and was given statutory status in the National Security Act of 1947. Its members are the chairman, the chief of staff of the army, the chief of naval operations, and the chief of staff of the air force. The commandant of the marine corps sits as an equal on the JCS whenever a matter of direct concern to the corps is under consideration.

The second corporate role of the JCS is to serve as the military operational staff for the secretary of defense. If there is some ambiguity and lack of clarity as to the first JCS role, the role of the JCS in the chain of military command is clear. The secretary exercised his right under the 1958 reorganization legislation to specify the chain of command beneath him, and a Department of Defense directive accordingly provided that the chiefs as a corporate body would serve as a staff link in the chain between the secretary and the unified and specified commands. Inasmuch as a committee is seldom an efficient vehicle for transmitting military command, the JCS has occasionally, in time of crisis, designated a single chief to monitor a unified command in its name —but only in a specified field or for a specific purpose. It must be stressed that the particular chief who performs in this capacity does so as the agent of the JCS as a whole, which in turn is serving as the military staff of the secretary.

The third role of the JCS, closely related to its other advisory functions, is in planning and programing the military forces and matériel it believes will be required in the future, given the policy objectives of the nation. The performance of this task results in advice to the secretary in his role as general manager of the department, because all forces and matériel must be provided for in the department's annual budget, which every year is the adjusted current increment of the department's five-year plan. The Joint Strategic Objectives Plan (JSOP) of the JCS is probably the most prominent planning document produced in this area; projected at least five years into the future, it is revised annually by the joint chiefs and sent to the secretary. (The JSOP is discussed in some detail later in this chapter.)

In contrast to the first three roles of the JCS, which are corporate in nature, the fourth function is their respective individual roles as the nation's senior soldier, sailor, and airman, each responsible to the secretary of his particular service. In this sense, the JCS traces its origin back to the kind of loose confederation improvised at the outset of World War II to deal with the organization of the British military chiefs of staff after President Franklin D. Roosevelt had decided to fight the war in alliance with Great Britain. The National Security Act of 1947 gave the JCS a statutory existence, but it did little to resolve some of the fundamental anomalies inherent in the JCS system. One of these anomalies was that the armed forces continued to be organized along traditional lines into armies and navies, supplemented by air forces as a result of the invention of the airplane but without any recognition that the true impact of the airplane in effect called into question the traditional way of organizing armed forces. Moreover, there still remained problems inherent in the fact that the separate armed forces, as traditionally constituted, were rival tribes complete with separate tribal customs, philosophies, professional styles, and life sytles—who really knew very little about each other.

Nevertheless, it still requires the better part of a man's career to train him to command a division of troops in the field, a fleet at sea, or a wing in the air. As long as this remains true, there will be men who are soldiers or sailors or airmen, with all their differences in custom, tradition, and outlook. The evolution of the Joint Chiefs of Staff in recent years, along with the growing support for "joint thinking" within the separate armed services, may well be the best way to proceed toward the best solution in practice, but these trends will require constant stimulation if the nation is to be served in the future by senior professional military officers whose experience will have fully qualified them to participate actively at the highest interdepartmental levels of the policy-making process.

ROLES OF THE CHAIRMAN OF THE JOINT CHIEFS OF STAFF

The chairman of the Joint Chiefs of Staff (CJCS), like the President, the secretary of defense, and the chiefs themselves, also wears several hats. Unlike the others, however, little of his authority derives from statutes and directives. In terms of formal written charters, he is merely one among equals within the JCS, but in terms of precedent and practice, he has come to enjoy a substantial range of powers. The precedents include the ways in which several extremely able chairmen—especially Admiral Arthur W. Radford under President Eisenhower, General Maxwell D. Taylor under President Kennedy, and General Earle G. Wheeler under President Johnson—were able to make themselves highly useful and valuable to the Commanders in Chief whom they served. The practices include the ways in which these recent Presidents and several secretaries of defense have responded to the contributions of notable chairmen by informally "institutionalizing" the latters' important functions. The practices also include the way in which the other chiefs have in some respects gradually come to defer to the chairman and have even explicitly delegated some of their collective authority to him.

A certain degree of authority inheres in the very designation as chairman of any collective group. It often provides a man with a constituency and a power base from which to operate. This is less true of the CJCS than of other kinds of chairmen, because he is not elected or appointed by the collectivity which he represents. Moreover, he has no service or other "constituency" from which he can draw support but must borrow his help from the other chiefs. In short, he is appointed by the President, presumably in most cases with the concurrence of the secretary of defense, yet he would serve the President and the secretary rather poorly if he did not have or acquire the confidence and trust of the other chiefs. He is thus in the difficult position of holding office because of an appointment from above, but being effective in office only if he can acquire the support of the peers over whom he presides. It is a tribute to the personal abilities of a number of CJCS that this office has gradually increased to a very considerable position of power and prominence.

The first of the chairman's roles is that of the officer serving as senior military adviser to the President and to the secretary of defense, and in some cases, also to the secretary of state. This is a *de facto* role, almost wholly unsupported by *de jure* authority, and yet it is extremely important. Partly for the same reason that recent Presidents have turned for advice more and more to their secretaries of defense—the simple fact that it is easier to deal with a single individual than with a faceless institution such as the Department of Defense or the Office of the Joint Chiefs of Staff —the Presidents have also tended to turn to the CJCS as a primary military adviser in uniform.

The most noteworthy of the chairman's informally "institutionalized" roles have perhaps been his regular membership in
President Johnson's Tuesday lunch group, the highest-level policy
forum in the national-security field during the Johnson Administration, and his membership on the State Department-chaired
Senior Interdepartmental Group (SIG). In recent years, the chairman has also accompanied the secretary of defense on important
trips and has participated with the secretary in many—perhaps most—of the latter's informal and formal policy-making
tasks.

The Chairman is not formally a member of the military staff
of the secretary–commander, except insofar as he is a member of
the joint chiefs. In practice, however, he has occasionally been
deputized by the chiefs to serve as their agent for certain operational and advisory matters. To that extent, he has from time to
time exercised a role of senior officer on the military staff that is
the JCS.

As the chairman's position has evolved under recent incumbents,
perhaps his most important role is to serve as an "ambassador"
between the secertary of defense and the joint chiefs. As suggested
above, the chairman's role is anomalous in that he is subject to
the President and to the secretary, although much of his actual
power derives from the respect and trust that he enjoys among
his fellow chiefs. In earlier years some chiefs tended to view the
chairman with the suspicion that he was "one of them, and not
one of us," that he was primarily loyal to the President and the
secretary, and that he therefore was not enthusiastic about defend-
ing views held by the chiefs. This suspicion has been largely overcome in recent years because the chairman has been able to act
as a goodwill messenger and ambassador between the secretary
and the JCS, helping both to establish effective rapport and cooperation between the central civilian and military leadership
within the Pentagon. This has been a constructive and useful
development, although it has depended in large part on the nature of the personalities involved. Like other developments, however, it may have become sufficiently institutionalized to survive
changes in key personnel.

The Planning, Programing, and Budgeting System (PPBS)

Two features of the "McNamara Revolution," the Planning Programing, and Budgeting System (PPBS) and the related systems-analysis techniques, merit further discussion. Both were basically intended to help answer the perennially central question of Defense Department programing: How much is enough—i.e., what amounts of what kinds of defense (*not* how much army or navy or air force) are we buying?

The main elements of the PPBS were the so-called program packages, the Five-Year Defense Program (originally called the Five-Year Force Structure and Financial Program), and the use of cost-effectiveness studies. With the possible exception of the five-year-program concept, these devices were not in themselves novel. The distinctive feature of the program packages, for example, was that they focused on broad functional areas such as strategic forces, continental-defense forces, and general-purpose forces, rather than on the traditional service categories. The army had previously studied such an approach, and the air force and navy had already developed functional programs for their own use. The services had also pioneered in the use of operations research and systems-analysis techniques. There was even some precedent for the five-year concept, in that Congressional committees had been urging the development of programs that would extend beyond the annual-budget cycle. The really innovative feature of the PPBS was that the secretary elected to make the functional programs major vehicles for his decisions. The Five-Year Defense Program focused on functional categories that were broader than the responsibilities of any single military service or department and thus tended to shift the initiative to the secretary.

One of the objectives of the PPBS was to develop additional analytical capability in the OSD. The budget had previously been the secretary's principal managerial tool, and a substantial capability for fiscal analysis already existed in the comptroller's office. Projections of the long-term as well as the immediate costs of various proposals became an important feature of the five-year projection and of the specific programs. What proved to be the most controversial feature of the new system was the extensive use of systems-analysis techniques to review and evaluate the force proposals of the JCS and the services on a substantive as well as a budgetary basis. Such techniques also were used by the comptroller to provide the secretary with independent analyses of a broader range of force levels and mixes than the alternatives specifically proposed by the JCS and the services.

Under the current system, the JCS still provides a basic statement of military requirements. Its vehicle for this purpose is the Joint Stategic Objectives Plan (JSOP), which projects military needs for five to eight years into the future. It, too, was changed to the functional-program format, a change which tended to place emphasis on *joint* planning and to shift the initiative from the service departments to the Joint Chiefs of Staff.

The submission of the JSOP starts the planning, programing, budgeting cycle.[3] It furnishes a military input into the development of the five-year program and of the defense program and budget which is submitted annually to Congress. In both cases, the secretary's staffs start by evaluating the proposals of the JSOP on a program-by-program basis, that is, strategic forces, general-purpose forces, and other broad, mission-oriented categories. A major step in the process is the use of systems-analysis techniques to carry out cost-effectiveness studies aimed at comparing the military utility and cost of various alternative ways of accomplishing the basic missions. More traditional techniques are used to develop necessary cost estimates and fiscal data. Until 1965, both types of analysis were carried out by the comptroller. Since then, the comptroller and the assistant secretary for systems analysis have shared the responsibility.

It is worth suggesting that arguments in support of PPBS procedures for enhancing the control of the secretary can also be regarded as arguments in support of stronger and more effective

---

[3] The account of the role of the JSOP in this paragraph is largely theoretical. In fact, the JSOP did not play a very significant role in the budget process of the Eisenhower Administration or the PPBS system of the Kennedy–Johnson administrations.

control by the President as well. This does not mean that all arguments for PPBS are valid, but it does mean that the advantages and limitations of PPBS, reviewed below in terms of the secretary's interests and position, can also apply in a significant sense to those of the President.

The advantages of PPBS procedures from the point of view of the secretary of defense include the following:

The secretary's independence. Secretary McNamara's use of cost-effectiveness studies gave him a means of evaluating proposals independently from the categories of the separate services and other components of the Defense Department. He was thus able to require that discussion and deliberation take place on his ground, in his terms, and from a departmentwide perspective, rather than piecemeal from the limited perspectives of the separate department components.

The secretary's involvement in substantive issues. Pre-PPBS procedures tended to limit the secretary to approving or disapproving proposed budgets submitted by department components, without providing him an opportunity to become engaged in the substantive issues underlying the budget proposals. The PPBS procedures gave the secretary an effective means of involving himself in these fundamental substantive issues, requiring justifications based on merit.

More useful budget categories. The program-package concept, based on functional rather than service-connected categories, provided the secretary (and the President and Congress) with a means of ascertaining exactly how many of what kinds of military forces the United States was buying and maintaining for any particular purpose (such as strategic-nuclear attack, continental defense, and so on). This kind of information was more useful than merely how the army, navy, and air force were "making out" in a given budget.

Better financial management. In a world of finite resources, any technique that improves a manager's ability to assess costs and then to compare the costs of two or more different ways of accomplishing the same objective (i.e., cost effectiveness) is obviously of great value.

Long-range planning. Many modern weapons systems and other hardware needed by the Defense Department require long-lead times for research, development, and production. Hence, decisions to go ahead with them will have a significant impact on not only the national budget but on the size and structure of the U.S. Armed Forces—and thus on U.S. military capabilities—for years to come. The Five-Year Defense Program helps keep these long-range considerations in the forefront of the thinking of government officials in the Defense Department and in the White House.

The limitations of PPBS must also be considered. President Kennedy told the joint chiefs at a meeting a few weeks after the Bay of Pigs that, when he asked for their views on national-security problems, he wanted them "to base their advice not on narrow military considerations alone but on broad-gauged political and economic factors as well." [4] But excessive commitment to a particular tool or technique can narrow people's vision just as intensely professional perspectives sometimes do, and this caveat applies to overreliance on PPBS. The PPBS procedures were primarily useful to the secretary in his role as general manager of the department rather than in his role as military adviser to the President or in his role as a principal in the chain of command. These procedures were presumably of little use, for example, in advising the President on expanding or contracting the Vietnam War or in deciding who would be the officer best suited to command U.S. military forces there. For questions such as these, the analytical and intellectual resources provided by PPBS are hardly relevant. Such questions do call for the kind of "professional judgment" developed by military officers in the course of lifetime careers.

Now that we have suggested the advantages of PPBS in a very

[4] Theodore C. Sorenson, *Kennedy* (New York: Harper & Row, 1965), p. 605.

general way and the major limitation on these techniques over-all, let us return to the five categories of advantages noted above and discuss the specific limitations inherent in each.

The secretary's independence. While everyone would probably agree that the chief executive officer of a large organization must have a staff responsible to him alone, lest he become the captive of some line faction within the organization, there is the ancient question: "Who guards the guards?" The traditional way of offsetting privileged access to the king's ear is to structure the organization so that the king has to listen to others as well. This is not easy to do, but ideally there should be at least two groups of equal status working directly under the defense secretary, sharing the same departmentwide perspective that he must exhibit, yet representing quite different professional backgrounds, analytical skills, and mental sets.

The matter of the secretary's independence, especially from the professional military leaders, raises another issue. He must have independent means for evaluating their proposals and indeed for generating his own, lest he become too dependent on them. At the same time, the posture of political neutrality, on which the long-term credibility of the professional military corps rests, can depend in no small degree on their maintaining a discernible independence from an incumbent secretary and administration. The difficult question is thus how these two partners in the same enterprise —the civilian secretary of defense and the uniformed military leaders—can maintain some independence from each other and yet work cooperatively toward shared goals. This calls for the understanding on the part of a secretary that he will be the loser if he exerts too many controls over the professional military leaders; it calls for a JCS that fully appreciates the secretary's need for a staff of his own that can evaluate and propose; and it calls for a secretary and a JCS who work very hard not only to avoid abrasiveness toward each other, but who go out of their way to establish and maintain attitudes of cordial cooperation.

The secretary's involvement in substantive issues. Few would disagree that the secretary of defense must be able to involve him-

self in substantive issues if he is to maintain effective control of
his department. The real question is how and where he acquires
a staff to give him substantive competence in this respect. The
secretary will presumably be a civilian with little previous familiarity in the field of technical military knowledge and information
necessary to make decisions at the top of the Defense Department.
It is worth stressing that the professional military officers assigned
to the OSD must be of the highest order of competence. Ex-
hortation, however, will not change the inclination of the respective military services to assign their very best officers to their own
service staffs. It is desirable that the tours of duty of professional
military men in the OSD come to be regarded as choice assignments. The best and perhaps the only way to bring this about is
to see that the promotion system offers clear inducements and
rewards for these assignments.

More useful budget categories. The functional categories associated with PPBS in program packages have been very useful, but
the emphasis on them may have crowded out other valuable approaches. One of the real complexities of any accounting system
results from the fact that, though there are many ways to "cut
the pie" for the purposes of accounting, once it is cut it cannot
be put back together and cut a different way. Also, an accounting
system based on cost-effectiveness analysis of functional categories
tends to consider weapons and forces as having a single function,
when, in fact, many of them serve multiple purposes.

Better financial management. The PPBS can be best applied to
decisions about alternatives which can be quantified in cost dimensions. Many decisions in politics, strategy, and even economics
involve values, considerations, objectives, and the like which cannot be translated into dollar terms or other quantified data. Financial management is by no means the sum of management,
and fiscal decisions are not the only decisions, certainly for purposes of making national-security policy.

Long-range planning. One difficulty with the Five-Year Defense
Program is that, instead of giving policy-makers a clearer picture
of the future that they are deciding, it can tend to lock them

into a mental set in which they may feel that future options are largely foreclosed or that attempts to alter future programs through innovation are simply too expensive. An incremental change today may be tolerable enough, but, in the light of its potential long-range costs and implications, it may appear prohibitive. This fact can have salutary effects—working against casual decisions to go ahead with questionable innovations—but it can also make for excessive conservatism, inhibiting useful and imaginative innovations.

Systems Analysis (SA)

The Office of Systems Analysis in the early McNamara Pentagon was a unit within the Office of the Comptroller, closely associated with PPBS. In 1965, Systems Analysis was converted into a separate entity, its director becoming an assistant secretary of defense. The uniformed officers could see that McNamara was effecting important changes in the department quickly, and, like most officials in long-established organizations, they were not wholly receptive to sudden change. They naturally tried to determine where the power was gravitating among the offices close to the secretary. The rather rapid rise of Systems Analysis to a special status underscored its pre-eminent role next to McNamara, although it also underscored the fact that much of the professional military's criticism of Systems Analysis may in actuality have been tactfully off-target criticism of the policies and procedures of the secretary himself.

Precisely why did the military men regard Systems Analysis as the prime "enemy"? First, what *is* "systems analysis"? The concept of "system," so much in vogue in recent years, is one which links many disciplines of social science with natural-science concepts. But even experts on systems research do not provide much more than the following simple explanation: A system is any assemblage of parts and related links so that whatever is done to one part has some impact on all the rest. The systems approach is helpful in that it keeps us mindful of the complex ramifications of decisions about one part of an organism or an organization as these may affect the rest. Yet while there may be "natural systems" in nature—the physiology of an animal or the ecology of a forest—in human society, what we call "systems" are usually artificial constructs which are used, deliberately or not, by specialists to help in the study of something.

The word "analysis" literally suggests taking something apart for the purpose of studying it. Thus, etymology alone would suggest that "systems analysis" is a technique for looking at something in its broadest dimensions and then picking it apart. This, as it happens, is not a bad description of what systems analysis did for Secretary McNamara.

In the annual defense-budget cycle, substantive evaluations of force recommendations have been carried out for the secretary principally by the Office of the Assistant Secretary of Defense for Systems Analysis. The justifications and rationale for the proposals of the military professionals have often been challenged in the course of this review and alternatives suggested. This has led many military men to believe that the JSOP of the Office of the Joint Chiefs of Staff is not sufficiently reflected in the annual defense program, while the view at the OSD level is that JSOP's in the past have been largely irrelevant. Some of the difficulty no doubt stemmed from the character of the JSOP itself, which has often been regarded by the JCS more as a negotiating device than as a vehicle for assisting the secretary to make decisions about allocating limited resources.

The earlier tradition in preparing the JSOP was that it should be based on purely military considerations, that the JCS should not compromise its professional judgment about military requirements by taking account of economic and political constraints. The practice in the 1950's was for the JCS to submit statements of military requirements which far exceeded the administration's budgetary guidelines—leaving it to the secretary to reconcile the two. In that period, it is generally agreed, the JSOP was noted by the comptroller and the other OSD staffs in preparing the annual budget for defense, but it was given very little real attention.

The JSOP's of the early 1960's were prepared in similar fashion by the JCS, but Secretary McNamara rejected the idea of defining military requirements without reference to cost. He proceeded on the assumption that the allocation of scarce resources must always be central in developing the defense program and that the objective must always be to acquire maximum military capability for the funds expended. The PPBS was predicated on that approach, and the function of Systems Analysis within the system was to develop measures of military effectiveness that could be related to cost and used as a basis for comparing the utility of different force levels and mixes.

In adopting the PPBS, McNamara served notice to the JCS and the services that he intended to take these considerations into account in arriving at decisions. It was, in effect, an open invitation for the JCS to include in the JSOP supporting analyses that would permit him to consider its force recommendations in these terms. The JCS was slow to accept that invitation, in part because the joint staff initially had a limited capability to respond, as well as the normal institutional resistance to change.

The nature of the problem has changed somewhat in the intervening years. The JCS has undertaken to improve the JSOP and to make it more responsive to the secretary's demands, while the joint staff has come to accept systems analysis as a useful method for subjecting proposals to sharp scrutiny. A significant, recent innovation has been the introduction of costing out the force proposals included in the JSOP. These changes have helped bring the joint staff and the OSD staff closer to a common approach. Nevertheless, the military staffs have continued to regard Systems Analysis with some misgivings. They recognize that many of its techniques are valid, but they argue that it has not always been used as an analytical tool and that occasionally it has been used as a device to support the secretary in reducing military expenditures. It is sometimes charged, for example, that the Systems Analysis staff selects program areas in which it believes military expenditures can be reduced, and then it performs analyses to demonstrate that there is a quantitative justification for such reductions. Military critics concede that this may make economic sense but not military sense.

Many of the advantages of systems analysis are similar to those of PPBS. The techniques give the secretary a means of evaluating and generating proposals independent of the particular interests and perspectives of constituent Defense Department components; they help the secretary to involve himself in substantive issues at a very early stage in their consideration, long before crystallization into budgetary statements; they provide more useful categories for comparative analysis than are ordinarily provided in proposals coming to the secretary from department components; and they generally contribute to long-range perspectives.

In short, Systems Analysis (along with PPBS) has provided the secretary with critical support for integrating major plans and programs in a more rational way, so that what emerges is a coherent whole rather than a grab bag of disconnected bits and pieces. It has helped to define the several elements of major defense programs much better than before, making it easier for decision-makers to understand interrelationships, and revealing more fully the ramifications of various policy options.

Systems Analysis can appear very mysterious to the layman, and it is indeed a complicated matter. Yet some of its techniques are in reality quite simple. One is to try to make sure that all of the Defense Department agencies which participate in developing a particular plan or program work from the same factual base. Another technique is to try to uncover the assumptions underlying the positions of the participating groups; in this way—by identifying basic disagreements as to the facts and by examining underlying assumptions and interests—Systems Analysis has helped to focus attention on the issues worth arguing about as policy was translated into plans and action programs. Anyone who has ever studied major problems of policy, planning, and programing in U.S. defense management would agree that factual inconsistencies and unexamined assumptions have often played a large part in creating difficulties.

Some of the criticisms of Systems Analysis from staff levels in the JCS organization and the separate services reflect little more than disagreement with particular policy decisions by those who were overruled in the process of decision. Other criticisms appear more fundamental and substantial. Indeed, one important argument against Systems Analysis does not involve any criticism of its general methods nor of the importance to the secretary of having his own group to study issues on an across-the-board basis; rather, it is argued that Systems Analysis involves a fusion of incompatible functions. For example, one official interviewed for this inquiry, a man very favorably disposed toward the work of Systems Analysis after 1961, stated that it was particularly important for Systems Analysis to be "honest" when playing the role of the "devil's advocate." But this is a contradiction in terms if "honest" is taken to mean being an objective gatherer and presenter of facts. A devil's advocate plays the role of adversary for the sake of contention, the idea being that somebody else makes the decision after hearing both sides. The distinction is similar to that between a judge and jury on the one hand, and the opposing attorneys on the other. It is understandable that the secretary of defense should feel a need for someone on his staff to "make the secretary's case," i.e., to be his prosecuting attorney, or, if he himself is being prosecuted in the Congress or elsewhere, then to be his defense attorney. But if he uses Systems Analysis for this purpose, then others can hardly regard it as a dispassionate and objective source of analysis. One is reminded of the flustered young lawyer who, in opening his summary statement, told the judge: "Your Honor, here are the conclusions on which my facts are based." Because Systems Analysis occasionally performed studies to establish objective and "quantitative" arguments for conclusions reached earlier on other grounds, there was bound to be some "credibility gap" about *all* of its work. The roles of the partisan advocate and the neutral analyst do not mix.

THE DRAFT PRESIDENTIAL MEMORANDUMS (DPM's)

Early in the McNamara period, the preparation of what were called Draft Memorandums to the President (DPM's) on each of the major programs in the defense budget became an important means of reaching and promulgating major decisions by the secretary. Each DPM sets forth national-security policy guidance, develops a rationale based on that guidance, and examines alternative ways of accomplishing the program's purpose. After extensive coordination and revisions, the secretary's decisions on the major elements of the program are announced in a final version of the DPM, late in the annual budget cycle. The DPM's have provided a specific way of defining the main issues, exchanging views, and eventually ariving at key decisions on each program. It is from these decisions that the development of each program and its budget thereafter proceeds.

The initial version of a DPM, usually but not always drafted by Systems Analysis, is technically the secretary's response to the recommendations of the JCS as presented in the JSOP. The initial DPM defines and describes the program that the secretary tentatively proposes to support; when released by the OSD, it is sent to the JCS and to the service chiefs and secretaries for comment. The comments on the DPM's are vigorous and forthright, and they serve several purposes. They identify the main issues between the secretary, the JCS, and the service chiefs and secretaries. They provide an opportunity for OSD assumptions and analyses to be challenged, for additional analyses to be recommended, and for alternative program proposals to be made. When these comments reach the OSD, the DPM is revised to reflect them to the extent that the secretary considers appropriate. A new version is then circulated in the same manner. This process may be repeated several times before the major issues are resolved. Then, when the JCS and service views have been taken into account and accepted, rejected, or modified, coordination with other departments and agencies begins—including informal checking out with appropriate staff officers in the White House.

After final coordination within the Defense Department of the version incorporating the secretary's decisions, the DPM is revised for formal submission to the White House. The President has not usually given his explicit approval to the DPM's, although he has often studied the key ones very carefully. The practice of continuing to label them "drafts" tends to identify the secretary, rather than the President, with the decisions on controversial issues. In any event, at the end of the annual cycle, the President does approve the total defense program and budget, which are derived from the DPM's collectively.

One advantage of the DPM procedure is that it provides a cumulative record, available throughout the department, on the background of each major decision. A second advantage is that the process of preparing, commenting on, and revising the successive versions of the DPM's provides regular occasions for extensive discussions and informal exchanges of views at all levels of the Defense Department. The exchanges between the senior civilian and military authorities on the issues are one of the most decisive parts of the process determining the final form of the defense budget.

The DPM's have assumed another kind of importance, only indirectly related to their function in the program-budget cycle. With the NSC system in a kind of abeyance during the Kennedy and Johnson administrations, the secretary of defense became the direct source of policy guidance for his department, and the DPM's became one of his major vehicles for disseminating it. Use of the DPM's for that purpose has caused some misunderstanding, particularly about whether the DPM's should be regarded as expressions of the secretary's personal views or as authoritative statements of national-security policy.

By contrast with the Eisenhower NSC system, the subsequent eight years witnessed a reversion to a more traditional relationship between the President and his Cabinet officers. It has always been customary for a Cabinet officer to be regarded as the President's principal agent for matters affecting his department. In principle, it is up to the President to decide whether he wants to provide general or detailed policy guidance for a department. If he chooses the former, in effect he makes the secretary responsible for the detailed guidance required for the department's operations. After 1961, the secretary of defense assumed that responsibility, clearly with the concurrence and support of the President.

SOURCES OF MILITARY ADVICE

The Military Service Departments

When the 1958 Defense Reorganization Act enhanced the powers of the defense secretary and reduced those of the separate service secretaries, it tended to make the latter, and their assistant secretaries and other civilian staff, extensions of the secretary of defense. Yet, despite the decline in their autonomy, the army, the navy, and air force, along with their civilian and military chiefs, retain far more prominence and subtle forms of power than one might expect from reading the 1958 legislation and the literature on the "McNamara Revolution." The continuing stature of the services derives partly from the reluctance of Congress to eliminate them as separate organizations, even though Congress has approved an increasing degree of centralized authority over them. Other anomalies persist. The rituals and symbolism of the armed forces and the organizational loyalties of their members continue to be largely service-oriented, whereas the operational forces in the unified commands are under the command of the secretary of defense. Only three of the major military educational institutions (the National War College, the Industrial College of the Armed Forces, and the Armed Forces Staff College) are not service-operated, and these three are for relatively senior officers. By contrast, all three undergraduate academies, three middle-rank staff schools, three war colleges, three Reserve Officer Training Corps programs, a variety of other training schools for officer candidates, and a number of other programs continue to be "owned and operated" separately by the traditional services. Perhaps of greater importance, promotions and career patterns are controlled by the respective services, and an officer's career prospects can be jeopardized if he stays away too long from his service "flagpole." For this reason, many officers have been reluctant to accept assignments in the Office of the Secretary of Defense, the State Department, or even the White House.

A service military chief has considerable latitude in deciding how best to support programs of particular interest to his service. Outside the JCS arena, he can make his case formally through his service secretary, or informally through the OSD staffs. The former tactic often has the advantage of getting service views before the secretary of defense in unfiltered form, while the latter provides somewhat greater assurance that when the OSD staffs deliver formal opinions later on, they will be favorable. The approaches of the different chiefs have tended to reflect the different traditions of their respective services. The navy has preferred to keep Systems Analysis and the other OSD staffs at arm's length and to work through its secretary; the air force has been inclined to establish and maintain close relationships with the OSD staffs; the army has tended toward an intermediate position in this respect.

The Chairman of the Joint Chiefs of Staff

The great enhancement of the authority and powers of the chairman of the JCS in recent years has been noted above. Of course, the chiefs collectively and individually still have the right of direct access to the President, but President Kennedy found it awkward to work out a suitable basis for meeting them as a body; and almost the only regularly scheduled meetings between President Johnson and the JCS as a group were the final budget reviews every December, conducted at the LBJ ranch. A service chief is understandably reluctant to exercise his right of direct access to the President; such action smacks of short-circuiting the chain of command by bypassing the corporate JCS, the chairman, and the secretary of defense. In practice, therefore, the chairman has become the effective working link between the JCS and the White House except in those instances when the President himself may request comments from one particular chief, usually on a matter relating primarily to the latter's service.

Over the years, the chairman has acquired considerable staff support. From the time his position was created in 1949, he has been served in his immediate office by about half a dozen outstanding officers of colonel–navy captain rank, who are collectively designated the chairman's staff group. He is also directly supported by a three-star assistant to the chairman and by a sizable special study group, which was established in 1961 to assist in responding to time-consuming requirements levied by the OSD. Finally, since 1962, the chairman's office has maintained an important, semi-institutionalized link to the White House through an officer of colonel or brigadier general rank who serves on the national-security staff there.

Some observers feel that the chairman's enhanced powers should be supported by statute or directive. Others feel that there is little point in formal directives, because the chairman's effective authority will always depend on his gaining the confidence of the President, the secretary, and his fellow chiefs. Furthermore, the history of centralized offices within the U.S. Armed Forces suggests that there is usually a natural concord of interests between the senior centralized civilian official and the senior centralized military authority.

The Joint Chiefs of Staff

The decade and a half after World War II was a period of severe strains within the JCS as the group sought to cope with new demands of the international environment. The Korean War temporarily reduced interservice tension because it relaxed the budgetary pressures of 1945–50, but the period was also considered in many quarters as an aberrational interlude. During most of the 1950's, the dominant military doctrine accepted the argument that a long-range strategic nuclear delivery force was about the only military capability the United States required. The acquisition of this capability began in the Truman Administration, was only slightly interrupted by the Korean War, and came to a climax in the Eisenhower Administration. The air force received approximately half the annual armed forces appropriations during the eight years of Eisenhower's Presidency; the army and navy were left to split the remaining half, with the navy ordinarily receiving a little more than the army. The Soviet Union was the only perceived enemy, and Europe was considered the likely war theater.

In this context, the JCS became an arena for interservice jockeying, with the air force trying to maintain the pre-eminence it had finally won, the navy trying to accommodate itself to the dominance of airpower thinking, and the army suffering through another of the frequent periods in United States history when military policy has been founded on the assumption that shortcut military solutions featuring massive hardware eliminate the need for trained ground forces.

President Kennedy's conviction that the world was a more complicated place than had been assumed in the military planning of the 1945–60 period and that the United States was therefore in need of rethinking its over-all military posture, led to important changes in the roles of the services and in relations between them. One point was clear to the new President: The U.S. military establishment required a wide variety of forces capable of response to a wide variety of conceivable situations. As noted before, Secretary McNamara immediately set in motion dozens of study efforts to help him lead the rethinking.

It has also been noted that the joint chiefs' initial contributions to many of these studies featured ritualistic rhetoric characteristic of their papers during the 1945–60 period, which in turn had tended to reflect the interservice differences of the pre-World War II period. Secretary McNamara's consequent loss of confidence in the joint chiefs' work led him to rely on the group of talented individuals and aggressive agencies with which he began to surround himself, including the Office of the Comptroller, Systems Analysis, International Security Affairs, and Defense Research and Engineering. These components within the OSD were almost exclusively civilian in their leadership and composition.

One result was to challenge or goad the JCS into a higher level of performance, in part because it was still required to respond to problems assigned to it by McNamara, and in part because the chiefs realized that only through improved performance could they expect to bring collective professional military judgment to bear on major decisions. The chiefs were handicapped, however, by the relatively small size of the joint staff and, even more, by the fact that the services did not always send their best people to OJCS duty. Both of these problems derived from the old view that any strengthening of the OJCS would be at the expense of the services.

In time, however, military leaders began to appreciate that the best way to strengthen the professional military voice was to strengthen the OJCS. By 1968, the OJCS had changed materially. The joint staff had significantly increased its capabilities, the services were assigning better-qualified officers to it, and, unlike the situation eight years earlier, it was able, through the National Military Command System, to handle the national-level military operations of a major war in Vietnam. The chairman's special study group had substantially strengthened the joint staff's analytical and technical capability. So, too, had several new special assistants' offices (particularly those for counterinsurgency and strategic mobility), new functional divisions throughout the joint staff itself, as well as the contributions of such civilian research groups on external contract as the RAND Corporation and the Institute for Defense Analyses.

As has been mentioned above, Secretary McNamara's dissatisfaction with the first JSOP, which he saw in 1961, helped persuade him that he needed to strengthen the analytical capability of his OSD staff. Some informed observers believe that the secretary would probably in any case have created his own groups, such as PPBS and Systems Analysis, and that he preferred the continuing appearance of some degree of unresponsiveness within OJCS in order to strengthen his own position. However, the OJCS sometimes appeared less concerned about effective participation in policy making than in stating its own positions (by means of the JSOP) for the historical record. One of these views is not especially flattering to the secretary, and the other is not especially flattering to the chiefs, but it does seem fair to conclude that into at least the early 1960's there was little cooperation between the OJCS and the civilian offices surrounding the secretary.

One sign of the growth and maturity of OJCS activities in the later 1960's was the erosion of the "closed shop" atmosphere and the notable increase in communication from day to day between OCJS officers and civilian or military officials elsewhere in the Pentagon and in Washington generally. The office of the chairman, the office of the director of the joint staff, and other elements became considerably more open to informal channels, and something like normal working relationships began to develop in which discussion could take place *prior* to, rather than *after*, official JCS positions were officially and solemnly reached. This cooperative and open atmosphere should allow the secretary to provide more usable policy guidance to the chiefs, and in turn, enable them to provide more useful military advice to him.

Military leaders during the McNamara years, like other U.S. military leaders throughout this century, tended to feel that they received too little (and insufficiently authoritative) policy guidance from their civilian superiors. In part, this criticism reflected the feeling of many military men that the secretary's policy positions (in his Draft Presidential Memorandums, his speeches, and the like) were not necessarily definitive versions of "national policy" as viewed by the President, the secretary of state, or the Congress. There was a tendency to lament the absence of something like the Basic National Security Policy (BNSP) documents of the Eisenhower Administration. This criticism no doubt also reflected a feeling that JCS views were inadequately reflected in policy pronouncements by the secretary.

The PPBS formulation helps illustrate some of the above issues. In the planning, programing, and budgeting cycle, the ideal theoretical sequence would begin with the formulation of a basic national-security policy and its transmittal to the OJCS, which would then devise military plans, from which would flow the programs that would in turn underlie the defense budget. Then, if the budget exceeded the limits allowed by the President and the Congress, the procedure would be repeated in accordance with budget guidelines until the budget reached was both politically acceptable and militarily sound. The OSD has sometimes felt that the services wanted to shortcut this procedure by asking for a BNSP document from which they could proceed directly to the submission of a "military requirements" document to the secretary. McNamara believed that such a document from the services would be little more than a "wish list."

It may be true that the JSOP force lists prepared by the JCS from service inputs did look like wish lists. Some military observers were surely on shaky ground, however, when they expressed reservations about the authority of the secretary's policy guidance, for example in the DPM's. Even if the secretary devised this guidance pretty much on his own (and not, as clearly was the case, through a variety of contacts with the President and the secretary of state), this was not for the JCS to question. An old rule of organizational behavior is that responsibility gravitates to the lowest level that will accept it. If the President and others, such as the secretary of state, are not inclined to provide definitive policy guidance, it necessarily becomes the duty of the secretary of defense to fill the gap by giving the Defense Department the policy guidance which, in his judgment, most nearly accords with objectives of the responsible authorities. A more understandable military grievance was the allegation that JCS views had not been adequately integrated into final Defense Department positions. Whatever the merits of these arguments, it is clear that the misunderstandings and misgivings on both sides of the fence underline the importance of opening up OJCS toward closer and more cooperative relationships with the OSD.

Intelligence in the Pentagon

In 1961, Secretary McNamara, building on work begun by his predecessor, Thomas Gates, established the Defense Intelligence Agency (DIA) to provide him (and the joint chiefs) with a centralized source of intelligence support, largely to replace the three separate service intelligence organizations. The DIA was in this sense analogous to the Defense Supply Agency and the Defense Communications Agency which were established at about the same time. At least the principle appears analogous. But procurement of hardware and maintenance of communication nets are different kinds of business than intelligence, and the effectiveness of the DIA is thus more difficult to judge than that of the other new, centralized agencies.

The interviews conducted during this inquiry make clear that a strong DIA is needed and desired not only by the civilian and military leadership in the Pentagon but by knowledgeable veterans of the White House national-security staff and of the Central Intelligence Agency as well. Bureaucratically, the latter might be expected to feel otherwise out of fear of competition, but they expressly do not. They have become accustomed to close cooperation with the DIA, and both organizations support and supplement one another through close and constant contacts. These working relationships may defy neat organizational charting, but they have proved very useful in practice. In addition, for the civilian professionals, the question is not one of either monopolizing the intelligence field or having to compete with the DIA; it is rather whether they deal with the DIA or with a fragmented array of military intelligence organizations.

By all testimony, then, the DIA stands as a salutary innovation. As government institutions go, it is still a young one—well under half the age of the CIA. Perhaps the first point to make is not that it needs strengthening, but that it has achieved a high degree of professionalism in a fairly short time. Nonetheless, most observers agree that it still suffers from several institutional handicaps. One is a corporate ambiguity about whether it works for the secretary of defense or the OJCS. It probably must work for both, because neither can do without it, but the need to do so means that it must serve two masters. Another institutional problem is that, for a number of reasons, the DIA still faces some competition from the service intelligence agencies, truncated as these agencies are. Finally, it is common testimony that the DIA is handicapped by the extent to which it must rely on short-term, rotating military officers—some of whom are not suited by training or inclination for intelligence—instead of a permanent corps of professionals.

There are no simple solutions to these problems, but certain ideas can be suggested. It might be useful, from the secretary's standpoint, to establish an assistant secretary of defense for intelligence in charge of assuring support for the secretary, helping the director of the DIA to deal with civilian intelligence offices outside the Pentagon, and freeing the director to give greater attention to the needs of the joint chiefs. Such an official could also assist the secretary and the director of the DIA in running various other intelligence operations conducted by the Defense Department. It might also be useful to strengthen the DIA's mandate and further extend its control of the service intelligence organizations—something that could be done by joint efforts of the DIA director and the OSD. And it would almost certainly be useful to strengthen the DIA's corporate capabilities by assigning more permanent civilian professionals to greater responsibilities and by making the tours of military officers longer and more rewarding.

IX

Prospects and Possibilities for the Department of Defense

The relationships between the Department of Defense and the White House were close during the Eisenhower years, when the President often worked directly with JCS Chairman Admiral Arthur Radford, and they grew even closer in the Kennedy–Johnson era, when Secretary McNamara became a key personal adviser of each President. McNamara personally participated in virtually all of the policy-making groups of the President or, if he did not himself attend, was personally represented. After General Maxwell Taylor became chairman of the JCS, Taylor also participated in the deliberations of that group and had, in addition, a representative on the White House staff. It would therefore be hard to argue that the interests of the Department of Defense were inadequately represented at the Presidential level through the Eisenhower, Kennedy, and Johnson years.

It should, however, be remembered that the White House national-security staff in 1961–69 concentrated mostly on foreign policy, in part because presidents Kennedy and Johnson felt they needed some personal staff support to compensate for perceived shortcomings in the State Department. By the same token, it is conceivable that the rise of critical defense issues or growing trouble in the Pentagon could persuade a President to build stronger Defense Department representation—either military or civilian or both—into his White House staff.

In theory and to some extent in practice, the Department of State provides foreign-policy guidance for the Defense Department and the armed forces, but its effectiveness in this respect has been limited. The ambiguity of its role was increased in the 1960's, after the NSC system was abandoned. However, the cordial and frank personal relationship between secretaries McNamara and Rusk, together with McNamara's close ties to the President, enabled the Secretary of Defense to transmit foreign-policy guidance with confidence, and the task was facilitated at lower levels by the growing contacts between officers of the State and Defense departments. Highly qualified State Department personnel were assigned to the Pentagon, where they helped in the making of defense policy, and outstanding military officers were assigned to comparable positions in the State Department. Civilian and military officers continued to attend each other's schools (the war colleges and the Foreign Service Institute), and they became better acquainted with each other's perspectives and problems. On the procedural side, as mentioned earlier, it became the practice for fairly early drafts of the secretary of defense's Draft Presidential Memorandums to be coordinated informally with the State Department through its Office of Political-Military Affairs and for a review by the State Department of the proposed Defense Department budget to occur later in the annual PPBS cycle. A more free and open spirit of cooperation also gradually developed between the joint staff and the State Department, with the over-all "opening up" of the OJCS.

Potentially, the most far-reaching innovation of recent years with respect to relations between the Defense and State departments in coordinating policy was the establishment, in 1966, of the SIG/IRG system.[1] Civilian and military leaders in the Pentagon have generally approved of the SIG/IRG arrangements and for the most part would retain and strengthen them. Many military men felt that the abandonment of the Eisenhower NSC procedures had brought needless confusion and that the subsequent *ad hoc* policy-making techniques had not provided adequate replacement. Hence, they welcomed the new plan, which was intended to bring more system into the process.

It is an interesting feature of the SIG/IRG system that the secretary of defense and the Joint Chiefs of Staff are separately represented as full members of the SIG by the deputy secretary

[1] For a detailed discussion of the SIG/IRG system, see Chapter VI.

of defense and the JCS chairman, both being members of the SIG, and the IRG's having representatives of both the OSD and the JCS. This contrasts with the general scheme under the Eisenhower NSC system, when the chairman of the Joint Chiefs of Staff merely accompanied the secretary of defense to NSC meetings as his adviser. Members of each IRG include the appropriate regional deputy from the Office of the Assistant Secretary of Defense for International Security Affairs and a corresponding officer from the OJCS. This separate representation encourages the trend toward openness in the joint staff, providing the opportunity for it to deal directly with the State Department and the other agencies represented in SIG/IRG and giving the professional military a way of speaking more clearly and directly on policy-making issues. Those who may be alarmed at the effects of giving the military a regular voice in these policy-making bodies can take comfort from the fact that the military voice has often spoken on the side of avoiding military commitment; there have been cases, for example, when State Department officers urged military measures and the military authorities opposed them because the requisite forces were not available, or were not adequate, or for other reasons.

There is nevertheless a question about whether the military voice may become too loud in policy-making councils. Some wonder, for example, if the OJCS might come to overshadow the OSD within interagency systems. Others wonder whether the separate military representation, together with increasingly direct contact between the military and the State Department might not encourage cross-cutting alliances between the State Department and the two sides of the Defense Department, which might undermine the authority of both the secretaries of state and defense. One reply to these misgivings is that the secretary of defense has sufficient authority to ensure a common Defense Department position within any other system, and in fact he has done so when he considered it important. Most knowledgeable observers at the OSD level are not really concerned; in fact, one has noted that McNamara had perhaps sat a little too heavily on the chiefs and that direct OJCS representation in the SIG/IRG network provided a needed "safety valve" for the military men.

SUGGESTIONS FOR THE FUTURE

Between 1961 and 1968, the number of civilians assigned to the Office of the Secretary of Defense increased by almost 1,000, and the number of military personnel assigned there almost doubled (to a strength of about 800). The civilians at the end of that period included eight with the rank of assistant secretary and more than forty with the rank of deputy assistant secretary—as compared to the 1961 figures of eight and thirteen, respectively. While some centralization was doubtless necessary to carry out the effective management envisaged by the defense legislation of 1958, many observers believe that the increase in OSD personnel went too far. As a short-term solution to getting the job done, the organizational accretions may have been necessary, but they probably merit review for the long run.

This does not mean that the OSD should be stripped back to where it was in the 1950's and 1960's. Some of the OSD assistant secretaries' offices perform functions necessary in any major department of government or certainly necessary to the mission of the Department of Defense; an example of the former is the Office of the Comptroller, and an example of the latter is the Office of the Director of Defense Research and Engineering. Among those that do invite attention is the Office of the Assistant Secretary of Defense for International Security Affairs (OASD/ISA). The secretary certainly needs in-house expertise in international affairs, especially in the administration of the military-assistance program, but the requirement for eight ISA deputy assistant secretaries, each with his own regional or functional "shop" of specialists, would appear to be somewhat doubtful. Because recruitment, training, and support (including housing) of military personnel are still functions of the separate services, there is question about the need for the assistant secretary of defense for installations and logistics to have in his office a deputy assistant secretary for family housing who, in turn, presides over four separate directorates. The purpose here is not to offer a blueprint for cutting the OSD; obviously any reorganization would have to be the result of detailed study. But it would be surprising if a hard look at the OSD did not turn up ways in which economy and efficiency could be promoted by the elimination of duplication and overlap.

Retaining Some Major Features of Recent Developments

By all testimony, two managerial innovations of enduring value are the mission-oriented approach to the defense program review process and the extension of the review process into a five- to eight-year future time frame. Two other innovations that merit retention, though probably in modified form, are the secretary's Draft Memorandums to the President and an OSD capability for independent analysis of the over-all defense program and budget.

The two features of the DPM's that commend them to most observers are their value in facilitating incisive communication within the Defense Department and between the Defense Department and other national-security departments and agencies and their usefulness in recording and reporting to the President the alternatives considered, the rationale followed, the decisions made, and the dissents registered in the review process. Independent analysis in the OSD should include, but not be limited to, systems analysis; indeed, the latter technique can and should be used more at JCS and service levels.

Modifying Some Major Features of Recent Developments

One of the most serious shortcomings within the Defense Department during the past several years has been the absence of an effective contribution by the professional military cadres to defense planning and programing. The Joint Strategic Objectives Plan, which was in theory supposed to provide the basic military "input" to the Five-Year Defense Program, has remained largely outside the arena where the real action takes place. Instead, military authorities, including the JCS, have often been placed in the position of simply reacting to Draft Presidential Memorandums produced by the OSD, with a kind of burden of proof imposed on their reactions.

There are two principal reasons for this. The OSD has not furnished the JCS the kind of political and economic guidance necessary to the development of sound military planning, and, the

JCS, for its part, has persisted in producing a JSOP that enunciates the best guidance it can pull together from a variety of sources and then recommends a single level and composition of forces identified as military "requirements." It is then virtually ignored in the OSD. This suggests modifying the process so that the OSD provides guidance appropriate for military-force planning by the JCS, so that the JCS, in turn, comes up with usable plans for mission-oriented forces. These plans would incorporate and compare alternative force levels and compositions and reflect the results of analysis—including systems analysis—performed in the JCS and the services.

These JCS force-planning memorandums would replace the JSOP. They would become primary vehicles on which other agencies (such as the OSD offices and the Department of State) could focus, perhaps with the burden of proof resting on comments from those agencies. After comments and revisions, the OSD would prepare draft program memorandums to the President, recording the entire sequence from the provision of guidance, through the evaluation of alternatives, to the recommended decisions on forces. In such a process, systems analysis would become a valuable technique at all echelons in the Department of Defense. It is likely that it would become less prominent than heretofore in the OSD, and it would be certain to become more prominent in the JCS and the military services.

Four Other Matters of Emphasis

A Stronger Personal Staff for the Secretary

Many observers believe that the secretary should have a stronger immediate staff of "generalists," as distinct from a proliferation of assistant secretaries. Such a staff would help the secretary to arrive at timely and effective decisions by collecting and organizing for him the relevant background material and the recommendations or alternatives on which he must act, aid him in assigning action and responsibility for coordination to the appropriate agencies of the department, and assist him in the monitoring of important subjects or activities.

The establishment of a group in the secretary's own office with the duties outlined above is not inconsistent with the proposition that a cutback in the number and responsibilities of some assistant secretaries' areas may be desirable. In fact, some decentralization of operational activities would reinforce the case for a group identified with the secretary's responsibilities and interests, because such a staff would be even more necessary in keeping the secretary abreast of important developments somewhat removed from his direct influence at a given time.

Greater Incentive for Innovation

A system which puts too much stress on cost effectiveness in selecting among alternative courses of action may, because of the estimated costs, tend toward conservatism; at least it does little to encourage innovation explicitly. This suggests the need for a built-in arrangement designed to emphasize innovation. Some believe that the best approach would be to allow more latitude for research and development programs by the military services and accept the increased cost of occasionally competitive programs as part of the price of technological advance, especially because the major costs are in any event not for research and development, but for production.

More "Joint Thinking" Among the Military

Virtually all observers favor more "joint thinking" in the activities of the military, but the record of progress is not in all respects encouraging. Each service continues to maintain large staffs for policy planning, operations, political-military affairs, and the like. Since the services were supposed to have begun phasing down these activities years ago, the case for reducing them now is even stronger. There is still a place for the perspectives of the separate services, but in matters related to the operations of the unified and specified commands, it should be up to the joint staff to incorporate these perspectives—as it sees fit—into the work that it does for the Office of the Joint Chiefs of Staff. Even now, the last thing a chief does before walking into a JCS meeting is to receive a thorough briefing by a senior member of his service staff, the operations deputy, who has earlier been briefed, with strongly supported recommendations, by working-level staff officers from his particular service. This custom has changed little, if at all, in over twenty years. It may still be necessary, given the way the JCS operates, but it is clearly an increasingly anachronistic practice, which helps perpetuate service parochialism.

Nothing is likely to promote joint thinking more effectively than making sure that an officer who performs well in an assignment away from his service will not only not suffer but may indeed earn preferment for advancement. Some steps in this direction have been taken, but much remains to be done, and it will require continued, forceful, and (preferably) tactful pressure by central OSD and JCS authorities over a period of time. It cannot, however, wait too long. For example, if, as proposed above, the JCS is to produce the basic force-planning memorandums of PPBS, the services of outstanding systems analysts will be required, including military officers. And outstanding military officers will not be interested in a career that almost forecloses opportunities for promotion to general rank.

An Additional Role for the Secretary of Defense

The functions of the secretary of defense described earlier should not obscure another, less-tangible, function that he could perform. It might be summed up in the description, "chief military philosopher." This function would call for the secretary to transcend details of budgets, forces, deployments, and other work-a-day aspects of his job, in order to take a philosophical look at his nation, at the world, and at the role of his nation in the world. It would call for him to relate military power to national purpose, not only as manager of his department, not only as military commander responsible for the troops under his command, and not only as primary defense adviser to the Commander in Chief, but also in a direct role with respect to the United States public. The secretary works for the President, of course, but both work for the

American people. Inspirational leadership is not yet outmoded by modern organizational procedures, and most Presidents would probably welcome the assistance of the secretary of defense in performing this task.

X

The President and Policy Guidance

The great executive departments and agencies covered in the previous chapters are essentially extensions of the Presidency. Their functions and powers are those which are delegated to them, under the law, by the President. They can assist in discharging the President's management burdens, but under the U.S. government system they cannot relieve him of his unique responsibilities. In national security more than in any other area of government, he is expected to speak and act for the nation. As already noted, law and custom have made him chief budget maker, chief commander, and chief diplomat rolled into one, and the nuclear age and the Cold War have greatly magnified and complicated each of these jobs.

FORMAL POLICY AS A MANAGERIAL TOOL

The President's foremost responsibility in managing national-security affairs is to define the courses of action that he expects his administration to follow. In textbook descriptions, this means selecting the objectives or goals that the executive agencies are to pursue and the general way in which they are to pursue them. This selection in turn is supposed to govern or "guide" the identification of subordinate tasks, the development of plans and programs to carry out the tasks, and, finally, the implementation of actions stemming from these plans and programs. Such a selection of over-all goals and methods and their dissemination is what is meant here by "policy guidance." It is supposed to provide the general framework of principles and rules within which the innumerable decision-makers and operators in the executive apparatus are called upon to make the innumerable determinations and take the innumerable actions required of them. It is supposed to enable the President to delegate work to subordinates and still have their decisions accord with the letter and spirit of his wishes. It is supposed to enable his subordinates to coordinate their interrelated decisions and actions with each other even in the absence of his direct intervention. In short, it is the crux of his management function.

It is easy to overidealize this policy guidance function, and it frequently has been so treated. In a perfectly rational setting, formulating national-security policy would involve a systematic examination of all the available national-security goals, arraying them as to importance and worth, analyzing the full range of alternative means for achieving them, weighing the relative utility of each, and finally linking the preferred means and ends in a neat and logical synthesis in which all the interactions and consequences are correctly accounted for. Such a synthesis would be a first-class management tool. The more comprehensive its coverage and the more detailed its provisions, the easier it would be to delegate the work of directing policy implementation, the more automatic and trouble free would be the coordination, and the more nearly the entire executive organization would operate as if with a single mind.

Unfortunately, it is impossible to construct such a perfect synthesis. In a dynamic world, which we do not fully understand and in which many events are inherently unpredictable, it is impossible to evaluate all of the competitive and conflicting goals and to predict the outcomes of all of the possible courses of action. It is extremely difficult to define and order goals except in a rough way, taken a few at a time, in specific contexts and with specific alternatives in mind. Ends are frequently inconsistent or incompatible. Means are entangled with ends and with each other. Costs and effects are difficult to trace and even more difficult to measure. Uncertainties and indeterminacies abound.

In the real world, the process of choosing—and subsequently pursuing—national-security goals and methods can at best be only a crude approximation of the ideal. It generally has to proceed in tentative, incremental steps, with imperfect logic and ambiguous information, with much trial and error, with considerable guesswork, with arbitrary choices, and with abundant room for legitimate disagreement. At any point in time, the process can look quite disorderly, more a matter of a struggle for power among competing interests than of cool reason. Within the government, it may seem more like political warfare among rival departments and agencies with minds of their own, striving for advantage, making deals with each other, negotiating bargains and compromises, and so on, behaving for all the world like medieval baronies. The President may often appear to be only a moderator or referee, a mere approver or disapprover of the *de facto* decisions of others. If he does not find ways to assert his will, he may find himself more a captive than the leader of the system: fought over, around, or even against; having to persuade, cajole, bargain, and maneuver like the rest, with no real power to command. The outcome of such a logrolling process would hardly be a very clear, consistent, or stable set of goals and strategies. Firm delegation in such a system would be chancy and difficult to control. To attend to problems of coordination would require unceasing vigilance at the top. Problems would have to be handled on a case-by-case basis, making it difficult to adhere to a steady course or accomplish a long-term objective.

How can a President exercise his management prerogatives in such a system, determine where to go and how to get there, confine himself to issuing general guidance without giving up the reins, enhance his ability to control matters without getting swamped with detail, maximize the opportunities and incentives for voluntary coordination in support of his purposes, and minimize the occasions and drives for discordant actions that cancel each other out?

There have been two recent schools of thought about how the President should proceed in formulating and issuing policy guidance. For sake of convenience, we can call them a formalized-codification approach and a pragmatic or *ad hoc* approach. Codification was approximated (but *only* approximated) in the policy documents produced in the rather formalized Eisenhower NSC system; the *ad hoc* approach was roughly the practice during the less formal Kennedy – Johnson period. As noted earlier, the Eisenhower system was not as thoroughly institutionalized as many commentators have suggested, but there was a clear intent to be as systematic and comprehensive as possible in formulating and disseminating Presidential policy guidelines; the Kennedy–Johnson administrations were more systematic than often met the eye, but there was a general intent to operate without formally prepared and promulgated Presidential policy papers, except as specifically required in given instances.

It is difficult to evaluate the experience with these two contrasting approaches without getting into substantive matters that are naturally highly privileged and highly classified. Many officials from both eras, however, have described and commented upon the strictly procedural aspects of the two approaches and have provided considerable information on the subject, together with their own thoughtful analyses. From their testimony, it is possible to identify some of the alleged virtues and drawbacks of each approach and to discern some of the implications of adopting one or the other, for it seems that the experience with each approach was mixed.

NATIONAL-SECURITY POLICY CODIFICATION UNDER PRESIDENT EISENHOWER

The salient features of the Eisenhower NSC system are well known. Its aim was to develop a simplified and cut-down approximation of the ideal synthesis—that is, as coherent a framework of principal ends and means as was practicable, in as comprehensive and detailed a form as prudence would allow. It was to be developed with the full participation of the responsible departments and agencies, promulgated after full discussion and debate—and formal approval by the President—as authoritative and explicit statements of U.S. policy, and disseminated for guidance as broadly within the government as security permitted.

The Eisenhower synthesis was produced in a series of documents, the most important of which was the Basic National Security Policy (BNSP) paper. The BNSP broadly defined U.S. interests and objectives, analyzed the major trends in world affairs that might affect them, and set forth a national strategy for achieving them, covering political, economic, and military elements thereof. The BNSP was an annual document. Although it was intentionally broad and general, it was a controversial and sensitive paper and became the basis for annual bureaucratic battles. Considerable drafting skill went into its preparation, for behind any small word might lurk a rather large issue. Thus, for example, whether strategic air power was *a* major deterrent to general war or *the* major deterrent made a world of difference to military planners. A disagreement over whether the concept of limited war included or excluded direct U.S.–U.S.S.R. military confrontations, or indeed whether there could conceivably be a limited war in the NATO area, was hardly just semantics. The exact wording of a policy statement on the use of nuclear weapons or a national commitment to go to war was not a trivial matter.

Amplifying the BNSP, and theoretically taking their cues from it, were a large number of documents that spelled out national security in fuller detail for various geographical or functional areas, down to individual countries or particular problems. There was never a fixed number or specified list of these subsidiary papers, but the intention was clearly to provide fairly complete coverage of all significant areas and issues.

The BNSP and its derivatives were processed through the National Security Council and the organs associated with it—the Planning Board and the Operations Coordinating Board (OCB). In fact, production or implementation of these documents was a large part of what the "NSC system" of the Eisenhower Administration actually did. Providing advice to the President "with respect to the integration of domestic, foreign, and military policies relating to the national security," which was legally the mission of the NSC, consisted primarily of advising him as to the substance of policy papers, and a sharp line was drawn between "policy," which always went through the NSC system, and "operations," which might not.

The NSC Planning Board was in charge of preparing the papers for NSC consideration and Presidential action. Although the system permitted papers to be produced on short demand, for the most part they were produced according to a schedule worked out months in advance. Phased with this schedule was the production of the so-called National Intelligence Estimates pertaining to the particular countries and problems involved. The policy papers were normally assigned to one of the departments for drafting—usually to the State Department, but sometimes to the Defense Department for predominantly military questions. Drafts were circulated among the various agencies and then taken up by the Planning Board, which would meet on each paper and revise it until it was considered to be in satisfactory shape. The paper was then circulated to members of the council, who met, discussed it, and acted upon it. The paper became an official statement of U.S. policy when approved by the President. After Presidential approval, if the paper dealt with foreign operations (and most of them did), it was assigned to the Operations Coordinating Board for monitoring of its implementation, a step which usually began with the translation of the paper into an "operations plan"—a summary of implementing actions. Although the President was apparently not much involved in it, the latter step represented a further refinement of the guidance available to departmental planners and provided a standard against which to evaluate performance.

How this processing of national-security policy documents actually worked in practice is subject to much controversy. It has been charged, even by certain insiders, that the BNSP and its offspring were so general that they were meaningless, full of compromises which papered over, straddled, or suppressed important issues, and virtually useless as guides to planning and action. Blame is usually placed on the committee procedures employed in preparing the papers for the National Security Council, in which pressures for consensus easily led to lowest-common-denominator positions. As former Secretary of State Dean Acheson has written, it is always possible to get agreement in a committee by increasing the vagueness and generality of a conclusion, and "agreement by exhaustion" is a favorite committee ploy. The result can be to provide the President with "agreed" papers, when what he needs is "disagreed" papers, and in the end to ask him to give his blessing to platitudes.[1]

The tendency of committees of delegates from departments to produce "treaties" written in watered-down language, if left to their own devices, is universally noted. There may be exaggeration, how-

[1] Dean Acheson, "Thoughts About Thought in High Places," *The New York Times Magazine*, October 11, 1959.

ever, in the charge that the BNSP and the other policy documents of the Eisenhower period were fully "agreed" papers when they went before the National Security Council. The Eisenhower special assistants—Robert Cutler, Dillon Anderson, and Gordon Gray—have written that despite all the efforts of the Planning Board, which clearly worked hard and long at its job, papers did go before the council with "splits" not only unresolved but specifically singled out for discussion and decision. Cutler, who invented the system and ran it longer than anyone else, has written that the Planning Board might take two or three months and a dozen meetings over an annual revision of the BNSP, and the document would still go to the council as often as not with six to twelve points of outstanding difference to be settled—a process which might in turn take the council as many as half a dozen meetings to resolve.[2]

The special assistants have also reported that, contrary to what many critics have alleged, discussions in the National Security Council were frequently vigorous—controversial stands were taken, and disagreements were expressed. President Eisenhower certainly asked for this; he has stated that he encouraged thorough staffing on problems to clarify and illuminate, not to suppress, the issues; and he asked to be informed about conflicting positions.[3] Again, historians will have to judge the question when all the facts are in. The importance of the issues at stake and the nature of any discussion about them are relative matters, and not all observers will agree as to what constitutes a lively debate about major alternatives clearly posed.

There are some indications that President Eisenhower himself was not entirely satisfied with the process. In 1957, according to Cutler, after President Eisenhower's second inaugural, the President said he wished to "open up" NSC procedures and make them more flexible; he particularly wished to move gradually from council consideration of policy *documents* to freer debate on policy *issues*, and he suggested that the Planning Board might be able to

[2] Robert Cutler, *No Time for Rest* (Boston: Little, Brown and Co., 1965), p. 312.
[3] Dwight D. Eisenhower, "The Central Role of the President in the Conduct of Security Affairs," in *Issues of National Security in the 1970's,* ed. Amos O. Jordan (New York: Frederick A. Praeger, Inc., 1967), pp 206–19.

draft the necessary policy papers for his consideration directly from council debates, without going through laborious interagency staffing.[4] Nothing much came of this apparently, but it shows that the President was aware of some of the drawbacks of the system.

In addition, of course, President Eisenhower made some use of special *ad hoc* instrumentalities outside the NSC system. Early in his first administration, in a high-level study-group effort, called "Operation Solarium," conducted at Fort McNair, he established specially chosen teams outside regular channels to work out the basis for his first BNSP. He also occasionally appointed committees of private citizens who were not encumbered by bureaucratic doctrine or interests, when he wanted a fresh look at national-security problems. These committees were not utilized to draw up policy papers as such (for example, the Gaither Committee of 1957, headed by Rowan Gaither, was charged with examining civil defense and related national-security matters), but their reports were presented to the council and discussed there, so that they did get into the ongoing stream of policy deliberations.

Some critics of the Eisenhower system do not fault it for trying to codify policy but for the way the officials in charge went about it. This was the criticism of the 1960–61 staff reports of the Senate Subcommittee on National Policy Machinery (Jackson Subcommittee), for example, which argued strongly in favor of a unified and coherent national strategy but claimed that the Eisenhower Administration had failed to produce one that mapped a clear course of action putting first things first, separating the necessary from the merely desirable, and distinguishing what had to be done today from that could wait until tomorrow—the very things which codification was supposed to accomplish. Some of the Jackson Subcommittee staff criticisms were that the committee processes of the Eisenhower NSC system were slow and cumbersome, resulted in compromises and generalities, prevented real issues from rising to the highest levels, smothered new ideas and innovations, and magnified obstacles to proposed new courses of action. Other criticisms were that the process was not sufficiently selective in concentrating on policy questions of overriding importance; the

[4] Cutler, *op. cit.*, pp. 347–50.

President and members of the NSC, it was argued, need not be asked to concern themselves with policy papers on every country or functional program in the world.

These criticisms in the Jackson Subcommittee's staff reports were based on an extensive examination of national policy-making procedures, but they were not accepted by the full subcommittee and have been strongly disputed by many members of the Eisenhower team. These officials argue that the authors of the staff reports were not privy to the substance of matters handled in the NSC system, that they obtained much of their information from secondhand sources, and that they used all of the information with which they were provided in a selective manner.

Be that as it may, the important point to note about the Jackson Subcommittee staff criticisms is that the deficiencies alleged are not inevitable concomitants of a formalized-codification approach to policy guidance. If some kind of coordinating operation is needed in preparing policy documents for Presidential decision, and few would argue that it is not, it need not be a collegial arrangement operating on a unanimity principle. It could be a committee under someone clearly responsible and clearly in charge, with decision-making authority. It need not be a committee of envoys from departments; it could be as much the President's own committee and as little captive to the bureaucracy as he wishes to make it—as President Eisenhower himself demonstrated by hand-picking the study teams in Operation Solarium. If the interagency staffing process threatens to blur and bury issues, the presence of the President's own man, say a staff assistant at the head of a planning group, could surface them in whatever degree of sharpness was desired. If the White House feels deprived of new ideas and suggestions, it has ways and means of encouraging them. If the process bogs down in routine and does not conserve the time of the top men for the top issues, they could see that it works otherwise.

A more basic question, even if the defects of committee-processing arrangements could be overcome, is whether a codification system could succeed in producing not just a coherent expression of lofty principles but one that is in fact useful as a management tool, one that is actually relevant in shaping real action in the real world. For the BNSP's and other national-security policy papers produced under President Eisenhower have been criticized on just those grounds—that they were not clear or specific enough to provide guidance for the actual work of executing national-security policy, the work of the budgeteers and planners and programers, or the work of the commanders and diplomats and project directors. And if they were not, of what use were they to the President in the conduct of his job, and of what use were they to his subordinates in carrying out theirs?

Care must be exercised to screen such criticisms for policy biases, because some of the criticism might amount to no more than that the President's policy statement did not resolve a particular issue to the critic's liking. Any President must also be granted the managerial prerogative of determining which issues must be resolved today and which can wait, which are ripe for resolution, and which had better be put off. In the world of policy making, there are always ongoing controversies and unresolved issues on which the President has not yet taken and may not want to take a definite stand. In the case of a major question that can be settled only after a great national debate, an unresolved issue can persist for years. In such instances, impatient bureaucrats will no doubt fret and fume and complain about the lack of clear guidance. And all they are likely to get from the President, who in the lore of U.S. politics is supposed to be decisive and have a definite opinion about everything, is a banality that does not commit him—or the country—to anything.

Even after making due allowance for the foregoing factors, it must be granted that a codification system may not necessarily produce useful policy-guidance instruments. To some extent this is because of the unavoidable nature of a codification approach when applied to difficult problems in a dynamic world, but it also depends on the particular procedures employed in producing the documents and the quality of the output.

It goes without saying that any policy statement contains elements of generalization and abstraction. The broader it is, the more remote it necessarily becomes from tangible realities, the more it is bound to oversimplify, and the more unsuitable it is in practical application. Any attempt to outline the complex problems of the world and the rules for dealing with them, especially in advance and in brief, is necessarily going to be crude and artificial to a considerable degree. In the knotty and fluid circumstances in which things are actually done, the best of such outlines will inevitably appear somewhat irrelevant, too simple by far, too inflexible, and too lifeless to fit concrete instances in all their rich variety. What may be put in a nutshell may be convenient, but it is often not very usable.

This point explains the inclination among many persons (including government officials) to put little stock in theory or doctrine of any kind in world affairs, to belittle planning, to count more on the discretion of the experienced operator playing it by ear in the midst of living circumstances at the scene of events than on any predetermined general guidelines. Those who share such views are no doubt correct in pointing to the limitations of policy guidance from on high and in the need for imaginative adjustment and adaptation (for genuine art, that is) in applying it. It is equally correct to stress, however, that people and organizations cannot function without simplifying concepts, that the effective conduct of organized activities on any significant scale over any significant period of time requires explicit concepts and norms, and that in very large and complex organizations there is no escape from having them laid down by remote executives without specialized or detailed knowledge and with more or less hypothetical circumstances in mind. But these weaknesses of the executive function do not belie its value. The man on the firing line may have the best grasp of what is happening there, but he may not be the best judge of what to do about it, especially if the required action is linked to other events and actions at other times and places, and no organized effort is likely to succeed if everyone in the operation is free to select his own destination and choose a path for himself.

If policy guidelines are necessary in managing large-scale and complex enterprises, yet are threatened with irrelevance and inappropriateness, one major antidote is to maintain an active and continuous dialogue between the policy-makers and the operators, so that abstract policy at one end is forced to come to grips with the challenge of hard facts, and action at the other end is forced to proceed toward definite and intelligible common purposes, with policy and action each conditioning and refining the other as they proceed. This is much easier said than done, of course, and it requires all the organizational art and skill that people can muster. It is bound to be imperfect, yet it is the crux of formulating relevant and useful policy. Otherwise, policy making is little more than an intellectual exercise carried out in a vacuum, and there can be no way to bend action to purpose.

Effective policy formulation requires a lively up-and-down flow of communications and is doomed to sterility without it. Dean Acheson has written that when the whole function of determining policy is gathered at the top, the resulting action is likely to be either ill adapted to reality or self-defeating. Policy-makers need information, ideas, and suggestions from below, from the cutting edge where policy is applied, where reality is faced in the raw, where problems are encountered and solutions tried and tested. "The springs of policy bubble up," according to Acheson's well-known aphorism, "they do not trickle down." [5] It may be added that the springs may also bubble uselessly if there is no coherent effort to channel and direct their flow.

Critics have alleged that in the Eisenhower system the interplay between the worlds of Olympian policy and pedestrian realities was not very effective. They have said that the world in which high policy was established was too ethereal, too insulated from action. It busied itself with the formulation of aspirations and attitudes, which were not really forceful prescriptions for doing things. It was emphatic on where it wished to go, but weak on how to get there, strong on what was desirable, but weak on what might be possible and, hence, not sharply focused on defining realizable goals toward which available actions could be oriented. General policy papers in the circumstances tended to be too vague to provide meaningful guidance; specific policy papers tended to be either inflexible or inappropriate.

These faults may be characteristic of the natural order of things

[5] Acheson, *op. cit.*, p. 292.

in a regimen of giant bureaucracy, but they may also to some extent be particular vulnerabilities of a formalized-codification system for policy formulation. It is not difficult for a codification system to produce ostensibly clear and coherent policy, which everyone in the government understands and dutifully bows to but which does not greatly affect what they have to do and, therefore, does not matter much. It is quite possible for a codification system to be only a conspicuous façade, with the important levers and controls not among the carefully processed policy papers but elsewhere in the daily pull and tug of bureaucratic politics. Thus, it is not impossible to have an administration that is for codification and system in principle but in which officials still make their action decisions on an *ad hoc* basis with no particular evidence of unified purpose. And in such circumstances, there may well be officials down the line who will feel the lack of clear and relevant guidance from above.

Whether this is a fair characterization of how the Eisenhower system operated or an exaggerated distortion will depend on the reader's viewpoint and need not be resolved here. The judgment that the policy documents of the Eisenhower system were not always manifestly useful is indirectly supported, however, by some of its foremost defenders. Almost to a man they state that the *process* of producing the policy documents was a more important contribution to effective policy making than the documents themselves. The process forced a large number of officials—both high and low, those who were responsible for managing operational matters—from the various agencies to interact and collaborate with each other. It put them through a series of intensive exercises in which they had to analyze world trends, explicitly confront questions of means and ends, identify problems, and consider the advantages and disadvantages of solutions. It provided a regular mechanism and set of procedures, sanctioned and supported by the President, for mobilizing the talents and ideas of the bureaucracy. It forced decision-makers, planners, and operators to look ahead and apply themselves to the challenge of achieving coherence and continuity in working toward future goals, instead of spending all their time attending to day-to-day brush fires. It brought them face to face with one another and with one another's perspectives, and if it did not always have harmonious results it at least clarified areas of agreement and disagreement and forced out the rationales behind them. It also legitimized and encouraged practices of workaday cooperation as the expected way of doing the President's business in national-security affairs. There is no question that the great majority of the participants found the process useful and, in the early years of the Eisenhower Administration, probably invaluable.

Plans are often useless, it is said, but planning is indispensable. It is possible that the benefits of a codification process greatly outweigh its costs in time and effort not because the resulting products have any great utility in directing the work but because the people who emerge from the experience do. With the documents, perhaps the most important thing they do is educate themselves. They are very likely to absorb the policy and be "guided" in the course of doing so.

Pragmatic Policy Guidance Under Presidents Kennedy and Johnson

At first glance, for all of its imperfections, a formal codification system for national-security policy formulation appears to make good sense. From the President's point of view, where the problem often is to get the word out correctly to every last person who can commit or involve him and the country, a document outlining where he wants to go and how he wants to try to get there would seem to be a good starting point in ensuring that the right things are done by the right people, at the right time and place, without his having to give all the orders himself. From the point of view of his subordinates, where the problem usually is to secondguess what the boss wants without having to ask him—and to do so in association with fellow officials whose close cooperation is necessary but who are likely to have their own strong opinions in the matter— a comprehensive compendium of policy guidelines would seem most useful. Even if it could not codify the final word as precisely as might be desired, it could at least cut down the range of uncertainty and perhaps give shape to an over-all policy "climate," which would help everyone understand what was generally desired of him, what the relative priorities were, and how the important problems should be handled. It could serve as a common frame of reference for the more detailed work of issuing whatever specific instructions were necessary in day-to-day management and for carrying out those instructions in a coordinated manner.

The desirability and utility of such a compendium is the subject of considerable argument, however. There clearly are some potential difficulties in having a compendium around and trying to use it. Presidents Kennedy and Johnson apparently felt that such difficulties outweighed the possible advantages, for neither of them saw fit to commission comprehensive BNSP's to incorporate their policy decisions, and both obviously preferred to issue policy guidance in other ways. The reasons in each instance may have been largely personal, but when we examine the case against a codification approach to policy formulation, it may suggest other considerations as well.

The most obvious argument against a codification process should be evident from the previous section. It is that a compendium of policy statements might not be relevant as a guide to action, especially if it is too general and not sufficiently operationally oriented. It may contain nothing but homilies, which everyone knows anyway. Yet, if it becomes specific and detailed, it runs the risk of either being too rigid or having to be constantly revised in the light of changing circumstances. In either case, it might not be considered worth the effort.

A second argument is that even if a useful policy compendium could in fact be produced, it might tend to commit the President to certain lines of action prematurely or to preclude alternatives. Precommitment may be necessary at times in national-security affairs, but it is easy to understand why a President might wish to keep his commitments to a minimum. He may view his policies not as hard and fast rules that he is prepared to swear by come what may but as tentative predispositions to be examined, when the time comes, in the full light of actual circumstances. He may see little value in trying to make important choices on the basis of hypothetical forecasts, "iffy" abstractions, and crude oversimplifications, when it is difficult enough to make them in concrete cases in which the realities are sharper and clearer. He may wish to retain maximum flexibility and room for maneuver, to make his decisions only when he must and not ahead of time, and—in the current idiom of the decision-making function—to keep his options as open as he can for as long as possible. He can gain this amount of elbow-room in a codification system only by keeping his policy statements so general that they cannot be used as prescriptions for action.

A third and similar argument has to do with what might be called a strategy of calculated ambiguity intended to maximize the President's personal power of decision. Clear and complete expressions of policy are instruments for delegating more detailed decisions downward, and delegation implies some surrender of direct control. If a President wishes to retain direct control in some matters and make certain that the detailed decisions come up to him, he may prefer to keep his real preferences somewhat to himself and keep his subordinates a little in the dark, as a way of forcing them to doublecheck with him before making some contemplated move. Every President and every executive who does not want to be led around by the nose must resort to deliberate ambiguity to some degree, and this may be another reason for avoiding clear and comprehensive codification of policy guidance.

A fourth possible argument is largely political and stems from the openness of U.S. society, the independence and energy of the press, and the practices of legislative and bureaucratic infighting. There are many legitimate reasons why a President should want to keep his policies and intentions secret: He has to concern himself with problems of domestic politics, relations with allies, the reactions of adversaries, and so on. Yet, discussions about the most delicate issues inside the most intimate circles within the government have a way of getting into the public domain, not necessarily because people want to betray trust but for all-too-human reasons, ranging from a desire to impress others with one's importance to a sincere dedication to a principle on which one is convinced the salvation of the nation depends. The result, abetted by the avid thirst of the news media for dramatic stories and by the easy accessibility of government officials, is the phenomenon of the accidental or deliberate information leak. Even extremely sensitive policy proposals can break out as front-page news, tipping the President's hand, spoiling his play, and compounding his political problems. The risks are considerable, and a President's caution in having his innermost thoughts and intentions put into writing is all too understandable.

A President who finds the foregoing arguments persuasive might prefer to adopt what can be called a pragmatic approach, issuing policy guidance where and when required, to suit whatever problems or situations he confronts. Such an approach has much merit in principle. It capitalizes on the fact that a President can often accept and live with much of his predecessor's national-security policy. It is the *changes* a new President wishes to make which clearly call for explicit direction, either because of the different values and perspectives he brings to the job, or because of new circumstances, or both. If these are marginal adjustments rather than fundamental changes in direction, they can often be handled satisfactorily on an *ad hoc* basis without having to reorganize the entire policy framework.

A pragmatic approach can also be a shortcut to promoting the relevance of policy decisions, in terms of the real will of the President as well as the actions of the departments and agencies. The decisions can be made on a case-by-case basis, empirically tested in concrete circumstances, and modified and refined as experience dictates. They can be made in incremental, experimental, and reversible steps. Presidential commitments can be kept under tight control, options can be kept open, and flexibility can be maximized. On the face of it, therefore, a pragmatic approach seems more fitting than a codification process to an action-oriented outlook, and to a rapidly changing or uncertain environment. In theory, however, it would appear to lessen the likelihood of consistency and coherence across the board and might well make delegation and coordination more difficult. A President who wished to follow an *ad hoc* approach might then have to assume heavier burdens and take a more active role in directing affairs than one who assembled an adequate compendium of policy statements, which permitted delegation and facilitated coordination.

For all that they discarded the idea of codification, presidents

Kennedy and Johnson did issue policy guidelines. Explicitly or implicitly, they had to set goals and make decisions on how the goals were to be attained; they had to define priorities; they had to see to coordination. The fact that they both chose to do these things on an *ad hoc* basis shows that the approach is entirely feasible.

There were important differences in the managerial styles of Presidents Kennedy and Johnson, but for purposes of the present discussion the differences can be largely disregarded. Both were quite informal, highly flexible, and very active in managing national-security affairs. Both utilized a variety of arrangements and channels without being tied to fixed patterns or set routines. Both improvised a good deal to suit themselves, the other personalities involved, and the problem at hand. These are the main characteristics with which we are concerned here, and they distinguished both Presidents, not so much from each other, but from President Eisenhower and his more institutionalized approach.

To admirers of regularity and systematic processes, both Presidents appeared disorderly. Their informality made it difficult to detect how they operated, and often the process by which something was decided or accomplished was not evident. Even in relatively formal and systematic administrations, the inner workings of government are not necessarily exposed to public view and may be quite different from what appears on the surface; in a deliberately informal administration, they can be even more of a mystery, difficult to spot, and even more difficult to describe.

Some who are uneasy about the dearth of formal, explicit policy documents in the Kennedy–Johnson administrations often overlook the many other ways in which any President, whether he authorizes such documents or not, can make his policies known. To begin with, by the time a President reaches office, most of his convictions have generally been publicly stated in speeches and writings, and his approach to things is pretty well understood. While some of his statements may be fairly elastic campaign oratory, others may contain well-developed views, preferences, and even proposals, particularly about what he would like to see changed. President Truman, it is said, began preparing his new legislative program after his 1948 victory by first reviewing his campaign pledges. President Eisenhower's principles about balancing the needs of defense and the long-run interests of the domestic economy were clear long before he was elected. Many of President Kennedy's over-all military policies were well developed and had been thoroughly expressed in public before he assumed office.

A President's policies are also reflected to some degree in the selection of his principal officers. A number of factors usually enter into this selection, of course, so that there is not necessarily a one-to-one correspondence between a President's policy views and those of his officials. We have even known of prominent members of the same official team who hold sharply diverging views and give the administration the advantages of internal debate as well as a decidedly schizoid appearance. Nonetheless, a President generally chooses his men with policy as well as other implications in mind.

Once he is in office, a President enunciates much policy guidance in the course of his normal activities as leader of the government and the nation. He is constantly being called upon to articulate and clarify how he sees things and what it is he is trying to do. There are such formal occasions as his inaugural address, his state-of-the-union messages, budget presentations, and the like. There are the things he must do to mobilize public support on an issue, to maintain public confidence in the government, or to keep in touch with popular attitudes—such as press conferences, speeches explaining and justifying some action or program of the government, and announcements and press releases of one kind or another. Within the government, these activities frequently force action, as situations are faced, alternatives considered, and positions developed, all to meet Presidential deadlines; thus, they can both stimulate and provide the occasion for policy guidance.

There are limits, of course, on public pronouncements as vehicles for national-security policy guidance. Many things cannot be said with everyone at home and abroad listening in, and the tone of such pronouncements must often be one of advocacy or persuasion rather than direction. Speeches and press releases are not always well staffed out, nor are policy alternatives always adequately considered in preparing them. Both are in fact often susceptible to "policy coups" by advocates of particular points of view. Most Presidents have nevertheless found it advisable to enunciate a great deal of their actual policy in the clear. It is important that Congress, the people, allies, and often national adversaries understand enough to feel assured that the President knows what he is doing, is pursuing a sensible and responsible course, and is in good command of what is going on. Without authoritative explanations of the meaning of events, the rationale for actions, or the values and purposes at issue, it is all too easy for governmental action to seem erratic and inconsistent, and for an administration to appear confused and uncertain. Presidents often favor a practice of frank disclosure, therefore, and this in turn makes the occasions of disclosure times in which large policy questions come to the fore and must be settled. A Presidential speech-writing process may therefore be a policy-making process as well, and for officials several layers removed from the President, the latest speech or press conference may often contain the best expression of current national-security policy available to them.

Within the government, major policy is often determined and issued in the course of conducting regular day-to-day business. A visit from a head of state or the appointment of a new ambassador may spur a reconsideration and perhaps a revision of policy toward a given country. The annual preparation of the budget prompts or requires major as well as minor policy decisions. As Secretary McNamara repeatedly insisted, a budget is merely a quantitative expression of a plan or a policy, and budgetary decisions and policy formulation are inextricably linked. In national-security matters, this is particularly true of the budgets of the Defense Department and the foreign-operations agencies. Programs must be reviewed, their value examined, priorities determined, and resources allocated. When it is all done, the President and his men have generally put themselves through an intensive reexamination of the whole framework of policy and have converted their policy preferences into the currency of hard cash.

Finally, the most important occasion and means for formulating and disseminating Presidential policy guidance is in the direct interaction of the President, his immediate staff, and his principal line officials. There is a flow of paper among them; there are telephone calls; and there is face-to-face conversation, in two's, small groups, large meetings. Officials come to the President with information, ideas, advice, suggestions, proposals; they seek reactions, "guidance," decisions. The President inquires, proposes, explains, requests, commands, all according to his manner and style. It is in the midst of this multifarious intercommunication, in the course of dealing with all the things in the President's "in" and "out" baskets, small and large, immediate and remote, all in whatever spirit of mutual assistance and mutual suasion prevails in a given administration, that the basic work of policy is mainly done, where in the final analysis the controlling "guidance" is delivered and where it is received.

It is difficult to depict this interaction between the President and his men as a "process." It is individual for each President, and it doubtless shifts and changes for different people and different things. What should be emphasized here is that from this interaction stems the stream of information and advice, of orders and directives, which makes things in government go in any direction other than that in which their own institutionalized momentum would carry them. It also should be emphasized that this interaction at the very top is only the center of the process. The President's men are themselves responsible for policy guidance in their own areas. Based on their own interaction with the President and their understanding of his desires and needs, they have the crucial job of explaining, clarifying, and amplifying policy for their subordinates, of converting the general word of the President into more specific directives for those below, of translating policies into programs, and programs into component activities. In this, moreover, they are not merely passive recipients and retransmitters of Presidential decisions. They can sometimes in large measure shape those decisions, as Secretary Dulles evidently did under President Eisenhower; and they can sometimes exercise wide latitude in elaborating them within their own realm, as Secretary McNamara did under Presidents Kennedy and Johnson. These are matters of degree, and each President works out his own terms with each man for the various aspects and problems in the policy field, but it is fundamentally a process in which there is considerable "give" from below as well as "take" from above.

That much of the "policy guidance" involved in these interactions is oral rather than written and occurs deep within the fastnesses of administrative privacy does not make it count for less in any administration. The Eisenhower Administration supplemented such interactions with a codified set of explicit doctrines, and the Kennedy–Johnson administrations did not, but both used the informal net extensively. As a result the comparative gains or losses in each case were perhaps not as great as the defenders and critics of each approach have made them out to be.

It is characteristic of the pragmatic approach that written policy guidelines are issued by a President when and where he believes they are needed, on a case-by-case basis. Under Presidents Kennedy and Johnson, there were three main formats for recording and communicating such guidelines: the National Security Action Memorandum (NSAM), the "functional" policy paper, and the geographical (country or regional) policy paper. In addition, there were various types of "departmental" papers, which may have lacked formal status as policy documents, but which had policy overtones and did reflect informal Presidential policy guidance.

The NSAM's were initially devised by the Kennedy Administration, not as statements of policy positions, but primarily as operational directives, instruments for issuing and following up on particular action decisions in national-security matters in which the President was especially interested. They were memorandums from the President's special assistant for national-security affairs, or even from the President himself, to the heads of respective departments and agencies. They were usually terse, generally only a page or two, purposely short on philosophy and doctrine, but loud and clear on what was to be done and who was responsible for doing it. There was no uniform pattern to their subject matter. Each was addressed to an individual problem, which might range from a change in jurisdictions in the intelligence community to the initiation of a multipoint program of political, economic, and military actions with respect to some critical country. They did not attempt to cover every problem in sight but were issued only as they were perceived to be required or expected. They were consecutively numbered, and the Kennedy series was simply continued and added to under President Johnson.

Although some NSAM's included formal statements of goals or objectives, for the most part they were reflections rather than expressions of policy. They certainly were not intended to add up to a global strategy or a unified conceptual framework in the manner of an Eisenhower BNSP, and they were no substitute for one. However, they were unquestionably important in managing national-security affairs. As their title implies, they were commands to do something. One major problem with them in this respect was that there were no regular procedures for reviewing, revising, or updating them. They remained on the books even if they were overtaken by events, rendered obsolete by new decisions or developments, or superseded by subsequent NSAM's.

The NSAM's generally originated in the President's NSC staff. They sometimes dealt with the kind of overarching matters discussed in the National Security Council, and some might even be passed through the council en route to ratification and promulgation, but they were not NSC documents as such. Their drafting might be coordinated and cleared by the President's special assistant with the relevant department and agency heads. Whatever the case, they were considered uniquely Presidential instruments and were meant to convey his personal imprint on something he particularly wanted done. Insofar as they did state or reflect general policy, they carried the full weight of his authority as few if any other documents in the national-security field did.

The "functional" policy paper, which covered some important subject or problem area, was another vehicle for explicit policy guidance during the Kennedy and Johnson administrations. An outstanding example of functional policy in both administrations was overseas "internal defense" (counterinsurgency) policy guidance with respect to less-developed nations. It had its genesis in President Kennedy's strong desire to assure full understanding and a common outlook throughout the government with respect to Communist "wars of national liberation"; to devise a strategy for preventing or resisting them which combined all available political, economic, and military resources in a concerted effort; and to promote close cooperation among the various departments and agencies in carrying it out. "Internal defense" was a politico-military policy area which President Kennedy obviously felt had been neglected and required elevating in priority; in which he felt all the major departments and agencies required indoctrination, reorientation, and even considerable revamping; in which effectiveness was vitally dependent upon an extraordinary amount of continuous interagency coordination at all levels; and in which, therefore, a detailed exposition of authoritative Presidential policy could be most beneficial. Similar viewpoints can be attributed to President Johnson, who carried forward Presidential policy-making concerns in the same field.

Under both presidents, overseas internal-defense policy was an outgrowth of special interagency arrangements and procedures that were typical of an *ad hoc* approach. A Special Group for Counter-insurgency—"Special Group (CI)"—was established in 1962, with membership consisting of a Presidential high-level representative plus deputy secretaries and agency heads whose responsibilities were related to the subject. The special group supervised the development of over-all policy guidelines and operational doctrines, made recommendations as to their application to selected countries, monitored the preparation of appropriate plans, and assisted in coordinating their execution. The President took an active hand in its business, and the special group's impact on the coordination of overseas programs was considerable.

Other illustrations of the resort to *ad hoc* policy papers and special-purpose policy machinery by presidents Kennedy and Johnson could also be cited. An outstanding example is found in the field of arms control and disarmament, a sensitive area in which coordination was critical although it was extremely difficult to hammer out sound positions that all departments and agencies could wholeheartedly support. Both presidents found it desirable to pay particular attention in developing explicit guidelines and in utilizing special arrangements for this purpose; in this case a so-called Committee of Principals consisting of the heads of departments and agencies whose responsibilities might be affected. (It is noteworthy that the Eisenhower Administration had also looked on disarmament questions as being in a category of their own and had carried out basic policy formulation outside the NSC system, in its own Committee of Principals.)

A third type of policy paper was designed to incorporate policy guidance with regard to given countries or regions. Both the Kennedy and Johnson administrations found uses for such papers and experimented with various formats, which evolved finally into a standardized series of National Policy Papers (NPP's). These papers, like many of the geographical policy documents under Eisenhower, were intended to be comprehensive, authoritative, unified statements of U.S. policy toward selected countries or areas, particularly where major expenditures or major security problems existed or were anticipated. By Presidential direction (via a National Security Action Memorandum), responsibility for promulgating NPP's was vested in the secretary of state. At the State Department, they were prepared under the aegis of the chairman of the Policy Planning Council, with the aid of *ad hoc* interagency working groups representing all agencies and bureaus (including the White House staff) with a substantial interest in U.S. policy and operations in the particular country. A special effort was made to avoid the weaknesses of "drafting by committee" by designating a senior officer to chair each working group and by charging him with responsibility for the product. There was provision for consultation with the ambassador and the country team in question, clearance by an interagency committee at the assistant-secretary level, and final review and approval by the secretary of state. The procedures allowed for taking unresolved issues that turned up in the course of preparing NPP's to senior levels—up to and including the President, if necessary.

Reports about the utility of National Policy Papers vary. The charge is made that they were not particularly useful in either planning or carrying out day-to-day operations. They were time consuming to prepare, and the resulting products are said to have been uneven in quality. Efforts to raise issues to higher levels for resolution were apparently not very successful. Agencies tended to ignore them except when they needed backing for something they wanted to do. In defense of the NPP's, it is pointed out that they superseded a variety of other country documents in the government which might contain their own statements of policy and strategy—special departmental guideline papers, internal-defense plans, military-assistance programs, information plans, and the like. It is also pointed out that what mattered was the *process* of analyzing U.S. interests and purposes and laying out the broad lines of action to be pursued over a substantial period by the various departments and agencies, even if the products themselves were not actually used for much.

These pro's and con's about National Policy Papers resemble those which were put forth in the case of the NSC policy papers and the plans of the Operations Coordinating Board of the Eisenhower era. But the most serious problem with the NPP's was that, despite the clear Presidential authorization for the program and the participation of the White House staff, there was no way to associate the President directly with their substance. They therefore were not regarded as authentic enunciations of Presidential policy that were binding on everybody as definitive guidance from the very top. They were not treated as reflecting a Presidential commitment to the courses of action with which they dealt.

There were still other documents with a noteworthy policy-guidance function, such as the defense secretary's Draft Presidential Memorandums (DPM's) and the statement of defense posture that accompanied the annual presentation of the military budget to Congress. Although the DPM's were memorandums to the President posing issues and making recommendations for Presidential decision, they generally incorporated statements of pertinent official policy and strategy, which were usually checked out informally with the State Department and the White House. In their final form, for example, the DPM's were generally treated as having tacit Presidential consent. The same was true of the annual "posture statement," which under Secretary McNamara became an exceptionally articulate analysis of the world situation, U.S. foreign-policy objectives, military strategy, and force structure, comparing favorably with the military portions of the old Basic National Security Policy papers. Although these documents were not intended to convey Presidential guidance in an official sense, in the absence of anything as formal and comprehensive as the former BNSP, the DPM's and posture statements tended to acquire considerable authority within the Department of Defense. Preparing them frequently provided an important occasion for reaching major decisions, and important decisions were in turn reflected in them.

It was characteristic of the pragmatic styles of the Kennedy and Johnson administrations to turn to specially tailored, special-purpose task groups as a means of dealing with crises or other urgent or difficult interagency policy problems in national-security affairs, rather than using the fixed, general-purpose interagency boards of the Eisenhower era. It was also characteristic of both Presidents to tackle the prime issues in smaller, more intimate, and more flexible meetings than the formal National Security Council. There were a bewildering variety of such groups during the Kennedy and Johnson years, with uncertain charters and fluid missions. They came and went with the ebb and flow of crises. Some critics have likened them to floating crap games, in which the locale, the stakes, and the players all churned about in perpetual motion. When they had names, they were called Ex Comm (Executive Committee of the NSC), task forces, coordinating committees, working groups. They were called upon to work out the strategy and tactics for dealing with such areas as Laos, Berlin, Vietnam, Cuba, the Dominican Republic—all the biggest and messiest trouble spots. They were supposed to review policy, develop courses of action, and manage crises. The most famous of them were the Ex Comm, which originated during the Cuban missile crisis, and the *de facto* council of war for handling Vietnam, which was irreverently labeled the "awesome foursome," and included President Johnson himself and the trio of Secretary Rusk, Secretary McNamara, and Special Assistant Bundy. The latter group subsequently picked up some other members, notably the chairman of the Joint Chiefs of Staff and the director of Central Intelligence, and it became practically institutionalized as the "Tuesday lunch."

To some, it appeared to be the fuctional equivalent of Eisenhower's National Security Council.[6]

The existence and activities of these task groups reflected whatever the ongoing Presidential priorities were at the time. Many of them were intended to embody his personal grip on a critical problem or situation, exercised through a hand-selected agent as the man in charge reporting directly to him. They were the President's mechanisms for expediting action, for bypassing the cumbersome processes of the system, for sweeping aside the layers of bureaucracy between decision and action, for obtaining real teamwork, for taking over the playing of his own hand, and for assuring privacy while doing so. They were used selectively, of course, and were usually for problems which required emergency treatment, but they were unquestionably major features of the national-security process.

The distinction between the Kennedy–Johnson and the Eisenhower administrations in the use of *ad hoc* groups rather than fixed-membership standing committees, although important, is nonetheless easy to overemphasize. When Eisenhower wanted speed and action he, too, went outside the NSC system. When the Quemoy–Matsu crisis broke, he met for strategy huddles with something closely resembling a tailor-made Ex Comm, although he did not call it that; and there were other similar occasions. Conversely, Kennedy's Ex Comm during the Cuban missile crisis may have been streamlined in that its members were chosen by name to suit the occasion, but it had thirteen members. The Special Group for Counterinsurgency was almost a general-purpose standing committee, and the Senior Interdepartmental Group (SIG), which came into being under President Johnson in 1966, was definitely intended to be one. In fact, the NSAM that established the SIG was intended as a new departure in managing national-security affairs, clearly delegating authority to the secretary of state for directing and coordinating overseas activities, and establishing a continuing interagency mechanism to assist him in exercising it. The SIG system did not completely replace *ad hoc*

[6] See Stewart Alsop, *The Center* (New York: Harper & Row, Inc., 1968), pp. 279–80.

instrumentalities (as the authors had hoped). Such bodies continued in use as required, sometimes independently of SIG and sometimes in association with it, as a method of expediting interagency coordination. Task forces and working groups often carried forward the business of policy implementation, although, like the SIG system, their role with respect to Presidential policymaking remained ambiguous.

The approach of presidents Kennedy and Johnson, with its premium on Presidential flexibility and operational control rather than on regularity and order, has been criticized for the alleged defects of its presumed virtues—failure to provide comprehensive, unified, intelligible guidance; preoccupation with the here and now to the detriment of the future; overburdening the top echelons with details; and inability to handle more than one crisis at a time. The latter has been cited as a major weakness. Preoccupation of the top leaders with a continuing, urgent problem like Vietnam can result in inadequate attention to other less immediate but no less important problems. Not all will agree that these criticisms are fully justified. It is fair to say, however, that they indicate the principal risks of an *ad hoc* approach, and hence suggest its potential disadvantages. Keeping explicit, written policy guidance to a minimum, issuing it only as required to suit particular situations, doing so in a variety of formats and through a variety of channels (without clear authentication in some cases), keeping many of the real plans, goals, and strategies in the heads of the chiefs or implicit in operational decisions, handling as much as possible on an oral and confidential basis—such practices decrease the visibility of any coherent theme in what is going on, of any sense of direction, of any rational link between means and ends. Thus, they increase the danger that long-term purposes will be neglected, overlooked, or lost sight of, not necessarily at the top but in the recesses of the system, where the tendency, anyway, is to respond to today's squeaky wheel. The less there is communication and understanding throughout the system concerning the common goals of action, the less possible it is for officials in all the various agencies to coordinate smoothly with each other on their own initiative. The more guessing they have to do, the more

they are forced either to "live dangerously," taking chances on
what the chiefs would like, or else pass more of the buck up to
them; and the greater is the risk of programs proceeding by zigs
and zags, with people setting their own courses without reference
to each other or to common objectives, dissipating their energies
in intramural conflict, expending resources in duplication and
waste, and generally working at cross-purposes.

At the same time, from the standpoint of the top echelons,
withholding clear and comprehensive national-security guidelines
from the view of those below generally means that there must be
more coordination by specific directive and more direct intervention into operational details, if there is to be any orchestration at
all of diverse and separate activities. Presidents Kennedy and
Johnson both chose to pay such a price. They personally immersed
themselves in the direct management of national-security affairs
to an exceptional degree. They and their principal officers led a
dizzying pace that was incomprehensible to many observers. They
may have gained flexibility in the process, avoided precommitment, and perhaps gotten more action where they wanted it than
if they had issued a comprehensive manual of what everyone was
supposed to do and let it go at that; but they had to work extremely
hard at trying to make sure that everyone did his job and that it
all added up to something in the end. To some, their approach
brought refreshing relevance to action and movement in the real
world; to others, it seemed more like action for action's sake with
no design at all. The important point to note here is that there are
not only some advantages but also some problems and pitfalls in
taking the informal approach to policy guidance in national-
security affairs, especially if carried to extremes.

What many critics missed in the Kennedy–Johnson administrations was systematic policy guidance—conspicuous machinery,
procedures, and products for imposing coherence in national-
security affairs and for offsetting the pressures and incentives to
play things by ear without regard to long-run objectives. In the
absence of systematic machinery and procedures, it seemed that
it was all too easy for the planning functions to disappear from
view or to suffer neglect, too easy for bureaucratic inertia to

operate against rather than for integration, too easy for the interests of the future to become lost in the daily shuffle. The President gained flexibility and enhanced his personal power of decision, but he paid a price. He kept his options open but ran the risk that energetic bureaucrats could use them as hunting licenses and end up closing them. In the final analysis, probably nothing short of assiduous monitoring of potential option-closers could adequately protect the President's interests.

THE MIDDLE RANGE OF CHOICES

The discussion above has contrasted two patterns for providing national-security policy guidance at the Presidential level, a formalized codification system and a pragmatic or *ad hoc* system. It has considered past experience with each, not in order to evaluate substantive performance, but in order to bring out the process implications of both and hopefully to shed some light on their advantages and disadvantages. In fact, as we have seen, neither the Eisenhower nor the Kennedy–Johnson administrations adopted one process to the total exclusion of the other. There was considerably more formal codification in the Eisenhower Administration, and considerably more informal policy guidance in the Kennedy and Johnson administrations, and there was a significant amount of each in both. The differences were important, but perhaps not as great in practice as partisans sometimes make out.

In principle at least, each system aimed at different benefits and tried to maximize different values; each was vulnerable to incurring certain difficulties, costs, and risks. Our purpose now is to review what such benefits and costs might be, to compare the two approaches with reference to specific criteria that a new administration might wish to consider, and to isolate the factors underlying some practical choices.

National-security policy guidance has been treated as a management "tool" in an area in which management is particularly important and difficult—important because of the intrinsic gravity of the activities in question, and difficult because of their sheer size, diversity, and complexity. It has been taken for granted that any President will therefore be interested in easing his management burdens, while still ensuring that the entire system is fully responsive to his direction. At first glance, these values seem to be in mutual conflict. Greater control generally calls for more active management, and less active management implies relinquishing some measure of control.

Fortunately, a number of factors combine to facilitate the task of a President in achieving at least a tolerable balance. One is that he is likely to find some ongoing national-security policy so institutionalized, so well defined and understood by those agencies which are charged with its implementation, that it requires little explicit policy direction from him unless he wishes to change it. Another factor is that he will have at his disposal an executive establishment experienced in taking the initiative in converting general guidance into effective action without normally having to bother the boss with all the details. Yet another is the existence of a great deal of working machinery, arrangements, procedures, and rules intended to facilitate the work of integrating and coordinating national-security activities at levels below the President, without requiring his direct intervention. It is well to note these factors, in order to keep matters in proper perspective. The President has the most difficult job on earth, but he also has a few things going for him.

The President may have even more going for him if he is fortunate in the choice of his principal lieutenants in national-security affairs—above all, his secretaries of state and defense, but also his chief White House assistant, and, although they are not "political appointees," the director of Central Intelligence and the chairman of the Joint Chiefs of Staff. The abilities of these officials help the President guide and manage national-security affairs, providing the advice and recommendations he needs, managing their departments and agencies well, and operating as members of a team in pursuit of shared goals—these are crucial elements in determining how well the President's job can be done. Probably nothing the President can do in organizing national-security procedures is as important as the choice of these officials. It is even conceivable that these choices may be *the* most important national-security decisions he makes.

A prominent school of thought about the Presidency argues that a President must divide in order to really rule and can best enhance his power of decision by adopting President Franklin D. Roosevelt's technique of mixing competitive personalities with ambiguous jurisdictions, in order to force the important choices to his own desk. This school tends to depict the President's Cabinet officers, in national-security as well as in other matters, as chieftains of self-centered and self-serving bureaucracies, bound to ride off in various departmental directions in defiance of the President's will unless he manages to impose it on them.[7]

There is more than enough truth in this image of intramural politics in the executive branch, and at times it has even appeared to be almost the whole truth. But the reverse can also be true, and it sometimes has been. Department heads need not always be advocates of purely departmental interests but can operate in broad support of the President, instilling his perspectives into departmental undertakings, working together to minimize mutual interference and to maximize mutual reinforcement and support. When this is the case, they can become the President's allies in helping to transcend parochial, departmental perspectives and synthesize departmental contributions in a unified framework. Their success or failure at such efforts determines whether the executive establishment is a loose confederation of relatively autonomous and freewheeling fiefdoms, as some observers would have it, or a real combination of departments with some kind of authority exercising a reasonable amount of central control.

To establish and clarify the over-all purposes of an administration and the general guidelines governing how it hopes to attain them calls for some kind of guidelines. Such guidelines are supposed to provide a common frame of reference for subordinate decision-makers, the planners and programers and the operators, so that they can perform their own duties in their own spheres, at their own levels, in a fashion consistent with the wishes of their superiors. The guidelines are supposed to enable the work of management to be delegated in a controllable manner, and to enable

[7] Perhaps the leading spokesman of this school is Richard Neustadt. See his *Presidential Power* (New York: John Wiley & Sons, Inc., 1960).

subordinates to cooperate with each other without having to buck all the questions to the top. Without such guidelines, explicit or implicit, complete or incomplete, centralized or decentralized, any large organization would run the risk of having everyone working at cross-purposes. There is no alternative to issuing guidelines. The question is how, in what form, through what procedures, and whether in fact they fulfill their mission.

The extent to which such guidelines can actually facilitate the work of coordinating related activities at lower levels, thus permitting considerable delegation from above without great loss of control, seems to depend in the first instance on how comprehensive and clear they are and how well they are communicated. In principle, the more complete their coverage of foreseeable problems and contingencies, and the more widely disseminated, the easier it should be for people throughout the system to be guided as to what they are to do, and the easier it should be for supervisors to confine themselves to an essentially monitorial role. What then would be more useful than a complete and accurate handbook of guidelines, spelled out in detail, eliminating as much guesswork as possible about who is expected to do what, where, when, and so on, and ensuring that whatever is done is coherent and consistent, in full harmony with the authoritative will at the top?

Unfortunately, as argued earlier, it is difficult in practice to be comprehensive, clear, and detailed in such a complex and changing field as national-security affairs without sacrificing other values that are also highly desirable. Guidelines serve no practical purpose unless they are relevant to real action in real circumstances, and unless they deal with means which are actually available and appropriate to realizable ends. Yet, fixed guidelines formulated hypothetically in advance of the circumstances to which they are intended to apply tend by their very nature to oversimplify; the more general they are the less useful in guiding concrete action in concrete situations; the more specific and detailed, the more difficult to fit to changing conditions and events. The criterion of relevance calls for the opposite of fixed guidelines: It calls for flexibility and improvisation—at the extreme, for guidance delivered in the midst of live situations in which the choices are vivid and specific and their implications clear and sharp. However, a lack of predetermined guidelines tends to defeat the aims of delegation; it throws more of the load on the top for assuring any kind of systematic coordination or coherent implementation.

It is these considerations which appear to underlie the basic dilemma of codification versus a pragmatic approach to policy guidance and which really eliminate exclusive reliance on one approach or the other. To sum up, comprehensiveness and relevance are competing values, and neither codification nor *ad hoc* policy guidance by itself, carried too far, can attain both of them. General policy guidelines are essential because delegation under control is necessary, but there must be flexibility if the guidelines are to be relevant to action. Where a sensible balance is struck depends upon how the priorities are weighed.

An examination of pro's and con's of the two approaches discussed above suggests several principles: First, if the President wishes to relieve himself of much of the burden of managing national-security affairs, particularly in terms of operational detail, he should consider emphasizing systematic policy guidance. The cost of *ad hoc* methods for maintaining order and continuity in national-security affairs appears to be exceedingly great in time and attention at the top, and what may be the President's gain in flexibility from such methods may be the system's loss.

Second, if an administration chooses not to issue explicit policy guidance across the board, it should still probably do so in select cases. Explicit guidelines can be particularly useful, and they may even be indispensable where major changes in direction or priority are intended, in order to overcome the inertia of obsolescent but institutionalized policies. There are also bound to be areas in which coordination among various departments and agencies is inherently difficult or particularly important. There are areas like defense in which there are long lead-time problems and in which continuity over time is exceptionally demanding. Other things being equal, in such cases, the more explicit the guidance, the lighter the management load at the top and the easier the coordination below.

Third, experience indicates that there is a special case for emphasizing explicit policy guidance during the early phases of a new administration. Bureaucratic uncertainty about the policies of a new President and his administration is likely to be greater at that time. Later, after familiarity sets in, explicit guidance may not be nearly as valuable or necessary. Moreover, the process of producing explicit policy guidelines may be a useful form of shakedown cruise for everybody concerned, both for the new officers at the top and the regular crews in the departments. The common experience shared by senior officials of clarifying objectives, analyzing trends, identifying problems, and evaluating ways of dealing with them may well pay off in subsequent performance, even if the actual products are not strikingly useful in themselves.

Fourth, experience with forms of explicit policy guidance suggests that certain pitfalls should be watched for and avoided. One is trying to be too global or encyclopedic at the cost of relevance; rigorous selectivity confined to the most important problems and issues is much more likely to produce useful results. Another is the risk of producing policy papers which are merely attitudinal essays or lists of wishes; policy papers are of little use as guides unless they are action-oriented and geared to the needs of the planners, programers, and operators who are required to do things. Yet another is the danger of staffing procedures that blur or bury issues; if the policy-formulating process is to be useful, it should smoke out issues, and if the policy-guidance products are going to be worth anything, they must define issues and take sides.

Finally, whatever a President does about issuing national-security policy guidelines, he is still faced with the problem of enforcing coherence in their implementation. The processes by which he chooses to manage national-security affairs and the pressures and incentives which these processes create throughout the government may serve to channel bureaucratic drives toward coherence, but he must take an active hand himself if he wishes to be sure that his ends are accomplished.

Epilogue

The New Administration and the National-Security Policy Process

The foregoing chapters have described the evolution of national-security arrangements during the past three administrations, and have analyzed the decision-making process, especially as it was being carried out in 1968, when the report was written. In preparing the report for publication as a book, we have made such editorial changes as would make it more useful for the student of government and for the general reader, but we have not attempted to take account of any changes in the institutions or process introduced since President Nixon took office. Nevertheless, a few necessarily preliminary observations on the first several weeks of his administration do seem in order at this point.

Every new administration in the first few months of its tenure tends to think of itself as poised at a watershed of history; there is always some truth in this belief, since a change of leadership in the United States is an important event. The Nixon Administration could, justifiably, regard itself in such a position, for the United States now faces an especially critical and challenging period. The end of the war in Vietnam would permit, indeed would require, a searching examination of our security requirements and interests in Asia. Urgent social and economic problems at home are already competing for attention and resources that have in the past two decades largely been devoted to the international arena. With the moon within our reach, the administration will face difficult decisions regarding the resources to be devoted to new frontiers of space. Other major crises, such as the Arab–Israeli confrontation, may preoccupy policy-makers even before the war in Vietnam is finally resolved. Questions of

251

nuclear proliferation, arms control, defense against ballistic missiles, the food-population race, dissidence and repression in some countries of Eastern Europe, and growing ferment in Latin America are but a few other major issues that demand the attention of the President and his national-security advisers.

The new administration has used its first precious few weeks in office to try to gain some degree of intellectual control over these somber problems and to explore the processes that could best provide the opportunities for choice and priorities. President Nixon, both before and since his election, has expressed his determination to participate personally not only in efforts to cope with international crises but also in the planning of longer-run national-security policy.

Working arrangements between the White House and the executive departments are still evolving and, indeed, will probably continue to evolve for months to come. Whatever the final arrangement, President Nixon has already indicated a desire to expose himself to an interaction of views among his chief advisers. In this, he is reflecting the experience of other presidents before him. Robert Kennedy put the point well in recounting President Kennedy's experience during the Cuban missile crisis of 1962: "I believe our deliberations proved conclusively how important it is that the President have the recommendations and opinions of more than one individual, of more than one department, and of more than one point of view." [1]

From informed press accounts and public documents that have appeared since January 20, it seems that the President is leaning toward a White House–centered system for national security, along the lines discussed in Chapters II, V, and VII. It would appear that his assistant for national-security affairs may not only play an active role in policy formulation but may also participate in, and perhaps even direct, the policy-planning process to a greater extent than did his predecessors. The National Security Council staff that has been assembled to serve the President's assistant is larger and

---

[1] Robert F. Kennedy, *Thirteen Days: A Memoir of the Cuban Missile Crisis* (New York: W. W. Norton & Co., 1969), p. 111.

more elaborately structured than that of either President Kennedy or President Johnson and, although President Nixon has reaffirmed the secretary of state's position as the "principal foreign-policy adviser" to the President, much of the task of coordinating inter-departmental national-security planning could be shifting to the control of that staff.

Perhaps the most important indication of the thinking of the Nixon Administration is its obvious determination to rely to a considerable extent on a structured approach to the process of national-security decision-making. An important element in this approach is the emphasis that the President has attached to the National Security Council. The President has said that he will use the NSC as the official forum for the consideration of major policy questions and has begun to hold regular, frequent council meetings. Indeed, there were five meetings of the National Security Council in the first two and one-half weeks of the new administration.

What may turn out to be a key element in the policy-planning and coordination process is a new NSC Review Group—chaired by the President's assistant for national-security affairs and consisting of representatives of the secretary of state, the secretary of defense, the director of Central Intelligence, the chairman of the Joint Chiefs of Staff, and other agencies as required. The review group, in composition and conception, bears some resemblance to the NSC Planning Board, which functioned as part of the NSC system during the Eisenhower Administration. A principal function of the group is to review interdepartmental or departmental papers prior to the council's consideration. Emphasis in the review is to be placed on examination of all feasible options and on the implications, including cost implications, of each option.

The former Interdepartmental Regional Groups (see Chapter VI) have been reconstituted as NSC Interdepartmental Groups. They are chaired, as before, by the appropriate regional or functional assistant secretary of state, and the secretary of state is authorized to delegate full power of decision to these chairmen on most matters involving interdepartmental activities overseas. The interdepartmental groups will address those issues cutting across more than one department or agency that can be resolved at the level of the assistant secretary. They will also prepare policy and crisis-contingency papers to be submitted to the review group prior to consideration by the National Security Council itself.

The Senior Interdepartmental Group (SIG), created by NSAM 341, has been transformed into the NSC Under Secretaries Committee, with what appears to be a more restricted role. The committee is chaired by the under secretary of state and consists, as did the SIG, of the deputy secretary of defense, the assistant to the President for national-security affairs, the director of Central Intelligence, and the chairman of the Joint Chiefs of Staff. Two agencies that were represented on the Senior Interdepartmental Group, the Agency for International Development and the United States Information Agency, appear to have been dropped as regular members of the new committee but will be invited to participate in discussions of issues that directly concern them. The Under Secretaries Committee will concern itself with matters referred to it by the NSC Review Group and with certain operational matters relating to interdepartmental activities of the U.S. Government overseas. The committee does not appear to have the formal responsibility for dealing with major security problems on its own initiative.

Although the interdepartmental groups and the Under Secretaries Committee seem to be tied closely to the NSC staff structure operating under the aegis of the assistant for national-security affairs, how far the shift of policy planning and implementation from the Department of State to the White House will go (or whether, indeed, a substantial shift will actually occur) is still uncertain. Although rescinding NSAM 341, the President has reaffirmed that memorandum's delegation to the secretary of state of the "authority and responsibility" for the "overall direction, coordination and supervision of interdepartmental activities of the United States Government overseas." In addition, the secretary of state is charged with the responsibility for the "execution of foreign policy"—a function not previously explicitly charged to the secretary and one that could make him the central figure, next to the President, in following through on NSC decisions.

These are but a few, first tentative steps in reshaping the existing institutions and past practices to conform to the desires and working style of the new President. Over the next many months, the new arrangements will be subjected to testing and evaluation, and additional new approaches will no doubt be tried. Some of the innovations may be modified or abandoned as events and key individuals make their influence felt. This is the shakedown period. If the postwar experience is any guide, the process tends to be especially fluid and dynamic during the first year of an administration. It is worth saying once again that, in the last analysis, the force of personality of the President and his principal advisers will have a more important influence on how major decisions are reached than will the organization procedures that have been set forth.

Appendix A

Excerpts from the National Security Act of 1947, as Amended

DECLARATION OF POLICY

SEC. 2. In enacting this legislation, it is the intent of Congress to provide a comprehensive program for the future security of the United States; to provide for the establishment of integrated policies and procedures for the departments, agencies, and functions of the Government relating to the national security; to provide a Department of Defense, including the three military Departments of the Army, the Navy (including naval aviation and the United States Marine Corps), and the Air Force under the direction, authority, and control of the Secretary of Defense; to provide that each military department shall be separately organized under its own Secretary and shall function under the direction, authority, and control of the Secretary of Defense; to provide for their unified direction under civilian control of the Secretary of Defense but not to merge these departments or services; to provide for the establishment of unified or specified combatant commands, and a clear and direct line of command to such commands; to eliminate unnecessary duplication in the Department of Defense, and particularly in the field of research and engineering by vesting its overall direction and control in the Secretary of Defense; to provide more effective

Intent of Congress.

257

and economical administration in the Department of Defense; to provide for the unified strategic direction of the combatant forces, for their operation under unified command, and for their integration into an efficient team of land, naval, and air forces but not to establish a single Chief of Staff over the armed forces nor an over-all armed forces general staff.

Title I—Coordination for National Security

NATIONAL SECURITY COUNCIL

SEC. 101. (a) There is hereby established a council to be known as the National Security Council (hereinafter in this section referred to as the "Council").

National Security Council Establishment.

The President of the United States shall preside over meetings of the Council: Provided, That in his absence he may designate a member of the Council to preside in his place.

President to Preside.

The function of the Council shall be to advise the President with respect to the integration of domestic, foreign, and military policies relating to the national security so as to enable the military services and the other departments and agencies of the Government to cooperate more effectively in matters involving the national security.

Function.

The Council shall be composed of—
    (1) the President;
    (2) the Vice President;
    (3) the Secretary of State;
    (4) the Secretary of Defense;
    (5)[1]   .   .   .
    (6) the Director of the Office of Civil and Defense Mobilization; [2]

[1] The original designee is no longer a member.
[2] The 1969 title is Director of the Office of Emergency Preparedness.

(7) the Secretaries and Under Secretaries of other executive departments and of the military departments, when appointed by the President by and with the advice and consent of the Senate, to serve at his pleasure.

(b) In addition to performing such other functions as the President may direct, for the purpose of more effectively coordinating the policies and functions of the departments and agencies of the Government relating to the national security, it shall, subject to the direction of the President, be the duty of Council— **Duties.**

(1) to assess and appraise the objectives, commitments, and risks of the United States in relation to our actual and potential military power, in the interest of national security, for the purpose of making recommendations to the President in connection therewith; and

(2) to consider policies on matters of common interest to the departments and agencies of the Government concerned with the national security, and to make recommendations to the President in connection therewith.

(c) The Council shall have a staff to be headed by a civilian executive secretary who shall be appointed by the President. . . . **Staff and Executive Secretary.**

(d) The Council shall, from time to time, make such recommendations, and such other reports to the President as it deems appropriate or as the President may require. **Recommendations and Reports.**

CENTRAL INTELLIGENCE AGENCY

SEC. 102. (a) There is hereby established under the National Security Council a Central Intelligence Agency with a Director of Central Intelligence who shall be the head **National Security Act of 1947, Amendment. Central Intelligence** thereof, and with a Deputy Director of Central Intelligence who shall act for, and exercise the powers of, the Director during his absence or disability. The Director and the Deputy Director shall be appointed by the President, by and with the advice and consent of the Senate, from among the commissioned officers of the armed services, whether in an active or retired status, or from among individuals in civilian life: *Provided, however,* That at no time shall the two positions of the Director and Deputy Director be occupied simultaneously by commissioned officers of the armed services, whether in an active or retired status.

Agency Director and Deputy Director.

.   .   .

(d) For the purpose of coordinating the intelligence activities of the several Government departments and agencies in the interest of national security, it shall be the duty of the Agency, under the direction of the National Security Council—

Duties.

(1) to advise the National Security Council in matters concerning such intelligence activities of the Government departments and agencies as relate to national security;

(2) to make recommendations to the National Security Council for the coordination of such intelligence activities of the departments and agencies of the Government as relate to the national security;

(3) to correlate and evaluate intelligence relating to the national security, and provide for the appropriate dissemination of such intelligence within the Government using where appropriate, existing agencies and facilities: *Provided,*

That the Agency shall have no police, subpoena, law-enforcement powers, or internal-security functions: *Provided further*, That the departments and other agencies of the Government shall continue to collect, evaluate, correlate, and disseminate departmental intelligence: *And provided further*, That the Director of Central Intelligence shall be responsible for protecting intelligence sources and methods from unauthorized disclosure;

(4) to perform, for the benefit of the existing intelligence agencies, such additional services of common concern as the National Security Council determines can be more efficiently accomplished centrally;

(5) to perform such other functions and duties related to intelligence affecting the national security as the National Security Council may from time to time direct.

.   .   .

Title II—The Department of Defense

SEC. 201. (a) There is hereby established, as an Executive Department of the Government, the Department of Defense, and the Secretary of Defense shall be the head thereof.

Department of Defense. Establishment.
Head.

(b) There shall be within the Department of Defense . . . the Department of the Army, the Department of the Navy, and the Department of the Air Force, and each such department shall on and after the date of enactment of the National Security Act Amendments of 1949 be military departments in lieu of their prior status as Executive Departments. . . .

Army, Navy, Air Force—Military Departments.

Other Agencies.

The Secretary of Defense

SEC. 202. (a) There shall be a Secretary of Defense, who shall be appointed from civilian life by the President, by and with the advice and consent of the Senate: *Provided*, That a person who has within ten years been on active duty as a commissioned officer in a regular component of the armed services shall not be eligible for appointment as Secretary of Defense.

Secretary of Defense. Appointment.

Eligibility.

(b) The Secretary of Defense shall be the principal assistant to the President in all matters relating to the Department of Defense. Under the direction of the President, and subject to the provisions of this Act, he shall have direction, authority, and control over the Department of Defense.

Principal Assistant to President on Defense.

.   .   .

(j) With the advice and assistance of the Joint Chiefs of Staff the President, through the Secretary of Defense, shall establish unified or specified combatant commands for the performance of military missions, and shall determine the force structure of such combatant commands to be composed of forces of the Department of the Army, the Department of the Navy, the Department of the Air Force, which shall then be assigned to such combatant commands by the departments concerned for the performance of such military missions. Such combatant commands are responsible to the President and the Secretary of Defense for such military missions as may be assigned to them by the Secretary of Defense, with the approval of the President. . . .

Responsibility.

JOINT CHIEFS OF STAFF

SEC. 211. (a) There are in the Department of Defense the Joint Chiefs of Staff consisting of—
    (1) a Chairman;
    (2) the Chief of Staff of the Army;
    (3) the Chief of Naval Operations; and
    (4) the Chief of Staff of the Air Force.

(b) The Joint Chiefs of Staff are the principal military advisers to the President, the National Security Council, and the Secretary of Defense.

(c) The Commandant of the Marine Corps shall indicate to the Chairman any matter scheduled for consideration by the Joint Chiefs that directly concerns the Marine Corps. Unless, upon request of the Chairman for a determination, the Secretary of Defense determines that such a matter does not concern the Marine Corps, the Commandant shall meet with the Joint Chiefs of Staff when that matter is under consideration. While the matter is under consideration and with respect to it, the Commandant has co-equal status with the members of the Joint Chiefs of Staff.

(d) Subject to the authority and direction of the President and the Secretary of Defense, the Joint Chiefs of Staff shall—

    (1) prepare strategic plans and provide for the strategic direction of the armed forces;

    (2) prepare joint logistic plans and assign logistic responsibilities to the armed forces in accordance with those plans;

    (3) establish unified commands in strategic areas;

    (4) review the major material and per-

Joint Chiefs of Staff.

Establishment.
Composition.

sonnel requirements of the armed forces in accordance with strategic and logistic plans;

(5) formulate policies for the joint training of the armed forces;

(6) formulate policies for coordinating the military education of members of the armed forces;

(7) provide for representation of the United States on the Military Staff Committee of the United Nations in accordance with the Charter of the United Nations; and

(8) perform such other duties as the President or the Secretary of Defense may prescribe.

.   .   .

(h) In addition to his other duties as a member of the Joint Chiefs of Staff, the Chairman shall, subject to the authority and direction of the President and the Secretary of Defense—

(1) preside over the Joint Chiefs of Staff;

(2) provide agenda for the meetings of the Joint Chiefs of Staff and assist them in carrying on their business as promptly as practicable; and

(3) inform the Secretary of Defense, and, when the President or the Secretary of Defense considers it appropriate, the President, of those issues upon which the Joint Chiefs of Staff have not agreed.

Appendix B
Consultants

Francis M. Bator
Harvard University

William Capron
Brookings Institution

Joseph I. Coffey
University of Pittsburgh

Vincent B. Davis
University of Denver

Paul Y. Hammond
RAND Corporation

Samuel P. Huntington
Harvard University

Carl Kaysen
Institute for Advanced Studies
Princeton University

Henry A. Kissinger
Harvard University

George A. Lincoln
U.S. Military Academy

Ernest R. May
Harvard University

Richard E. Neustadt
Harvard University

Don K. Price
Harvard University

Burton M. Sapin
University of Minnesota

Thomas C. Schelling
Harvard University

Richard C. Snyder
University of California at Irvine

Robert Tufts
Oberlin College

Howard Wriggins
Columbia University

Charles W. Yost
Council on Foreign Relations

Appendix C
IDA Definitions of Basic Terms Used in This Text

A *national interest* is an objective, the attainment of which is expected to contribute to the security or general welfare of the nation, and hence warrants the expenditure of resources to attain it.

Foreign policy (general) comprises the aggregate of the activities of a government conducted for the purpose of achieving its international objectives.

A *foreign policy (specific)* is a course of action for accomplishing a specific purpose in international relations and includes an objective(s) and the ways and means of attaining it.

National security is a condition which assures the protection of the nation, its institutions, and the sources of its power from foreign and domestic enemies.

National-security policy consists of the objectives and the ways and means of attaining and maintaining national security.

National-security process is the functioning and relationships of the governmental authorities and the departments and agencies responsible for national security.

National-security policy planning is the determination of the objectives of national security (objective planning) and the formulation of broad plans and programs for attaining those objectives (program planning).

Foreign intelligence is the information about the international environment needed by a government for the conduct of its foreign policy. In practice, the term is usually limited to those kinds of information which are obtained by government agencies specifically organized and equipped for its collection, evaluation, and dissemination.

Civilian control of the armed forces is accomplished through the policy guidance and lawful orders of the President and the secretary of defense. The responsiveness of the armed forces to this control implies loyal support of the policies of the President and the secretary of defense at home and abroad and a readiness to render an accounting to them for all actions of the armed forces.

Bibliography

NOTE: The following is a selected list of materials on government organization for national-security policy that have been published since 1962. Many of the classic works in this field do not appear in this list because they were published before 1962. For reference to these and other relevant materials from the pre-1962 period, the reader is referred to the very comprehensive, annotated bibliographies prepared for the Senate Committee on Government Operations, Subcommittees on National Policy Machinery in 1959 and on National Security Staffing and Operations in 1962. The second of these is listed below in the U.S. Government Documents section, under the title *Administration of National Security: A Bibliography*. The first may be found on pages 27–111 of the Committee Print of the U.S. Congress, Senate, Committee on Government Operations, Subcommittee on National Policy Machinery, *Organizing for National Security*, Volume II, "Studies and Background Materials," 1961.

BOOKS

ABEL, ELIE. *The Missile Crisis*. Philadelphia: J. B. Lippincott, 1966.

ABT, ROBERT J. *The TFX Decision: McNamara and the Military*. Boston: Little, Brown, 1968.

ALSOP, STEWART. *The Center*. New York: Harper & Row, 1968.

ANDERSON, PATRICK. *The President's Men*. New York: Doubleday, 1968.

BOWIE, ROBERT R. *Shaping the Future: Foreign Policy in an Age of Transition*. New York: Columbia University Press, 1964.

BROWN, SEYOM. *Faces of Power: Constancy and Change in U.S. Foreign Policy from Truman to Johnson*. New York: Columbia University Press, 1968.

BUNDY, McGEORGE. *The Strength of Government*. Cambridge, Mass.: Harvard University Press, 1968.

BURNS, JAMES MACGREGOR. *Presidential Government: The Crucible of Leadership*. Boston: Houghton Mifflin, 1966.

CARALEY, DEMETRIOS. *The Politics of Military Unification*. New York: Columbia University Press, 1966.

CATER, DOUGLAS. *Power in Washington: A Critical Look at Today's Struggle to Govern*. New York: Random House, 1964.

CORWIN, EDWARD S. *President: Office and Powers*. New York: New York University Press, 1967.

CUTLER, ROBERT. *No Time for Rest.* Boston: Atlantic Monthly Press of Little, Brown, 1966.

DULLES, ALLEN. *The Craft of Intelligence.* New York: Harper & Row, 1963.

EISENHOWER, DWIGHT D. *The White House Years.* Vol. I, *Mandate for Change, 1953–56.* Vol. II, *Waging Peace, 1956–61.* New York: Doubleday, 1963.

GEYELIN, PHILP L. *Lyndon B. Johnson and the World.* New York: Frederick A. Praeger, 1966.

HEREN, LOUIS. *The New American Commonwealth.* New York: Harper & Row, 1968.

HILSMAN, ROGER. *To Move a Nation.* New York: Doubleday, 1967.

HITCH, CHARLES J. *Decision-Making for Defense.* Berkeley: University of California Press, 1965.

HUGHES, EMMET J. *The Ordeal of Power.* New York: Atheneum, 1963.

HUNTINGTON, SAMUEL P. *Changing Patterns of Military Politics.* New York: Free Press, 1962.

JORDAN, AMOS A., JR. (ed.). *Issues of National Security in the 1970's: Essays Presented to Colonel George A. Lincoln on His Sixtieth Birthday.* New York: Frederick A. Praeger, 1967.

KAUFMANN, WILLIAM W. *The McNamara Strategy.* New York: Harper & Row, 1964.

KIRKPATRICK, LYMAN B., JR. *The Real CIA.* New York: Macmillan, 1967.

KISSINGER, HENRY A. (ed.). *Problems of National Strategy: A Book of Readings.* New York: Frederick A. Praeger, 1965.

KOENIG, LOUIS W. *The Chief Executive.* New York: Harcourt, Brace & World, 1968.

McNAMARA, ROBERT S. *The Essence of Security.* New York: Harper & Row, 1968.

MAZO, EARL, and HESS, STEPHEN. *Nixon: A Political Portrait.* New York: Harper & Row, 1968.

MOLLENHOFF, CLARK R. *The Pentagon.* New York: G. P. Putnam's Sons, 1967.

MURPHY, ROBERT D. *Diplomat Among Warriors.* New York: Doubleday, 1964.

NIXON, RICHARD M. *Six Crises.* New York: Doubleday, 1962.

PAIGE, GLENN D. *The Korean Decision, June 24–30, 1950.* New York: Free Press, 1968.

POWERS, PATRICK W. *A Guide to National Defense: The Organization and Operations of the U.S. Military Establishment.* New York: Frederick A. Praeger, 1964.

PRICE, DON K. *The Scientific Estate.* Cambridge, Mass.: Harvard University Press, 1965.

RAYMOND, JACK. *Power at the Pentagon.* New York: Harper & Row, 1964.

RIES, JOHN C. *The Management of Defense: Organization and Control of the U.S. Armed Services.* Baltimore: Johns Hopkins Press, 1964.

SAPIN, BURTON M. *The Making of United States Foreign Policy.* Washington, D.C.: Brookings Institution, 1966.

SCHLESINGER, ARTHUR M., JR. *A Thousand Days.* Boston: Houghton Mifflin, 1965.

SIDEY, HUGH. *A Very Personal Presidency: Lyndon Johnson in the White House.* New York: Atheneum, 1968.

SIMPSON, SMITH. *Anatomy of the State Department.* Boston: Beacon Press, 1968.

SORENSEN, THEODORE C. *Decision-Making in the White House: The Olive Branch or Arrows.* New York: Columbia University Press, 1963.

————. *Kennedy.* New York: Harper & Row, 1965.

STANLEY, DAVID T. *Changing Administrations: The 1961 and 1964 Transitions in Six Departments.* Washington, D.C.: Brookings Institution, 1965.

STEIN, HAROLD (ed.). *American Civil-Military Decisions: A Book of Case Studies.* University: University of Alabama Press, 1963.

TAYLOR, MAXWELL D. *Responsibility and Response.* New York: Harper & Row, 1967.

WEINTAL, EDWARD A., and BARTLETT, CHARLES. *Facing the Brink.* New York: Charles Scribner's Sons, 1967.

WICKER, TOM. *JFK and LBJ: The Influence of Personality upon Politics.* New York: William Morrow, 1968.

WILKAVSKY, AARON B. *The Politics of the Budgetary Process.* Boston: Little, Brown, 1964.

WISE, DAVID, and ROSS, THOMAS B. *The Invisible Government.* New York: Random House, 1964.

ARTICLES

American Foreign Service Association. "Toward a Modern Diplomacy," *Foreign Service Journal,* XLV, No. 11, Part II (November, 1968), 2–60.

BALDWIN, HANSON W. "The McNamara Monarchy," *Saturday Evening Post,* CCXXXVI (March 9, 1963), 8, 11.

————. "Slow-down in the Pentagon," *Foreign Affairs,* XLIII (January, 1965), 262–80.

BOBROW, DAVIS B. "Civil Role of the Military: Some Critical Hypotheses," *Western Political Quarterly,* XIX (March, 1966), 101–11.

BROGAN, D. W. "The Presidency," *Encounter,* XXII (January, 1964), 3–7.

BROWN, HAROLD. "Planning Our Military Forces," *Foreign Affairs*, XLV (January, 1967), 277–90.

BUNDY, McGEORGE. "The End of Either/Or," *Foreign Affairs*, XLV (January, 1966), 189–201.

———. "The Presidency and the Peace," *Foreign Affairs*, XLII (April, 1964), 353–65.

CUNLIFFE, MARCUS. "A Defective Institution?" [The Presidency], *Commentary*, XLV, No. 2 (February, 1968), 27.

DIEBOLD, JOHN. "Computers, Program Management and Foreign Affairs," *Foreign Affairs*, XLV (October, 1966), 125–34.

FALK, STANLEY L. "The National Security Council Under Truman, Eisenhower, and Kennedy," *Political Science Quarterly*, LXXIX (September, 1964), 403–34.

GILPATRIC, ROSWELL L. "An Expert Looks at the Joint Chiefs," *The New York Times Magazine* (March 29, 1964), 11, 71–72.

Ginsburgh, Robert N. "The Challenge to Military Professionalism," *Foreign Affairs*, XLII (January, 1964), 255–68.

———, and COLBERT, RICHARD G. "The Policy Planning Council," *U.S. Naval Institute Proceedings*, XCII (April, 1966), 73–81.

HAMMOND, PAUL Y. "A Functional Analysis of Defense Department Decisionmaking in the McNamara Administration," *American Political Science Review*, LXII (March, 1968), 57–69.

HUGHES, THOMAS L. "Policy-making in a World Turned Upside Down," *Foreign Affairs*, XLV (January, 1967), 202–14.

McNAMARA, ROBERT S. "Managing the Department of Defense," *Civil Service Journal*, IV (April–June, 1964), 1–5.

NEUSTADT, RICHARD. "Approaches to Staffing the Presidency: Notes on FDR and JFK," *American Political Science Review*, LVII (December, 1963), 855–64.

———. "Kennedy in the Presidency: A Premature Appraisal," *Political Science Quarterly*, LXXIX (September, 1964), 321–34.

NITZE, PAUL H. "Office of the Secretary of Defense: International Security Affairs," *Armed Forces Management*, X (November, 1963), 73, 76.

RICHARDSON, HUGH F., and AUSLAND, JOHN C. "Crisis Management: Berlin, Cyprus, Laos (Executive Decisionmaking and Policy Implementation: Role of the State Department and the Military in Three Security Crises 1961–63)," *Foreign Affairs*, XLIV (January, 1966), 291–303.

RUSK, DEAN. "The Anatomy of Foreign Policy Decisions" (Address before the American Political Science Association, Washington, D.C., September 7, 1965), *Department of State Bulletin*, LIII (September 27, 1965), 502–9.

————. "Science and Foreign Affairs," *Department of State Bulletin*, LVI (February 13, 1967), 238–42.

————. "Secretary Gets New Responsibility for Conduct of Foreign Affairs: Texts of a White House Announcement and a Message Dated March 4 from Secretary Rusk to His Colleagues in the Department of State and Abroad," *Department of State Bulletin*, LIV (March 28, 1966), 506–9.

TAYLOR, MAXWELL D. "The Development of State's Role in Coordinating Foreign Affairs" (Address before the American Foreign Service Association), *Department of State Newsletter* (May, 1966), 2–5.

WHEELER, EARLE G. "The Joint Chiefs of Staff," *Armed Forces Management*, XI (November, 1964), 32–38.

YARMOLINSKY, ADAM. "How the Pentagon Works," *Atlantic*, CCXVII (March, 1967), 56–61.

U.S. GOVERNMENT DOCUMENTS

ARGYRIS, CHRIS. *Some Causes of Organizational Ineffectiveness Within DOS*. Washington, D.C.: Government Printing Office, January, 1967.

U.S. Congress. Senate. Subcommittee on National Security and International Operations of the Committee on Government Operations. *Conduct of National Security Policy:*
　　Hearings, Part 1, May 13 and 25, 1965. 89th Cong., 1st sess., 1965.
　　Hearings, Part 2, June 16 and 17, 1965. 89th Cong., 1st sess., 1965.
　　Hearings, Part 3, June 29 and July 27, 1965. 89th Cong., 1st sess., 1965.
　　Hearings, Part 4, August 30, 1965. 89th Cong., 1st sess., 1965.
　　Initial Memorandum. 89th Cong., 1st sess., 1965.
　　Selected Readings. 89th Cong., 1st sess., 1965.
————. *Planning-Programing-Budgeting:*
　　Hearings, Part 1, August 23, 1967. 90th Cong., 1st sess., 1967.
　　Hearings, Part 2, September 27 and October 18, 1967. 90th Cong., 1st sess., 1967.
　　Initial Memorandum. 90th Cong., 1st sess., 1967.
　　Official Documents. 90th Cong., 1st sess., 1967.
　　Selected Comment. 90th Cong., 1st sess., 1967.
　　Budget Bureau Guidelines of 1968. 90th Cong., 2d sess., 1968.
　　Hearings, Part 3, March 26, 1968. 90th Cong., 2d sess., 1968.
　　Interim Observations. 90th Cong., 2d sess., 1968.
　　PPBS and Foreign Affairs, Memorandum (by THOMAS C. SCHELLING). 90th Cong., 2d sess., 1968.

Program Budgeting in Foreign Affairs: Some Reflections, Memorandum (by FREDERICK C. MOSHER). 90th Cong., 2d sess., 1968.
Uses and Abuses of Analysis, Memorandum (by JAMES R. SCHLESINGER). 90th Cong., 2d sess., 1968.

U.S. Congress. Senate. Subcommittee on National Security and International Operations of the Committee on Government Operations. *The Secretary of State and the Problem of Coordination: New Duties and Procedures of March 7, 1966.* 89th Cong., 2d sess., 1966.
———. *Specialists and Generalists: A Selection of Readings.* 90th Cong., 2d sess., 1968.

U.S. Congress. Senate. Subcommittee on National Security Staffing and Operations of the Committee on Government Operations. *Administration of National Security: A Bibliography.* 87th Cong., 2d sess., 1962.
———. *Administration of National Security: Staff Reports and Hearings.* 88th Cong., 2d sess., 1964.
———. *The Ambassador and the Problem of Coordination.* 88th Cong., 1st sess., 1963.
———. *Staffing Procedures and Problems in Communist China.* 88th Cong., 1st sess., 1963.
———. *Staffing Procedures and Problems in the Soviet Union.* 88th Cong., 1st sess., 1963.